Crossroads of Change

CORI KNUDTEN
AND MAREN BZDEK

*The People and
the Land of Pecos*

UNIVERSITY OF OKLAHOMA PRESS : NORMAN

Library of Congress Cataloging-in-Publication Data

Names: Knudten, Cori Ann, 1983– author. | Bzdek, Maren Thompson, 1968– author.
Title: Crossroads of change : the people and the land of Pecos / Cori Knudten, Maren
    Bzdek.
Other titles: People and the land of Pecos
Description: First edition. | Norman, OK : University of Oklahoma Press, 2020. | Series:
    Public lands history; volume 4 | Includes bibliographical references and index. |
    Summary: "A history of how people and cultures interacted with and changed the
    environment in the area of Northern New Mexico that became Pecos National Historical
    Park from 1540 into the twenty-first century"—Provided by publisher.
Identifiers: LCCN 2019057917 | ISBN 978-0-8061-6624-7 (paperback)
Subjects: LCSH: Pecos National Historical Park (N.M.)—History. | New Mexico—
    History—To 1848.
Classification: LCC E99.P34 K58 2020 | DDC 978.9/55—dc23
LC record available at https://lccn.loc.gov/2019057917

Crossroads of Change: The People and the Land of Pecos is Volume 4 in the Public Lands
History series.

The paper in this book meets the guidelines for permanence and durability of the
Committee on Production Guidelines for Book Longevity of the Council on Library
Resources, Inc. ∞

For my grandmother, who also loved writing
For Justin, who helped me see it through

CONTENTS

Preface   ix

Acknowledgments   xiii

ONE   A Powerful and Prosperous Pueblo,
Pre–European Contact to 1598   1

TWO   Sowing the Seeds of Dissent, 1598–1680   18

THREE   Strife and Settlement on the Borderlands,
1680–1821   36

FOUR   Claiming the Land and Contesting Its Future,
1821–1916   58

FIVE   Making a Living in the Land of Enchantment,
1916–1941   93

SIX   Management and Mythology in a Postwar Landscape,
1941–1980   112

SEVEN   Enduring Spirits, Enduring Environment,
1980–2019   131

Notes   151

Bibliography   181

Index   199

PREFACE

WE FIRST VISITED PECOS in the autumn of 2007. At the time, both of us worked as researchers at Colorado State University's Public Lands History Center in Fort Collins. We drove down to New Mexico, following I-25 over Raton Pass, and the spacious, undeveloped land that opens on either side of the interstate in northern New Mexico presented a stark contrast to the morning rush-hour crowds of Denver. The National Park Service had hired us to write an environmental history of Pecos National Historical Park. As soon as we crossed into New Mexico, we began eagerly scanning the landscape and speculating about the historical forces that had shaped the environment we saw. Our interest only increased as we took the exit for Pecos. Had the stands of piñon and juniper always been this thick? Was there a water course by the pueblo ruins? Could you still see the ruts of the Santa Fe Trail? What did this place look like when the Pecos Indians lived here? What about during the Civil War Battle of Glorieta Pass?

An environmental history is a specific type of historical narrative. Many people assume it is simply a history of the environment. But it is more than that—an environmental history seeks to retell our familiar human stories through a new perspective and ask new questions about the relationship between people and nature. Environmental historians approach our understanding of the past from the perspective that there is no divide between humans and the places we inhabit. Humans live in a reciprocal relationship with the environment—our actions affect it and, in turn, environmental conditions and transformations affect us. At heart, history is about change. How and why did things change in the past to shape our current world? Every landscape has a history; every environment has changed and is continuing to change. Humans are part of those changes. No place remains untouched by anthropogenic influences. To understand the history of a place and of people, we need to investigate the many complex interconnections between people and the land, water, forests, and climate in which they live.

Uncovering these interconnections is not always easy. When we arrived at Pecos on that autumn afternoon, it appeared to be a sleepy, tranquil place. The Pecos River wound past lazily, the occasional bird sang in the piñons, and the distant peaks of the Sangre de Cristo Mountains rose up beyond the pueblo ruins. It seemed off the beaten path, and yet, for much of its history, Pecos had been involved in significant historical events. Pecos Pueblo had been an important trading center where Pueblo Indians, Spanish soldiers and settlers, and Plains Indians all confronted each other, sometimes peacefully but often not. Pecos stood right on the Santa Fe Trail in the 1800s, and later the first railroads in New Mexico steamed past the area. During the Civil War, United States and Confederate forces clashed at Pecos in a battle that halted the Confederates' western advance. In the twentieth century Pecos became a tourist destination, and two federal agencies—the National Park Service and the U.S. Forest Service—managed the new historic site and the nearby national forest. Over the years, different peoples, from the Pecos Indians to Spanish settlers to Euro-Americans, contested ownership and use of the land. Pecos had been a crossroads, constantly transforming.

This book tells the story of those transformations through the lens of environmental history. We begin our story in the 1500s when the Spaniards first arrived in New Mexico, but we also consider how the Pecos Indians lived before encountering Europeans and how they adapted to their arid environment and built a prosperous and powerful settlement. We investigate how Spanish conquest and settlement altered those adaptations. How did Spanish perceptions of the environment differ from those of the Pecos Indians? What changes did disease, warfare, and forced labor set in motion? By the late 1700s, Hispanic settlers had moved into the area, building new homes and planting crops. How did they lay claim to the land, and how did their way of life and their large herds of cattle and sheep affect the environment? By the mid-1800s, the region had become United States territory, and we consider how that shift placed Pecos in a precarious position as Americans fiercely debated whether the Southern slave system should expand westward. The Civil War eventually reached the inhabitants of Pecos, and we look at the changes that followed. How did Pecos residents and the descendants of the Pecos Indians assert their claims to the land under American legal systems? What were the environmental consequences of railroads, logging, and mining in the late 1800s? With the turn of the twentieth century came new relationships between humans and their environment at Pecos: tourism and preservation. A rodeo star operated a dude ranch and a Hollywood actress created a vacation home at Pecos. How did they alter the landscape to create their idyllic retreats? The designation of the Pecos Pueblo ruins as first a state monument, then a national monument, and finally a national historical park also brought change, in the name of preservation and protection of the remnants of the region's past. How did the National Park Service manage the environment as its staff interpreted the park's history? Even as things changed, older connections between people and the land endured. How did Pecos Indians and Hispanic residents continue to debate land use and ownership with these newcomers to Pecos? How did the Pecos environment assume the shape that greets visitors to the park in the twenty-first century?

As we researched the answers to those questions, we saw more and more clearly the complex interconnections and past transformations that lay beneath Pecos's deceptively calm appearance. We finished the environmental history report for the park in 2010.[1] We have now revised the original report into this book and added some information to bring the story up to the present. Since we did our original research, climate change has become a more pressing issue for park managers, yet park staff and Pecos residents alike are still seeking to build a resilient future for the Pecos environment. The people of Pecos—whether they reside in the village, visit to pay tribute to their ancestral home, work at the park, or stop by as curious tourists—are still changing the land and are changed in turn by their experiences in this place. People and the environment will remain intertwined at Pecos as the future of this dynamic place unfolds.

ACKNOWLEDGMENTS

WE BEGAN THE FIRST ITERATION of this project over a decade ago. In producing both the initial report and then this monograph, we relied on the help, advice, and feedback of two important mentors and friends. Mark Fiege, then the faculty council chair of the Public Lands History Center at Colorado State University, oversaw the initial project and provided invaluable guidance as we researched and wrote the report. We fondly remember our wide-ranging discussions of environmental history as we drove to and from Pecos with Mark. When we later turned the report into a monograph, Jared Orsi, current faculty director and council chair of the Public Lands History Center, provided an insightful review of the manuscript and also helped us receive a generous grant from the Public Lands History Center to cover publication-related expenses.

We relied heavily on the expertise of staff and volunteers at Pecos National Historical Park. In both phases of research for the original report and this book, they helped us with research, guided us through the park, provided comments on the draft report, and shared their knowledge of the landscape's history. We would like to thank Kathy Billings, Heather Young, Christine Beekman, Daniel Jacobs, Sue Eininger, Cheri Dorshak, Eric Valencia, Joe Dalton, Eluterio Varela Jr., Rhonda Brewer, Eric Sainio, and Claudia Floyd. In particular, Heather Young helped us navigate the extensive files in the park archives. Other National Park Service personnel who worked in the Southwest Region also provided insight, feedback, and encouragement for the project, in particular Robert Bennetts and Jill Cowley. Gilbert Ortiz generously shared his memories of the Forked Lightning Ranch.

We would also like to thank staff at various archives and research libraries. These include the New Mexico State Archives, the Museum of New Mexico, the Santa Fe National Forest headquarters, the Pecos–Las Vegas Ranger District in Pecos, the New Mexico State Engineer's Office, the National Archives and Records Administration regional office in Denver, the National Cowboy and Western Heritage Museum in Oklahoma City, the Center for Southwest Research and Special Collections at the University of New Mexico, and the Jake and Nancy Hamon Arts Library at Southern Methodist University.

Turning the original report we produced for the National Park Service staff into a shorter and more reader-friendly book for a general audience presented a number of challenges. It would have been much more difficult without the detailed and thoughtful suggestions from the anonymous reviewers who read and commented on both the original report and the shortened manuscript. Our editorial team at the University of Oklahoma Press, including Charles Rankin, Adam Kane, Steven Baker, and Tim Bryant, helped us create a stellar final product. We would also like to thank Erin Greb for creating the maps for the book.

As we learned about Pecos and its people, we came to care deeply about the history of this special place tucked into the Glorieta Pass. Sharing the many intertwined stories of Pecos with our inner circle of families, friends, and colleagues and seeing their curiosity piqued provided the encouragement we needed to see the project through to publication. We thank each of them for their enthusiastic, unwavering support, questions, and suggestions. We know that all who take the time to learn more about Pecos will be equally enriched.

ONE | A Powerful and Prosperous Pueblo
Pre–European Contact to 1598

CICUYE, 1540—YELLOW WILLOW LEAVES swirled in the water of the Pecos River as it wound its way past the fields of corn. The people of Cicuye moved through the fields in the autumn sunshine, bringing in the harvest. Some of them may have glanced to the southwest, where a party of their friends and relatives had disappeared some days past. Word had reached Cicuye, known as Pecos by others in the region, that "strange people" had entered the Puebloans' land.[1] The Pecos, who had previously pondered the dim rumors of conquest to the south, now faced the potentially dangerous reality of the interlopers arriving in their own territory. Pecos leaders decided to send a delegation to meet the newcomers. At best, the foreigners might prove to be strong allies—at worst, enemies. As they brought in their crops, the Pecos wondered which way events would turn.

Some 250 miles southwest of Pecos Pueblo, the delegation from Pecos had arrived at the Zuñi pueblo of Háwikuh in the late summer of 1540. The Spaniards they met called the leader of the delegation "Bigotes" ("Whiskers") because he sported a distinctive mustache. Bigotes was probably a war leader among the Pecos or occupied some equally prominent position within Pecos society. He may often have traveled away from Pecos Pueblo on trading expeditions and probably knew at least one other dialect besides his own.[2] At Háwikuh, Bigotes met Francisco Vásquez de Coronado, who had come north from Mexico chasing rumors of wealth that rivaled the riches of the Aztec empire. To his dismay, Coronado had not found any fabulous cities of gold. Instead, he encountered a land whose Puebloan inhabitants struggled against the aridity of their environment to raise enough crops for subsistence and trade. Corn, hides, feathers, piñon nuts, pottery, turquoise—these were the resources the inhabitants of Háwikuh and the other pueblos valued. They promised small returns to the Spaniards, who hoped to find wealthy cities whose inhabitants they could conquer and then tax, extracting large tribute payments.[3]

1

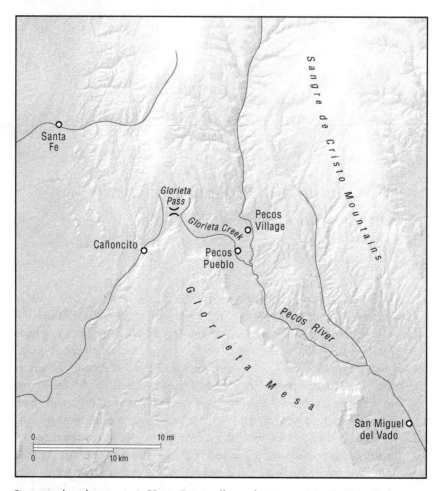

Sites noted in chapters 1–3, Upper Pecos valley and environs. Map by Erin Greb.

But the Spaniards did not intend to simply give up and leave empty-handed. Even if the Puebloans did not possess an abundance of wealth in silver and gold, the Spaniards could still conquer them and levy more modest tributes. The Franciscan friars who accompanied Coronado also reminded him that the Spaniards had a duty to bring Christianity to the Puebloans and save their immortal souls. And Coronado had not quite given up on his dreams—cities filled with wealth enough to satisfy any man's ambitions might still wait beyond the horizon. After overcoming the resistance mounted by the Zuñis at Háwikuh, Coronado set about subduing other pueblos in the region—preferably peacefully, but resorting to force if necessary.[4] When Bigotes and Coronado met, Bigotes assured him the Pecos wanted to be friends with the Spaniards and presented him with several gifts, including bison hides. Intrigued by the curly pelts, Coronado appointed Captain Hernando de Alvarado to travel with

Bigotes to Pecos Pueblo to formally establish relations with the Pecos and learn more about the region.[5]

Bigotes led Alvarado and a small detachment to Pecos Pueblo, arriving in September or October. The Pecos were busy bringing in the autumn harvest. Coronado's men studied the pueblo carefully, determining how much of a threat the Pecos would pose if they suddenly turned hostile. In a history of the expedition, Pedro de Castañeda de Nájera recorded that Cicuye, the Spaniards' original approximation of the name for Pecos Pueblo used by its inhabitants, had "as many as five hundred fighting men. It is feared throughout that whole land."[6] Another description from Coronado's expedition mentioned that Pecos was "larger" than all the other pueblos and "very strong." The pueblo itself was "four and five stories high" and "surrounded by a low stone wall."[7] The environment around the pueblo also captured the men's interest. Castañeda stated that "Cicuye is in a small valley between mountain ranges and lands forested with great stands of pine. It includes a small stream which has many fine trout and beavers. Many large bears and excellent falcons flourish around there."[8] To the Spaniards, Pecos appeared to be a pueblo that, if not filled with gold, was still a valuable prize, particularly because it offered a gateway onto the eastern plains.

Located on the border between the Puebloan peoples and the inhabitants of the southwestern plains, particularly the Apaches, Pecos was in a position to broker trade between the various communities. Available evidence suggests that Bigotes and other inhabitants of Pecos did indeed occupy a powerful pueblo. Although Spanish accounts of the Coronado expedition and other Spanish forays into New Mexico provide the only written sources from the period, and inevitably reflect the Spaniards' cultural biases, other evidence, including archaeological and ethnological data, supplements these sources. Therefore, we can reconstruct a semblance of life at Pecos Pueblo in 1540 when Bigotes cautiously brought the Spaniards within its sandstone and cobblestone walls.

"The Best and Most Populous of the Pueblos":
Settlement and Subsistence at Pecos Pueblo

The Pecos's way of life developed over thousands of years as their ancestors adapted to the environment and crafted strategies and techniques that allowed them not only to survive but to prosper. In Puebloan oral tradition, a divine being granted the Puebloans their southwestern homeland at the beginning of time. This same being also taught them how to plant crops and identify useful wild plants. The Puebloans trace the movements of their ancestors through songs that describe the locations of deities, such as mountain peaks and lakes.[9] Modern-day archaeologists turn to physical evidence of habitation, such as lithic scatters and arrowheads, to uncover the movement of the Southwest's first human inhabitants, who appear in the archaeological record around 11,500 BCE. It was not until the period from 600 to 1200 CE that humans built habitations in the Upper Pecos River valley meant for sedentary, long-term use. Pit houses and a few small structures of indeterminate purpose, dating to the eleventh and twelfth centuries, have been unearthed in the vicinity of Pecos Pueblo.[10] From 1325 to 1450 an influx of people came to the valley, and habitation sites increased in number. The ancestors of the Pecos built several pueblos within a five-mile radius of Pecos Pueblo, including the Forked Lightning Ruin, Dick's Ruin, Rowe Pueblo, Arrowhead Ruin, Loma Lathrop, the Hobson-Dressler site, and the Black-on-White House, which occupied the later site of the northern section of Pecos Pueblo. By the mid- to late-1300s, people began to vacate these various nearby habitation sites and congregate at Pecos Pueblo, which was the only village in the valley by 1450. All other pueblos had been abandoned.[11]

Why the Pecos chose to consolidate their community in one location is open to debate. The decision may have been made for reasons of defense. The location of the pueblo, on an isolated, steep-sided *mesilla* providing a view of the surrounding valley, afforded its residents a protected vantage point to spot enemies at a distance. The location on the ridge also provided the advantage of southerly exposure to offset the cold air flowing from Pecos Canyon upstream. Competition for resources also may have encouraged aggregation. As habitation sites proliferated in the Upper Pecos valley, competition for fertile soils, hunting territories, and gathering areas increased as well. Consolidating into one pueblo may have been an attempt to share resources communally. A larger and stronger pueblo could have forced other, smaller groups away from resources.[12]

Climatic trends may also have played a key role in population aggregation. Today, two precipitation regimes characterize the Southwest. The Upper Pecos River valley sits just below the line dividing these two regimes. Pecos and areas to the southeast are within a pattern characterized by unimodal, summer-dominant precipitation. To the northwest a bimodal pattern dominates. Due to this pattern, the Upper Pecos valley receives most of its moisture during the monsoon months of July and August. Evidence suggests that this pattern also existed in the past, at least as early as 750 CE. Between 1250 and 1450 CE, however, the northwestern regime collapsed into a number of variable patterns. The monsoonal pattern of the southeast persisted.[13] Thus, people may have migrated to the area that provided more climatic stability.

Of course, amounts of precipitation and average temperature varied over time, including in the Upper Pecos valley. In general, the Southwest grew warmer and drier over the course of centuries. During the Paleo-Indian period (10,000–5500 BCE), the climate was drier than it had been previously, yet still wetter and cooler than today. During the Archaic period (5500 BCE–600 CE), the climate continued to grow warmer and drier. Desert species established themselves as woodland species withdrew.[14] Any discussion of the role of climate, however, must consider local variations. Climatic conditions can vary dramatically from place to place, and broad generalizations may not accurately depict the climate of a specific area. Evidence for the climate of the Upper Pecos valley includes data from tree rings in the area south of Santa Fe. Multiple periods of low precipitation occurred periodically, but the area experienced times of increased precipitation as well. Higher than average spring moisture prevailed from 1400 to 1415, for example, while a severe drought occurred in the years around 1420.[15] Although the population aggregation at Pecos Pueblo occurred during a period of stable rainfall, as the Pecos population grew, they depended ever more heavily on the surrounding resources, thus increasing their impact on the local environment.

Bigotes lived at Pecos during the height of its population and power, when it had been established for approximately one hundred years. Population within the pueblo peaked between 1450 and 1475.[16] Spanish accounts stated that the pueblo was "enclosed and protected by a wall and large houses, and by tiers of walkways which look out on the countryside."[17] Expedition member Castañeda de Nájera explained that "the buildings are all of the same height, [which is] four stories. At that height one walks through the whole town without there being a street which might hinder that." No doors opened on the ground level; instead "ladders that can be raised up are used" and "in time of war [the people] communicate with each other by means of the interior doors."[18] Baltazar de Obregón, who wrote a history of the Coronado expedition in 1584, related that Pecos had "the greatest and best buildings of those provinces and is most thickly settled by *gente vestida* [clothed people]."[19] Here, Obregón compared the Pecos to the nomadic Chichimecas of central Mexico, hunter-gatherers who reportedly practiced cannibalism and thus were feared and loathed by the Spaniards. In contrast, the Puebloans' settled, agrarian lifestyle reminded the Spaniards of the sedentary natives of Mexico, as well as villages in Spain.[20] To the Spaniards, settled communities and farming signaled civilization. The Spaniards' admiration in some ways predetermined their conviction that the Pecos could be converted to Christianity—and also that the Pecos's stores of resources would provide suitable tribute to the Spaniards.

The strategic location with connections to a wide trading network provided the Pecos with impressive resources, even compared to other pueblos. The Pecos were not necessarily allies with the other Puebloan groups, even the Jemez pueblos located to the west, with whom the Pecos shared the Towa language.[21] Castañeda de Nájera reported that the Pecos "boast that no one has been able to subjugate them and that they subjugate [whichever] *pueblos* they want to."[22] Bigotes did not meet the Spaniards as a supplicant but rather as an emissary from a powerful community that commanded the surrounding region.

The Pecos's success rested on their ability to cultivate and maintain a plentiful food surplus, allowing them to survive inevitable periods of drought. Long before the formation of Pecos Pueblo, societies in the Southwest began experimenting with agriculture, eventually transforming from mobile, hunting-and-gathering cultures into sedentary, agrarian cultures. Indigenous species, particularly agave and little barley, may have been the first cultivated plants.[23] People swiftly replaced these species with maize (corn), which was probably introduced to the Southwest from Mexico during the Archaic period (5500 BCE to 600 CE).[24] Farming soon became integral to Puebloan life, and corn provided the foundation of their communities.[25] Indigenous communities in areas such as California, with more fertile soils and wetter climates, did not adopt corn, but it thrived in the Southwest's arid environment.

Even if corn could grow with limited moisture, it still needed at least some rain, and so when Puebloan communities adopted corn as their main crop, they placed it and rain at the center of their daily rituals. Farmers selected the seeds of plants that performed well in their local conditions, receiving new varieties of corn seeds, including flint, dent, flour, sweet, and popcorn, through trade networks.[26] The carefully planted and tended fields, along with the stone pueblos, became integrated among the piñon and juniper woodlands and open grasslands of the Upper Pecos valley. But the wide distribution of a new plant species and the activities associated with farming, including clearing fields, also altered the local environment. Farming encouraged the spread of other edible species. Corn replaced native plants, and disturbed soil and abandoned fields supported interloping species of weeds.[27] The introduction of cultivated corn also changed human society. Corn required an input of human energy and technology in order to flourish.[28] Puebloan society transformed as the individual pueblos developed strategies for successful cultivation and incorporated corn into their daily lives.

Over time, the Puebloans developed a number of practical strategies and religious rituals to cope with the undependable moisture and temperature extremes of their environment. Several methods existed to take advantage of ephemeral moisture from rain and snowmelt. Check dams retained water, and diversion dams channeled water to garden plots. The Puebloans used terracing extensively to prevent rapid water runoff. They also employed grid garden systems, in which borders made of earth or stone formed cells that captured moisture. Gravel mulching of plots also increased the moisture retention of the soil. Proper location of a plot was essential for success—a plot situated at the head of a ravine behind a check dam ensured that an adequate supply of water would reach it, but at a slow enough rate to avoid damage to the plants. Some plots may have been located inside gullies, where the surrounding walls trapped daytime heat, keeping the soil warmer overnight.[29]

The Pecos conducted a variety of agricultural activities and used these terraces, check dams, grid gardens, and reservoirs to capture and manage rainfall and snowmelt and maximize the available moisture in the soil.[30] They irrigated fields in the deep, moisture-retaining alluvial sediments of Glorieta Creek, the small water course that flows directly beneath the western slope of the mesilla on which they built their large pueblo. But the majority of irrigable land lies to the northeast by the Pecos River in a low, swampy area known to later Spanish settlers as a *ciénega* (spring).[31] A large expanse of well-watered soil, the ciénega was a coveted resource. As the Pecos population grew, the pueblo residents put marginal soils into production as well. Over time, the distance increased between habitation sites and non-habitation sites, such as fieldhouses and other places associated with subsistence activities. The Pecos may have located fields along Glorieta Creek extending quite a distance from the pueblo, utilizing any small patch of fertile ground they found.[32]

As a trader who traveled frequently away from the pueblo, Bigotes may not have spent much time in the pueblo's fields, but many Pecos labored there throughout the year. They anxiously watched for signs of rain in the summer, for although the Pecos developed agricultural strategies enabling them to thrive in their arid environment, growing a successful crop of corn each year was never a certainty. If the rains did come in sufficient quantity, the corn was ready for harvest in about 120 days. With an average of approximately 127 growing days, the Upper Pecos valley offered marginal conditions for corn agriculture.[33] Living at an elevation of about 7,000 feet, farmers in the valley also faced the threat of frost in the spring, which could kill seedlings. Colder temperatures could also prevail through the spring months, inhibiting growth. Moisture was critical. A lack of moisture later in the growing season put greater stress on corn.[34] In order to avoid famines in years when the harvest was poor, the Pecos stored crop surpluses during good years. Spanish observers recorded that they had stored "quantities of maize, cotton . . . beans, and squash."[35] The pueblo had "such an abundant supply of corn that everyone marveled," a later Spanish expedition in 1591 commented and added, "Each house had two or three rooms full of [corn], all of excellent quality. . . . [I]t seemed that some of the corn was two or three years old."[36] The Pecos thus managed their food supplies to withstand periods when their crops failed.

Although we know Pecos Pueblo supported a large population, determining exactly how many people lived there is challenging. No firm agreement exists regarding the population when the Spaniards arrived in 1540.[37] Spanish sources described it as approximately 2,000.[38] The Spaniards had reason to overestimate the population—a higher number made a potential conquest sound more impressive. However, the first detailed census of the pueblo, conducted in 1694, recorded 736 inhabitants at the pueblo after almost a century of close contact with the Spaniards and exposure to disease epidemics, suggesting that a higher earlier population estimate for Pecos Pueblo may be correct.[39] Regardless of the actual population at Pecos Pueblo, the Spanish observation that it was "the best and most populous of the pueblos" was probably accurate as a relative indicator of population.

Maintaining a substantial community meant the Pecos made use of all the resources at their disposal. A varied diet was important, because corn alone provided little iron or calcium. Farmers grew a variety of the "three sisters"—beans, squash, and corn. Squash, less nutritious than corn, was easily dried and stored, and the gourds provided useful containers. Beans were an important source of lysine, the amino acid missing from both corn and squash that allowed these staples to be more easily digested. Beans also replenished nitrogen in the soil while corn depleted it. Weedy annuals, such as goosefoot, amaranth, and beeweed, grew in disturbed soils, such as the borders of cultivated fields, and provided supplements to the Pecos diet. Amaranth grains, for example, can be made into flour. The Pecos could also use sunflowers, Indian ricegrass, and cactus fruits, among many other edible plants. The piñon nut provided an important source of protein in the Pecos diet. Substantial yields occur every four to seven years and, like corn, the nuts can be stored. Plants also possessed importance beyond their role as a food source. Puebloans used plants to make such diverse items as cordage, mats, sandals, and loom anchors. Yucca root could be made into soap. The Puebloans also boiled cota, a plant with bright yellow flowers, to make a tea with a sweet taste. Piñon sap, when combined with lard, formed a salve for skin abrasions.[40]

The pines, junipers, and other trees growing near the pueblo also formed a critical component of the Pecos's lives. The Spaniards observed that the Pecos possessed "plentiful supplies of firewood, and of lumber for building houses. Indeed, we were given to understand that whenever anyone wanted to build a house, he had lumber for that purpose ready at hand."[41] Although the primary building materials the Pecos used were sandstone and mud, along with gypsum quarried from Glorieta Mesa for windows and plaster, they used wood as well, particularly for roofs. Excavations of the north pueblo complex revealed beams of yellow pine, covered first with cedar or more pine, and then with small twigs of cedar, willow, wild cherry, or rushes.[42] Although wood was important for building purposes and for making tools and weapons, the Pecos used the greatest amount of wood to feed their fires. They collected all readily available wood, including piñon and juniper, for firewood. The Spaniards remarked that the mesilla was "cleared of trees" and that only half a league away did "a heavy growth of cedars, pines and oaks" begin. A league is 2.6 miles, and the term "cedar" probably referred to junipers. "Oaks" may refer to the native Gambel oak, a small tree or shrub, or may be a catchall term used by the Spaniards for deciduous trees in general. By 1540 the Pecos had inhabited the area for centuries, and the pueblo population had grown quite large. The Pecos searched for wood in an ever-widening circle around the pueblo.

The Pecos may also have affected forest density by using fire to clear away trees and brush. No evidence for the Pecos's use of fire for clearing exists. Any conclusions must rely on an extremely limited number of sources, many of them discussing indigenous tribes or locations far removed from the Upper Pecos valley. Probably any purposeful burning by the Pecos was limited in extent and did not affect the overall landscape. Instead, lightning provided the primary source for fire ignitions. Striking during dry spring weather and summer storms, these fires match the fire-scar record of the Southwest far better than anthropogenic causes do. If the Puebloans had been using fire to clear vegetation, the logical time to set such fires would have been in the fall or winter when conditions made the fires easier to control. Evidence, however, shows that most fires occurred in the spring and summer.[43]

For the Pecos, the piñon and juniper, interspersed with grassland areas, formed a familiar landscape. Walking around the pueblo, Bigotes and the other residents of Pecos passed under the boughs of piñon pines, encountered meadows where the sun shone brightly, and pushed through willows on the banks of the river. The Pecos valued piñon and juniper as well as the many other species that grew in these ecosystems and contributed to a diverse diet. The Pecos residents also probably enjoyed the sweet fruit of the prickly pear cactus, drank doveweed tea to cure a headache, and snacked on nodding wild onion bulbs as they worked.[44]

"Big Bears and Fine Falcons Multiply in This Region": Wildlife Populations and Hunting

While the Pecos had established an agrarian subsistence that allowed large settlements to form and persist in an arid climate, their meat came from hunting and trade. The Spaniards noted the "large bears" and "excellent falcons" around Pecos Pueblo, but mule deer, rabbits, foxes, and other species roamed the slopes of the mesas and nosed along the riverbank. The Pecos hunted many of them, often with the assistance of the companion dogs they kept to guard the fields from wild animals.[45] The Pecos not only incorporated wild game into their diets but also utilized many parts of animals for other utilitarian needs and for decorative and ceremonial purposes. When Alvarado arrived at the pueblo, the Pecos offered him turkey feather robes and animal skins. The Pecos also valued grizzly bear teeth and eagle claws, and they used eagle bones to make musical instruments such as flageolets and whistles.[46]

The Pecos River and Glorieta Creek afforded the Pecos plentiful fishing opportunities. The Spaniards mentioned "a brook which abounds in excellent trout and otters."[47] The description could refer to either the Pecos River or Glorieta Creek. The trout was probably the Rio Grande cutthroat trout.[48] In 1540 the riparian ecosystems of both the Pecos River and Glorieta Creek would have possessed diverse vegetation, although the presence of agricultural fields as well as the harvesting of useful plants, such as willows, may have resulted in a less dense riparian growth near the pueblo.

Evidence for the types and amount of meat in Puebloan diets survives in the midden heaps surrounding the pueblos. Animal bones discovered in the large midden heaps on the east slopes of Pecos Pueblo revealed that mule deer comprised the most substantial number of bones—over three-quarters of those found. Rabbit bones occurred in large numbers, followed by antelope, mountain sheep, and elk. Archaeologists also discovered bison bones, which increased in number after about 1470.[49] All of these species occur in the Upper Pecos valley or within a distance that pueblo inhabitants could travel easily.

A study of the Arroyo Hondo Pueblo ruins, located south of Santa Fe, examined animal bones in greater detail than any studies at Pecos Pueblo. This study recorded a number of species that currently inhabit piñon-juniper and grassland ecosystems, such as desert cottontail rabbits, white-footed mice, coyotes, and foxes. Spotted ground squirrels, Gunnison's prairie dogs, and Ord's kangaroo rats clambered about prehistoric Arroyo Hondo in large numbers but they rarely appear today. Black-tailed prairie dogs, yellow-faced pocket gophers, white-tailed jack rabbits, and Richardson's ground squirrels also were present in greater numbers in the prehistoric period. Grizzly bears and gray wolves also appear at Arroyo Hondo Pueblo—species that faced local extinction in the nineteenth and twentieth centuries. Arroyo Hondo residents raised corn-fed turkeys, and some evidence exists that turkeys may have been raised at Pecos Pueblo as well. Domesticated turkeys provided a source of feathers for blankets, clothing, and ceremonial purposes, as well as supplemental meat when wild game was less abundant.[50]

Social, religious, and practical considerations influenced the methods of Puebloan hunting societies which, like those societies dedicated to warfare, were exclusively the realm of male members of the community. Men hunted deer, elk, and antelope whenever food reserves were low and for ceremonial purposes, including when the kachinas were about to visit. The kachinas were the ancestor dead who lived underneath lakes and on mountaintops and brought rain and sustenance for the people. Communal hunts conducted by hunting societies required intensive purification and preparation rituals. After completing the rituals, the hunters, dressed in deerskins with head and antlers still attached, traveled to the hunting ground, where they encircled their prey and carried out a carefully prescribed killing. For example, the hunters suffocated deer to allow the animal's breath and spirit to be reborn and replenish the herd. The deer meat could not enter the home and provide sustenance for the family without another ritual process that involved the women "feeding" the carcass with cornmeal to adopt it symbolically into their household.[51] These rituals were based on carefully organized production and distribution of resources among the people and an emphasis on reciprocity that recognized mutual obligation through gift giving. That obligation extended to all elements of the natural world and to the ancestors.

But the arid region had limits on what it could produce and sustain. Due to the concentrated nature of the population at Pecos Pueblo, it is likely deer in the immediate area were over-hunted, requiring hunters to travel greater distances to find game.[52] At Arroyo Hondo, hoofed mammal bones declined over time, while small mammals and bird species both increased and diversified. This trend suggests that the population of hoofed mammals near the pueblo fell due to overhunting, which forced people to broaden their subsistence strategies.[53] Social factors also impacted large mammal hunting. Other Puebloan groups in the area, in the Galisteo Basin or on the other side of Glorieta Mesa, may have controlled their own hunting territory, limiting the reach of Pecos hunters. Once again, evidence concerning hunting among Puebloan groups is limited, but we should not assume that the Pecos could freely make use of all the resources in the area.[54]

"They Worship the Sun and the Water":
Pecos Religion and Culture

Religious rituals and social expectations impacted not only hunting but all facets of the Puebloans' relationship to their environment. On a reconnaissance mission at Taos Pueblo, Hernando de Alvarado, the same member of Coronado's expedition who visited Pecos with Bigotes, remarked that "they worship the sun and the water." Although neither Alvarado nor anyone else on the Coronado expedition commented on the religious practices of the Pecos in particular, all of the Puebloans shared a belief system and similar religious practices and myths based on the relationships between people and nature in its various forms. Natural landforms, such as lakes or mountains, possessed specific spiritual significance and meaning, as did animal and plant species. Clans were associated with animals and natural elements. A 1904 interview with Se-sa-few-yah, who had lived at Pecos Pueblo before migrating to Jemez Pueblo in the early 1800s, collected a list of fourteen traditional clans. The clans were Wâ-kah (Cloud), Pe (Sun), Se-peh (Eagle), Kyu-nu (Corn), Whâ-lu (Bear), Shi-añ-hti (Mountain Lion), Wa-hā (Squash), Pâh-käh-täh (Sand), A-la-wah-ku (Elk), Al-lu (Antelope), Pe-dâhl-lu (Wild Turkey), Fwah (Fire), Mor-bāh (Parrot), and Hä-yäh (Snake). During interviews with Pecos descendants in the 1990s, one elder recounted an ancient story of the Pecos, wherein a bull emerged from a lake in the mountains above the Upper Pecos River Canyon. The Pecos brought the bull back to the pueblo and chained it, but the bull broke the chains and returned to the lake. The Pecos Bull ceremony and many others continue today, carried out by the Pecos in their new community at Jemez Pueblo. They continue to practice ceremonial dances and rituals at certain times of the year that were created by their ancestors as a tribute in conjunction with planting, harvesting, and other activities.

In the Puebloan world, nothing was more important than rain, and the rain chief in every village was powerful because he could conjure precipitation by calling kachinas. He could also stage the Snake Dance to call the Horned Water Serpent, which created abundance and brought rain by joining together male and female, life and death, sky and earth, and earth and underworld. Knowing when to offer a certain prayer, plant corn, or expect the first snows required attunement to astronomical cycles. The stars, sun, and moon also figured into Pecos spirituality.[55]

With agriculture such a mainstay for their society, it is no surprise that corn was at the center of Puebloan daily rituals and identity. As the Pecos population grew, community members would have competed for fertile soils, and those with greater social power, such as religious figures, may have controlled larger amounts of land. Possibly, land acquisition was similar to current systems of land control among the Puebloans. For example, clan affiliation can determine access to land. In a matrilineal society such as the Jemez, land is passed down to both sons and daughters. Stores of dried corn and prime agricultural fields had to be defended against enemies, as well. But the system of irrigated agriculture also demanded cooperation in non-kinship groups that relied upon group ceremony and ritual to mobilize collective labor and celebrate the success of their efforts and their respect for the rain, sun, and earth.[56] The Pecos achieved equitable distribution of resources by bartering for services with food and sharing surpluses with less-fortunate community members.[57]

Agriculture also influenced gender roles and family composition within Puebloan society. Farming encouraged larger families because it provided a more plentiful food supply but also demanded more labor. Therefore, women began having more babies with less spacing between them. From the Puebloan point of view, a successful harvest required a complex system of ritual that began at birth, when every Puebloan child received a corn fetish representing the Corn Mothers, from whom all life and spiritual sustenance emerged. Boys also received a flint arrowhead, representing the hunt. The sound of two pieces of flint struck together suggested the crash of thunder and lighting, the harbingers of rain. Male members of the pueblo possessed religious knowledge, practiced and taught to others in their kivas, the ceremonial spaces for powerful rituals. Murals of kachinas covered the kiva walls, and kachina dancers dressed as the ancestors in community rituals that created common identity beyond ties of kinship. The *cacique* (village chief), as a descendant of the sun, was the keeper of sacred time and in charge of maintaining the cosmic balance. It was he who determined the dates for planting and harvest.[58] The dynamic ideology and rites of the Puebloans recognized the feminine generative patterns latent in the earth and seeds and the masculine generative powers of rain. Historian Ramón A. Gutiérrez notes, "To the Pueblo Indians, flint, rain, semen, and hunting were to male as corn, earth, and childbearing were to female."[59] Division of labor reflected these symbolic roles. Women planted "kitchen gardens," which contained more specialized plants such as greens and herbs for culinary use and religious ceremonies. The importance of the gardens may have bestowed greater cultural status on their caretakers, as did the gathering of women in groups to grind corn. Men farmed the land farther away from the pueblo. In these ways and in others, the Pecos's society and culture influenced their interactions with the environment.

"Very Heavy Hair like the Mane of a Wild Lion": Pecos Pueblo's Connections to the Southwestern Plains

From the moment Bigotes brought bison hides to Coronado, the Spaniards wanted to know more about these strange "cattle." When they reached the plains to the east of the Upper Pecos valley, the Spaniards encountered bison directly. Pedro de Castañeda de Nájera, the official chronicler of the expedition, struggled to describe the animal. He related it to animals familiar to his audience: "They are bearded like very large he-goats. . . . From the middle of the body back they are covered with very woolly hair like that of fine sheep. From the belly to the front they have very heavy hair like the mane of a wild lion." Just as the indigenous people of the plains before them, the Spaniards quickly realized the utility of bison hides for warm clothing, sturdy tents, and other items.[60]

The Pecos relied upon bison hides and meat acquired through trade to supplement the fruits of their own hunting and farming activities. Trade allowed them to transcend the limits of their environment, accessing food and materials they could not produce locally and supplementing their diets when local resources were scarce. The pueblo's strategic position at the gateway to the plains situated them within an extensive trading network. Puebloan trading connections extended to the Pacific Ocean, eastward onto the Great Plains, and south to Central America.[61] At Pecos, tribes of Southern Athabaskan nomads—ancestors of the Indians who became known as Plains Apaches—arrived each autumn from what is now eastern New Mexico and west Texas to trade. The Pecos traded corn, pottery, turquoise, and other items for bison meat, fat, and hides. Archaeological evidence suggests this interaction began at Pecos Pueblo in the mid-fifteenth century—about one hundred years before the Spaniards arrived. At this time artifacts attributed to Plains groups began to appear at Puebloan sites with greater frequency, particularly at Pecos Pueblo and other eastern pueblos, which monopolized the trade.[62] The trade testifies to the success of Pecos agriculture as well as the importance of meat in their diet. The Pecos had enough corn to trade without threatening their own supply. Through trade they obtained protein that corn did not provide.[63]

Although trade with Plains Apaches provided both groups with needed resources, the relationship between the two peoples was complicated. When Apaches came to Pecos Pueblo to trade, they remained outside the pueblo, camping in the wide meadow to the east, and were perhaps only invited into the pueblo in small numbers. But trade could also foster social ties between the two groups. Intermarriage gave both sides more reasons to keep their relationship peaceful and strengthened strategic alliances. For example, later in the 1700s some of the Pecos joined Jicarilla Apache bands, and Apaches sometimes joined the Pecos Pueblo. These interactions probably occurred during earlier periods as well.[64]

In addition to trade and intermarriage, both the Puebloans and native groups on the Plains took captives during raids and enslaved them. A boy called Sopete was part of the delegation led by Bigotes that met Coronado at Háwikuh. Sopete had been born among the Wichitas, nomads who lived in present-day Kansas, an area the Spaniards called Quivira. The Pecos pointed to a tattoo of a bison on Sopete when they attempted to explain the origin of the bison hides to Coronado. Later, when Coronado set out from Pecos Pueblo to try and locate Quivira, the Pecos gave him two other Wichita captives, a man the Spaniards called El Turco and another young boy called Xabe, to serve as guides.[65] The Pecos may have captured Xabe and the others themselves or purchased them from their original captors, perhaps the Apaches. Captives were a source of labor but were also usually incorporated into the social structure and community of their captors. In this respect and others, slavery among the indigenous peoples of the Southwest was different from the chattel system of slavery that later developed in the Southern United States, which included extensive legal, social, and cultural barriers to prevent enslaved black people and free blacks from assimilating into white society.

Enslaving people from other groups was one more element of the lucrative trade with Plains nomads that the Pecos profited from and apparently controlled to some extent. Farming corn had proven to be successful as well. The diverse environments around their pueblo provided numerous other resources. For a time, Pecos society supported a high population, including numerous warriors who gave the pueblo a formidable reputation. Although by the mid-1500s Pecos Pueblo had already begun to decline from its peak population, it was still one of the most important pueblos in the region. The Spaniards recognized the importance of Pecos when they entered the scene in 1540.

"We Shall Forcefully Enter Your Country":
Early Spanish Expeditions to New Mexico

Bigotes brought Hernando de Alvarado to Pecos in the autumn of 1540. While the Pecos watched and listened, Alvarado read aloud the *requerimiento* to the assembled crowd and pueblo leaders, informing them of their new status as subjects of the Spanish crown and promising death and destruction if the Pecos resisted Spanish rule. If the Pecos refused to submit, "We shall forcefully enter your country," the requerimiento proclaimed, "and shall make war against you in all ways and manners that we can." The Spaniards, in their strange clothing with prayer-sticks and lightning sticks (crosses and guns), riding atop unfamiliar large animals (horses) presented a spectacle that mystified the Pecos. We can only speculate on the reaction of Bigotes and the other Pecos to Alvarado's belligerent pronouncement. But after dispatching with such formalities, Alvarado and Fray Juan de Padilla, the Franciscan who accompanied him, pursued the topic that truly interested them—did the Pecos have any gold and, if not, did they know anyone who did? The Pecos brought forward their captives El Turco and Sopete, urging them to tell the Spaniards about their homeland. El Turco claimed that in his homeland of Quivira, a journey of some days to the northeast, gold and other fantastical sights abounded. El Turco told Alvarado that Bigotes possessed a gold bracelet from Quivira.[66]

When Alvarado questioned him, Bigotes replied that El Turco had lied. He refused to accompany Alvarado back to Coronado's main encampment. Alvarado seized Bigotes, clapped him in chains, and returned to Coronado with word of his discoveries in the east. After a winter spent fighting and slaughtering the inhabitants of various pueblos along the Rio Grande in the region around present-day Albuquerque and forcibly taking supplies to feed his hungry men, Coronado returned to Pecos Pueblo in the spring of 1541, accompanied by his large expeditionary force. Although about 300 Spaniards led the expedition, the vast majority of Coronado's followers consisted of about 1300 native allies from central and western Mexico. An unknown number of servants and enslaved people also accompanied the expedition. Although the expedition's records mention only two women by name, they probably formed a substantial contingent as well, either accompanying their husbands or working as servants and companions. New people joined the expedition as it went along, too—for example, an unnamed Puebloan woman married one of the expedition's members, becoming the third and last woman to be explicitly noted in the records. The expedition also herded thousands of horses, cows, and sheep along with them. An unusually wet period in the early 1540s that improved the quantity of native grasses along the route allowed many of the livestock to survive the journey.[67] Although sheep and cattle had proliferated in large numbers in the colonial settlements of northern Mexico by that time, the Pecos would never have seen such animals, not to mention such vast numbers of people traveling en masse, including Europeans of unfamiliar appearance. Although some Spaniards and native allies entered the pueblo, the majority of the expedition and its livestock camped in the surrounding area, completely transforming the quotidian landscape with strange sights, sounds, and smells.[68]

Hoping to regain the Pecos's favor, Coronado freed Bigotes in a gesture of good faith. The Pecos once again gave El Turco to the Spaniards to serve as a guide to Quivira, along with the young captive Xabe. The expedition set forth, pausing after about four days of travel to build a bridge over the Pecos River to allow the passage of the large party and livestock.[69] But when they at last reached Quivira, it proved to be no more than a settlement of Wichita villages on the Arkansas River. Although the Wichita prospered in their subsistence culture, they possessed no gold. Coronado ordered El Turco strangled, but before he died, El Turco claimed the Pecos had told him to mislead the Spaniards by drawing them out to the unfamiliar environment of the plains, where their forces would become less of a threat to Pecos as they weakened due to lack of provisions and faced potential attack from the Apaches.[70]

Captain Tristán de Arellano returned with a contingent of forty men to Pecos Pueblo ahead of the furious Coronado and the rest of the expedition and found the pueblo's inhabitants in wait, armed and ready to resist. It is possible that Bigotes stood among the warriors, perhaps eager to take revenge on the Spaniards after his long winter in captivity. A prolonged battle ensued, but the Spaniards emerged the victors. Arellano and his men waited near the subdued pueblo until Coronado arrived, and the expedition returned to camp near the Tiguex pueblos, along the Rio Grande near present-day Albuquerque. But Coronado's power over the Puebloans was extremely tenuous, limited by distance and the necessity of dividing his force among the various pueblos if he wished to try and remain in control of those he had subdued. Undoubtedly the Pecos began planning new ways to contest the Spaniards' claim on their territory. But whatever plans they made proved unnecessary. By the following spring, Coronado's disillusioned men convinced him to return to Mexico to subdue a new rebellion by the indigenous people of Sonora. Fray Juan de Padilla, leader of the Franciscans on the expedition, and an older lay brother, Fray Luis de Úbeda, decided to stay. Captain Juan Jaramillo, in an account of the expedition, recorded that Úbeda asked that a young enslaved person of Jaramillo's called Cristóbal remain with him.[71] Padilla was determined to return to Quivira, but Úbeda and Cristóbal remained at Pecos, along with a flock of sheep that Coronado gave them. The fate of Úbeda and Cristóbal is unknown, but the sheep did not survive.[72] The Pecos did not convert to Christianity, nor did they retain the flock to use as the basis for their own foray into sheep herding. Instead, as Coronado's expedition disappeared over the horizon, Bigotes and the other Pecos resumed their normal activities, although they stayed alert for any news of the invaders' return.[73] They were granted several decades of reprieve. In 1546, silver was discovered near Zacatecas in Mexico, and the Spaniards became consumed with establishing mining operations and warring with the Chichimecas near the frontier towns that grew up around the mines.[74]

Two more Spanish expeditions eventually arrived at Pecos Pueblo. Captain Antonio de Espejo, a cattle rancher who had been traveling through the pueblos with a small *entrada*, arrived at Pecos with a party of eight soldiers in July 1583, by which point Bigotes would have been an old man if he still lived. Like Coronado, Espejo resorted to force to obtain needed provisions. The Pecos did not offer Espejo a warm welcome, but when the Spaniards forced their way into the pueblo, the Pecos relented, offering provisions for the return journey to Mexico in the hope that Espejo would do no harm. When he departed, Espejo took with him two captives from Pecos, and one made it to Mexico City, where he taught his native language to four indigenous people under the direction of Fray Pedro Oroz, in preparation for one day carrying the gospel back to the Pecos in their own language. In 1590, don Gaspar Castaño de Sosa led a colony to New Mexico and once again turned to the Puebloans for food and shelter—perfectly willing to resort to violence if help was not offered freely. Again the Pecos resisted with arrows and rocks from their fortified positions in the housing blocks and fled the pueblo when Castaño captured it.[75] For all the violence and disruption these Spanish expeditions brought, all three failed to establish a permanent Spanish presence in New Mexico. Defeated by the harsh and arid environment and resistance of the Puebloans, the Spaniards all returned to Mexico. But their brief encounters, however limited, demonstrated the vast differences between the two societies.

Bigotes experienced firsthand the cultural gulf separating the Spaniards and the Pecos. The insistent Spanish demands for gold, a metal the Puebloans had little familiarity with and did not value; the tame Spanish horses and bleating sheep, both animals the Pecos had never seen before—these were integral elements of the Spaniards' culture. Under Coronado and his successors, the first horses left their hoofprints in the ground around Pecos Pueblo, and the Spaniards and the Pecos fought over the food supplies the Pecos had spent many arduous hours coaxing to grow or hunting in the forests. These early contacts between the Pecos and Spaniards were brief, but they hinted at how contentious the conflicts over resources could become when two diverse cultures encountered each other. The Pecos had spent centuries adapting to life in the Upper Pecos valley. Now the Spaniards had arrived and with them came a host of new animals, plants, and microbes. For the moment, the effects on the Pecos and their environment had been limited. But the Spaniards had not given up on colonizing the vast region north of Mexico. They would return, and the Pecos would face the challenges of trying to survive in a transformed environment.

TWO | Sowing the Seeds of Dissent
1598–1680

EL PUEBLO DE LOS PECOS, 1635—Fray Andrés Juárez stood by the banks of the Pecos River, watching as his charges carried out their daily tasks. He noted with approval the stalks of wheat growing next to the traditional fields of corn. One of the Pecos boys who worked as a herder wandered by, urging sheep from the mission flock to drink in the river. In the distance, Juárez heard the bells pealing in the imposing Catholic mission church that now stood side by side with the pueblo on the mesilla.

As Juárez presided over the daily Mass in that church, he looked out over the faces he had come to know during his thirteen-year ministry at Pecos Pueblo—the longest of any Franciscan friar at the pueblo. Juárez had arrived at Pecos in 1622, following his first assignment at Santo Domingo. Now he was preparing to leave Pecos for a new mission at Nambé Pueblo, northwest of Pecos. Reflecting on his thirteen years at Pecos, Juárez must have felt a sense of accomplishment. He had overseen the Pecos in the grueling labor required to complete the massive adobe church that now dominated the mesilla. He had taught the Pecos about the Christian God and encouraged them to live as *gente de razón* (rational people) who had adopted Hispanic cultural traits—growing wheat, tending cattle, herding sheep, attending Mass, and speaking Spanish. Although many still rejected his ministry and resisted the Spanish way of life, Juárez would leave behind a tangible legacy, reflected in the changes to the pueblo settlement and the landscape of the valley.

Juárez hailed from the southern Spanish town of Fuenteovejuna, near Córdoba. He crossed the Atlantic in 1611 to serve as a missionary in the remote Province of Santa Fe de Nuevo México, where, in 1598, the conquistador and later colonial governor don Juan de Oñate had established the first successful colony for the Spanish Empire. At least Oñate called it a success, but his cruelty to both the native Puebloans and the Spanish colonists led many of the colonists, struggling to survive in the new province under his leadership, to revolt and try to return to Mexico. The Franciscans pleaded with the Crown not to abandon this new territory, and so royal officials replaced Oñate with a new governor, Pedro de Peralta. For Peralta, Fray Andrés Juárez, and other Spaniards who drifted north in the early 1600s, New Mexico appeared to be an isolated, alien environment. While the pueblos functioned as small agricultural villages, no horses, cattle, or sheep grazed around them. Corn, not wheat, grew in the fields. Few of the vegetables and fruits familiar to the Spaniards ripened in the sun-drenched earth. The Puebloans gave unintelligible names to the surrounding landforms. They worshiped strange gods. To the Spaniards, the Puebloans appeared as both heathens ripe for conversion and as potential slaves who could serve the settlers' households or be sold in Mexico to work in the silver mines.[1]

The Spanish colonists soon set about trying to turn this unfamiliar environment into a familiar one. They herded domestic livestock from Mexico. They planted wheat, grapes, onions, chiles, and radishes, often claiming the best land around a pueblo for their needs. The Franciscan friars not only planned to instruct the Puebloans in the tenets of Christianity, but they also expected them to embrace a Spanish lifestyle. At Pecos, Fray Andrés Juárez made sure his charges planted wheat and tended his kitchen garden filled with European herbs and vegetables. Sizeable herds of livestock now grazed around the pueblo, supplying Juárez with meat and revenue. The Spanish settlers, less committed to transforming the Puebloans into Christians than the Franciscans, sometimes abandoned Spanish ways and adopted Puebloan ones. Many, particularly the poorer members of the colony, ate corn, learned to speak Puebloan dialects, and intermarried with the Puebloans. But to the Spanish officials and Franciscans, such accommodation spelled certain ruin and loss of Spanish identity. They tried to keep Puebloans and Spaniards separate, while attempting to erase the Puebloan way of life and substitute a Spanish one in its place.

Their efforts bore varying degrees of success. Puebloan foods, medicine, and clothing styles influenced Spanish colonists, and many Spanish men fathered children with Puebloan women. In the remote province, where the Puebloans far outnumbered the Spanish colonists, miscegenation and acculturation between the two groups became the norm in a matter of decades, and mestizo people served as cultural intermediaries.[2] On the other side of the coin, the Puebloans did plant wheat and raise cattle under Spanish direction. Some Puebloans learned to speak Spanish. Some incorporated Christianity into their beliefs. But overall, the Puebloans resisted Spanish domination and enslavement, often in subtle, nonviolent ways. While a Pecos might attend Mass in Fray Andrés Juárez's church during the day, he also participated in a traditional Pecos ceremony in a kiva during the evening. While the Pecos might bring their required tributes of corn, piñon nuts, and hides to the governor at Santa Fe, they also exploited the adversarial relationship between Spanish secular and religious officials to their own advantage. Although the Spaniards tried to turn the Puebloans' world into a European one, a hybrid culture and environment resulted instead.

"The Friar Makes Them Sow Some Grain and Raise Some Cattle": *The Introduction of Exotic Species*

Fray Andrés Juárez came to New Mexico expecting to suffer deprivations and hardships, but he did not intend to forego all the trappings of a civilized life. For Fray Andrés, this meant enjoying wine, olive oil, and fine linens transported to New Mexico every few years via a lengthy wagon train from Mexico. He also expected the Pecos to sow wheat and tend the mission herds of cattle and sheep. Fray Alonso de Benavides, in an account of New Mexico written in 1634, recorded that every friar ordered the Puebloans at his mission to "sow some grain and raise some cattle" in order to "support . . . all the poor of the pueblo."[3] Although some produce was distributed to the poor and held in reserve for times of famine, the Franciscans never allowed the Pecos to begin herds of their own. Like all the missions in New Mexico, the Pecos produced crops and livestock controlled by the priests.

By introducing new species of plants and animals to the New Mexican environment, Fray Andrés Juárez and other Spaniards perpetuated what historian Alfred Crosby has termed "ecological imperialism."[4] The Spaniards already had reaped the benefits accrued from introducing European species to American shores in their conquest of Mexico, Central America, and South America. They discovered that possessing a self-propagating food supply freed them from some of the burdens of feeding exploratory missions in an often-hostile environment. The Spaniards brought cattle and horses (*ganado mayor*) and sheep, pigs, and goats (*ganado menor*)—all previously unknown in the Americas—across the Atlantic. The animals swiftly adapted to their new surroundings. Pigs, in particular, reproduced quickly, and the Spaniards deliberately left the animals on various islands or locations on the mainland to serve as food for other Spaniards following in their footsteps. Spanish *Criollo* (Creole) and Black Andalusian cattle breeds provided a source of food and leather, could be driven long distances, and also served the critical role of beasts of burden for agricultural work and transporting goods.[5] The Spaniards introduced horses as well, which initially gave them tremendous psychological and physical advantages over the natives of the Americas, although eventually many indigenous nomadic groups also adopted horses and gained their own advantages in subsistence, trade, and warfare. Sheep, although requiring more care, adapted well to arid environments and quickly became an important component of Spanish settlement in South America and eventually North America as well. The Puebloans' experience with animal domestication was limited to turkeys and dogs, and the power of the Spaniards' "animal magic" over the many unfamiliar species awed them.[6] The new livestock herds crowding the landscape disrupted the existing Puebloan social order as well as their environment. For example, the livestock marginalized the Puebloan chiefs in charge of hunting societies that previously supplied their people with meat.[7]

The Spaniards understood that livestock needed to be part of any successful colonizing force. In 1596 when don Juan de Oñate received approval from the Crown to lead a settlement expedition northward, he brought with him over 500 settlers and also 7,000 head of stock. The livestock included 1,300 horses, 100 donkeys and mules, 3,400 sheep, 1,600 cattle, 300 oxen, 1,000 goats, and 60 pigs. Oñate, born in colonial Mexico, was the son of Cristóbal de Oñate, who discovered and made his fortune in the Zacatecas silver mines. Oñate possessed the fortune to fund an expedition, and the Crown instructed him to bring along sufficient supplies so that settlers and soldiers would not be driven to demand corn from the Puebloans. The previous expeditions of Coronado, Espejo, and Gaspar Castaño de Sosa had forcibly taken food from the Puebloans to sustain themselves through the winter. Inevitably this policy caused friction and conflict. Memories of the harsh measures used by the Spaniards to procure supplies remained vivid in the minds of the Puebloans throughout the subsequent decades.[8]

The Spaniards recognized the self-defeating effects of these uncontrolled expeditions. By the time Espejo was traveling to New Mexico, the Crown officially had switched from a policy of conquering natives to a policy of pacifying them, as set forth in the 1573 Comprehensive Orders for New Discoveries. The orders attempted to reduce indigenous fatalities associated with the process of empire building. In reality the orders were ineffective. Few on the frontier enforced them; most colonizers and explorers did what they deemed necessary for survival and exploited indigenous labor for their immediate needs and to profit from the demand for labor in the silver mines.[9]

When Oñate prepared his colonizing expedition, he tried to follow the spirit of the orders, but bureaucratic delays kept him in Mexico for two years. In the meantime, the colonists that had already assembled consumed the food meant to sustain them on the road and during the first months in their new home. By the time they—and the cadre of Franciscan friars who joined Oñate—reached New Mexico, their circumstances compelled the settlers to demand corn from the Puebloans' food stores once again.[10] The settlers did so only reluctantly— they had planned to grow European crops such as wheat, as opposed to adopting a Puebloan diet.

The dispersal of new plant species had begun immediately after the Spaniards arrived in the Americas. When Columbus returned in 1493, he brought with him "seeds and cuttings for the planting of wheat, chickpeas, melons, onions, radishes, salad greens, grape vines, sugar cane, and fruit stones for the founding of orchards."[11] Oñate's settlers carried many of these same seeds with them when they traveled north in 1598. They also probably introduced clovers, used to feed livestock, and mullein, a medicinal plant, to New Mexico.[12] The colonists envisioned a future where they grew and consumed familiar European grains, fruits, and vegetables in their new environment.

In attempting to recreate European diets, recipes, and ingredients in the Americas, the Spaniards undertook what historian David Weber calls a "cognitive conquest" of the American environment.[13] The encounter with entirely new continents, people, plants, and animals that bore little resemblance to anything in Europe or Asia had potentially devastating ramifications for Spanish practitioners of Catholic theology because these new species and peoples cast doubt on biblical theories of creation. How could such different people and animals exist in the Americas when God had created all life in the same time and place? Although the discoveries in the Americas did lead some to question their beliefs, the majority of people accepted the conclusion that made the most sense to them: the Indians were heathens whose souls would be lost if they were not converted. The Spaniards placed unfamiliar animals and plants into preconceived categories as well. Explorers described the new species they found by relating them to European flora and fauna and even European myths. Europeans fit not only Native Americans but also the environment into their traditional worldview without substantially changing it.[14] The Puebloans experienced a familiar world slowly being made unfamiliar, while the Spaniards made an unfamiliar world familiar.

Despite the biological and psychological tools at their disposal, Oñate's colony faced an uphill struggle. Colonists, unused to the cold temperatures of winter and the opposite extremes in summer, described the climate as "eight months of winter and four of hell."[15] The Puebloans accepted the settlers and friars grudgingly, if at all. Many of the things the Spanish settlers must have viewed as necessary for a civilized life—iron tools, bread, linen cloths—did not exist except for what they managed to bring themselves. Although Oñate immediately drafted 1500 Puebloans to dig irrigation canals (acequias) at the newly established capital of San Gabriel de Yunge, the fields of the Spaniards were not immediately fruitful.[16] The colonists took food stores from the Puebloans instead, and in just three years had used up a six-year supply of corn that the Rio Grande Pueblos had stored for emergency rations.[17]

Clinging to a precarious existence, the Spanish settlers began to consider abandoning the colony. Fray Francisco de San Miguel supported leaving, stating that "if we stay any longer, the natives and all of us here will perish of hunger, cold, and nakedness." But Oñate was determined to stay. He repressed dissension among his colonists and the Puebloans. For example, when the Acoma Pueblos resisted Spanish control in 1598, Oñate's men seized the settlement and murdered, mutilated, and enslaved its inhabitants. Finally, when Oñate was away in 1601 on an expedition onto the eastern plains, most of the colonists fled south. The Crown investigated the situation. Although many favored abandoning the colony, the Franciscans protested, claiming they could not forsake the thousands of baptized Indians and the thousands more awaiting salvation. The Crown relented and declared New Mexico a colony of the Crown, supported by the royal treasury, not wealthy individuals like Oñate. More friars, settlers, and supplies trundled north under the leadership of Governor Pedro de Peralta, planning to continue transforming the northern territory of their incipient empire into a civilized, fruitful region.[18]

"They Do Not Die Because of Us":
Disease Epidemics among the Puebloans

The Spaniards deliberately introduced numerous species to the Americas, but they unknowingly introduced other plants and animals as well. Weed seeds traveled in the mud on human and animal feet and in their waste products. Rats, which the Spaniards would have happily left behind, also came in the ships to the Americas. But the species with the direst ramifications were common European disease pathogens, which had devastating consequences for Indians encountering them for the first time.[19] Disease became the darkest shadow of the Spaniards' experiment in ecological imperialism. In New Mexico some diseases may have preceded Spanish arrival, transported through existing trade networks. The long-term presence of Spanish colonies and constant contact between Spaniards and Puebloans made exposure far more likely, however. A Jesuit priest, Juan Bautista de Velasco, commented in 1593 that the natives "do not die because of us." He claimed that even the natives did not blame the friars because they assisted the sick during epidemics.[20] Despite the priest's rationalizations, many natives and Spaniards probably connected the arrival of the Spaniards to the epidemics despite their ignorance of the source of pathogens and the means of transmission. Fray Andrés Juárez hoped to baptize every Pecos before death, and during the seventeenth century burials became distressingly common. The presence of new diseases and their shocking effects shattered the Pecos's world as much as Spanish demands for tribute, labor, and religious conversion. Indeed, these effects were interrelated because enslavement and conflict inhibited the Pecos's ability to recover from epidemics. When the Black Death decimated European populations in the fourteenth century, those populations eventually recovered and surpassed their previous numbers. But the Pecos and other natives in the Americas faced constant traumas of warfare and dislocation that prevented them from recovering from the initial waves of epidemics.[21]

Smallpox was the most deadly, but other diseases such as typhus or measles also were effective killers. Confronting new diseases for which they had no cure disrupted Puebloan societies. The sudden loss of numerous members of a pueblo overturned social networks and hierarchies. The epidemics also affected the Puebloans' ability to gather, hunt, and farm food. Starvation could follow the plague when too few remained healthy to harvest or plant crops. Europeans, who had already formed immunities to these diseases, watched as thousands of Puebloans perished. Like their animals and technologies, the seeming invulnerability of Europeans to disease also gave them a psychological advantage in their conquest.[22]

Records of specific epidemics at Pecos Pueblo before the Pueblo Revolt do not exist, but the pueblo surely suffered the effects of disease. In 1622 Fray Andrés Juárez claimed that he ministered to "2,000 souls, a few less," at Pecos. Although Juárez had the time and ability to conduct a detailed census at the pueblo, he either did not do so or the records do not survive. Not until 1694—after the Pueblo Revolt and the Spanish Reconquest—does a record exist of a careful census, conducted by Fray Diego de la Casa Zeinos at Pecos. Zeinos recorded a total of 736 inhabitants. From the time of the permanent Spanish presence established by Oñate, and possibly before, the Pecos lost people to smallpox, measles, and other illnesses.[23] By disrupting Puebloan society and compromising the Puebloans' physical ability to resist the Spaniards, disease gave Europeans an advantage.

The presence of other introduced European species also benefitted the Spaniards. The ability to eat mutton and beef, to grow wheat and make it into bread, and to harvest familiar fruits from nearby orchards allowed them to feel more comfortable and in control of their environment. Of course, not every settler enjoyed equal benefits. Wheat, for example, did not grow well everywhere and could be difficult to obtain. Many settlers subsisted on a corn-based diet, just like the Puebloans. Spanish officials discouraged eating like the Puebloans, adopting Puebloan customs, and engaging in sexual or conjugal relationships with them. For example, only wheat could be used for communion bread. Officials wanted to maintain Spanish culture, but they also hoped to use their cultural distance to maintain authority among the Puebloans. The Spaniards realized that their control of certain resources and tools—guns, cattle, horses—gave them an advantage that would be lost if the Puebloans gained free access to them. Laws prohibited mission Indians from traveling to Spanish towns and forbade Europeans, blacks, mestizos, and mulattos from spending more than three days at a pueblo.[24]

In the seventeenth century, the small size of the Spanish population and the Franciscans' policy of intolerance towards Puebloan religion prevented much of the accommodation and cultural interaction that became a hallmark of the colony in the eighteenth century. But despite Spanish attempts to keep the borders between their culture and the Puebloans' firm, their encounter with a new environment meant that change and compromise were inevitable. The Spaniards tasted bison meat and realized bison hides were a valuable resource. Piñon nuts, too, became a coveted food item. Bison hides and piñon nuts traveled down the trail to Mexico to mingle with goods from other countries and continents. The Spaniards also adapted to life in a new place. Although they may have planted wheat and grazed sheep, they could not completely transform the New Mexican environment into a copy of Spain or Mexico. Instead, the Spaniards incorporated the environment into their own culture—giving Spanish names to mountains and rivers, enjoying the warmth of piñon wood fires, and identifying new birds, plants, and animals. During his thirteen years at Pecos Pueblo, Fray

Andrés Juárez became intimately familiar with thunderclouds piling over the slopes of Glorieta Mesa in the summer, the hard ground that changed to mud as the snows melted in the spring, and the sound of the Pecos language.

"Devoted to the Service of the Church":
The Franciscan Ministry at Pecos Pueblo

The Franciscan friars who resided at Pecos Pueblo induced many changes in the environment of the Upper Pecos valley, and they did so by persuading, manipulating, indoctrinating, intimidating, and coaxing the Pecos themselves to undertake these transformations. The Pecos Indians tended the herds of sheep, cattle, donkeys, and horses owned by the Franciscans. The Pecos—not the priests—also planted the fields of wheat and the kitchen gardens filled with European herbs and vegetables. A few served as cooks and personal servants. Fray Alonso de Benavides claimed that at every mission, "more than twenty Indians, devoted to the service of the church," labored for the friar.[25] The Franciscans did not establish a mission at Pecos Pueblo until 1617, but once they did, change followed rapidly. Fray Pedro Zambrano Ortiz served as the first friar at the pueblo, and he began construction of a small church away from the village on the north end of the mesilla, which was abandoned before it was completed. The archaeological record at Pecos reflects large numbers of European artifacts, specifically "domestic animals, china dishes, and metal implements" by 1620 to 1630.[26] The growing European influence coincides with Fray Pedro de Ortega's and, particularly, with Fray Andrés Juárez's ministries. Governor Peralta designated Santa Fe as the Spanish provincial capital in 1610, but settlers did not move beyond Santa Fe—and closer to Pecos Pueblo—until late in the eighteenth century. In fact, Spanish settlement in New Mexico remained low throughout the seventeenth century. By the time of the Pueblo Revolt in 1680, probably only about 2,500 members of the non-Puebloan Hispanic community—composed of Spaniards, Mexican Indians, and other integrated native people—lived in New Mexico.[27] The governor in Santa Fe demanded tribute from Pecos Pueblo, but it was the Franciscans who spearheaded the primary changes in the Pecos environment and Puebloan culture through religious conversion and subjugation.

Both Spanish officials and Franciscans entertained high hopes for the colony initially, but as the seventeenth century progressed it became apparent that they would obtain poor monetary returns from New Mexico. The human labor of the Puebloans proved to be the most profitable resource, and one that both Franciscans and governors used to their advantage. Although the Spanish Crown issued a decree of emancipation in 1672, forced labor did not disappear. Settlers, clergy, and local officials routinely ignored the law and continued to exploit the Puebloan settlements through various quasi-legal arrangements. Slavers also continued to transport captives south to the silver mines, although in diminished numbers. Historian Andrés Reséndez uses the phrase "the other slavery" to reflect the reality and scale of coerced, unpaid servitude experienced by many native peoples. While the system differed from the chattel slavery practiced in the Southern United States in later years, its impacts were no less severe and pervasive.[28]

The construction of the large mission church at Pecos Pueblo under the direction of Fray Pedro de Ortega and Fray Andrés Juárez exemplified one aspect of the onerous labor demands the Spaniards often made of the Puebloans. The most obvious manifestation of Spanish influence at Pecos, the Nuestra Señora de los Ángeles de Porciúncula church exhibited an awe-inspiring presence with six bell towers and walls forty-five feet high and ten feet thick. Its construction required about 300,000 adobe bricks, each weighing around forty pounds. Local timber provided wood for scaffolding and roof construction. Pecos laborers cut and hauled the wood, formed the bricks, and laid them in place to create the massive walls on a bedrock foundation. The Franciscans' living and teaching quarters, known as a *convento,* were attached to the church. The convento was also a monumental architectural addition to the built environment on the mesilla that demanded an equal amount of labor, raw materials, and time. As the primary site of activities associated with religious and social indoctrination, it was also critical for the mission's goal to transform the Pecos people and their way of life.[29] Because building construction occurred within the domestic realm of the village, the Pecos considered the task of laying adobe walls to be the province of women, but the Franciscans enlisted both genders in the church and convento construction. Fray Alonso de Benavides recorded how when the priests forced a man to do the work, "he runs away from it, and the women laugh."[30] While the Pecos were building the church, and before they built the convento, the friar occupied rooms in a structure located to the south of the main pueblo. Probably during the early 1600s, the Pecos added rooms and stories to the structure until it stood as a second pueblo on the mesilla. Historian John Kessell speculates that Pecos sympathetic to the Christianizing mission of the Franciscans may have inhabited the south pueblo, which was closer in proximity to the new church.[31] Building the church kept both men and women away from their own subsistence labor and other traditional activities and forced them to contribute to the establishment of a power center for the Catholic Church in their midst.

While the Pecos toiled for the Franciscans, debates over the merits of resisting Spanish control probably consumed many of the Pecos's private councils and personal conversations during the seventeenth century. The Puebloans were by no means a conquered people. Revolts flared up occasionally in response to the onerous demands for labor and tribute, although the Spaniards succeeded in suppressing them.[32] Even if the Puebloans did not actually fight the Spaniards, they resisted adopting Spanish religion and culture on a daily basis, and they maintained a cultural barrier when they spoke their own language to each other. The Franciscans failed to master the Puebloan languages, which incurred criticism from Spanish officials and kept them at a disadvantage. The Puebloans' ability to communicate without censorship in their own language and perpetuate their traditional religious practices allowed them to preserve their own customs and individual and collective identity despite the watchful eyes of the friars.[33]

At the same time, the friars were able to capitalize on the Puebloans' religious beliefs as well as divisions within Puebloan society to gain converts. The friars used their knowledge of the Puebloans' cosmology to impersonate the rain chiefs and medicine men by staging dramatic, symbolic events that conveyed the suggestion of spiritual power to bring rain and heal the sick and injured. Their facility with a range of unfamiliar domesticated animals underscored the "animal magic" they possessed. To the Puebloan men who abstained from sex during the practice of ritual magic, the friars' vow of chastity conveyed unusual strength. The Franciscans also played upon the Puebloan system of interdependence through gift giving and reciprocity, which was particularly effective for gaining the loyalty of youths. Offering knowledge of animal husbandry and the meat from domesticated livestock in exchange for their submission to baptism and obedience to the Christian God was akin to the traditional hunt chief teaching hunting magic and techniques in exchange for payments of corn and meat. For some young Puebloan men, whose typical path to social standing and food accelerated under the friar's tutelage, the authority of the hunt chief and the necessity to continue to hunt wild game no longer held the same importance. Hunting, an inherently masculine activity, important in the winter and linked also to warfare, was further co-opted by the friars in their portrayal of Christ as a war god, surrounded at his wintertime birth by animals in the manger. This and many other examples illustrate how the friars used the Puebloans' inextricable spiritual relationship with their natural world to compete with the Puebloan chiefs for the loyalty and physical labor of the people, and why they readily achieved some degree of success.[34]

At the same time, the Puebloans believed harmony could only be restored through the power of their ancient ritual and prayers, and resistance was ongoing if well-hidden. Franciscans were particularly concerned with suppressing the power of women in Puebloan society, and the patriarchal friars forbade and suppressed the women's fertility societies and interfered with their control of the household domain and corn production.[35] Many women resisted these attacks on their authority and expressed their defiance in the symbols they applied to pottery. Some of the people, including many native chiefs, remained skeptical of the friars' apparent spiritual powers. Like all densely populated and highly organized communities, factionalism was a longstanding reality in the pueblos, reflecting the interests of farmers versus traders or those more inclined by position and psychology to embrace change versus those more inclined to defend tradition.[36]

But even those Puebloans who continued to reject Spanish religion could see the material advantages of many Spanish goods and possessions. The Puebloans began to employ Spanish iron-bladed axes and hand tools along with their traditional fire-tempered digging sticks, deer scapula, and stone hoes for cutting firewood or hoeing weeds.[37] Spanish draft animals such as oxen, along with the introduction of the wagon and the plow, changed agricultural practices and production significantly and eased human labor demands. The Pecos could now use *burros* (donkeys) to haul wood—cut with Spanish metal axes—from the slopes down to their settlements, which increased the efficiency of tree harvesting and accelerated deforestation in woodlands along rivers and at higher elevations in the region. Cottonwood trees became wheels and wine barrels. Piñon trees became plowshares. Douglas fir was used for bridges and *vigas* (roof beams).[38] Horses transported goods and people quickly and easily across vast distances. Cattle and *Churro* sheep, a lean Spanish breed well adapted to arid conditions, provided new sources of food and clothing. By 1680, the Puebloans had converted from cotton to sheep wool for textile production.[39]

These advantages of Spanish goods and livestock were obvious to the Pecos but not always available to them for their own personal benefit. The Franciscans, who owned some of the largest herds of livestock in the colony, kept tight control over their animals. Controlling the livestock gave the Franciscans leverage in their constant fights with secular officials, and the friars probably also sold some back to the silver-mining communities in northern Mexico for their own profit. Governor Luis de Rosas complained in 1641 that "every convento is a livestock operation and general store owned by the friars."[40] As a source of food, the friars' livestock only benefitted the Puebloans and Spanish settlers when famine demanded the friars distribute meat to the poor. The sheep herds may have offered another benefit to the Puebloans, however, as sheepherding provided an opportunity to maintain traditional patterns of movement across the landscape even as the Franciscans attempted to limit and control Puebloan mobility beyond the village.[41]

At Pecos Pueblo the Franciscans ordered the construction of several corrals adjacent to the church to hold the mission's livestock. The Pecos probably built "two corral-like courtyards" immediately. Later, between 1640 and 1670, the friars oversaw the construction of another large corral complex to the south of the convento. This corral included three pens for stock against its east wall.[42] Existing accounts do not reveal what kinds of animals the friars kept at Pecos, but it was probably a mixture of sheep, cattle, oxen, horses, pigs, and goats. Each mission, along with the settlers, contributed to the rapid expansion of sheep herds in particular in the seventeenth century.[43] No specifics exist for the numbers of livestock, but evidence from other missions suggests approximate numbers for Pecos. An account of an Apache raid in 1669 at Acoma Pueblo noted the loss of 800 sheep, 60 cattle, and an unspecified number of horses.[44] While it is unknown how much of the overall livestock population that represented, it provides the basis for a minimum number. As a large pueblo, Pecos likely had livestock in numbers equal or greater.

Just as the presence of the mission changed the visual landscape of the mesilla at Pecos Pueblo, the presence of livestock altered the surrounding environment as well. Although not in sufficient numbers to cause widespread damage in the surrounding region, the domesticated livestock kept at the Pecos mission must have affected the immediate surroundings, in particular the riparian vegetation around Glorieta Creek and the Pecos River, where the livestock were watered and grazed. Their presence on the mesilla and along the creek banks probably accelerated soil erosion. The Pecos herders pastured the friars' livestock in other areas around the pueblo as well, although it is doubtful the herders followed the late-nineteenth and twentieth-century practice of summering livestock in the mountains and herding them back to the valley in the winter. During the seventeenth century, threats of Apache raids increased, keeping both people and animals close to the pueblo.

The Pecos continued to cultivate the fields in the ciénega and elsewhere along the river as well as by Glorieta Creek and areas that required dryland farming techniques. As the population at Pecos Pueblo decreased throughout the century, the Pecos may have had to abandon some fields, as they now had too few people to work them. Additionally, the mission system relied upon the ability to control, at least in part, the rhythms of Puebloan labor to its own benefit. Because traditional dispersed farming in field camps at some distance from the pueblo allowed the Puebloans to elude constant supervision, Franciscans may have encouraged abandonment of such fields.[45] It is doubtful that any fields would have been abandoned by choice. If cultivated land did decrease, the first fields removed from production would have been those on marginal lands farther from the river and creek.

The Puebloans had long occupied the most fertile areas of the high, cold, and arid valleys of New Mexico, and so the Franciscans automatically gained control of this valuable land upon the founding of a pueblo mission. This action created further tensions in their relationship to the native inhabitants and also with the Spanish colonists. The crops raised in Franciscan-controlled fields during short growing seasons spelled the difference between starvation or survival for Puebloans and colonists alike. The Puebloans, in particular, had to turn to the Franciscans for food because the crops from fields they had formerly used now went straight to the mission stores.[46] They became more reliant upon trade, hunting, and harvesting to supplement their diet.[47] The Franciscan domination of arable land engendered bitter feelings among the Spanish settlers and officials who also desired the land and labor of the Puebloans, which they accused the friars of monopolizing.[48]

"From Pecos They Have Brought Only Twenty-Three Fanegas of Piñon Nuts": Spanish Demands for Tribute

Unlike his successor Fray Andrés Juárez, Fray Pedro de Ortega was born in Mexico to wealthy, aristocratic parents. Ortega renounced the wealth he stood to inherit and joined the Franciscans. He traveled north in 1617, accompanying a party that included the new governor for the New Mexican colony, don Juan de Eulate. Eulate took up the governorship five years after Pedro de Peralta and following Bernardino de Ceballos. Ortega and Eulate did not get along. While traveling north, Eulate supposedly extolled the virtues of marriage over celibacy. Ortega rebuked Eulate, who went on to comment that the "religious didn't work, that all they did was sleep and eat, while married men always went about diligently working to earn their necessities." Ortega stiffly replied "that the sleep of John had been more acceptable to Christ Our Lord than the diligence of Judas."[49] The other Franciscans disliked Eulate as well, and his tenure in New Mexico—like that of many other governors—was rife with discord.

Ortega and Eulate's relationship did not improve with time. When Ortega began construction of the mission church at Pecos, he requested the loan of oxen from settlers—probably those near Santa Fe, the nearest Spanish settlement to Pecos—to help with the work. Eulate disliked any indication that the friars were bettering their situation at the expense of his own, and he confronted one of the settlers who had loaned oxen to Ortega. Eulate demanded the settler retrieve his oxen immediately or face a fine of forty *fanegas* of corn (104 bushels, enough to feed twenty people for one year).[50] When Ortega smashed the idols of the Pecos and removed a dissident named Mosoyo from the pueblo, placing him in the service of a Spanish family, Eulate ordered the man released. Mosoyo claimed Eulate did not want the Pecos to follow the orders of the Franciscans. Although Eulate probably never stated the matter so plainly, he did what he could to undermine the Franciscans' authority.[51] His interference in the matter likely did not reflect a concern for Mosoyo's personal fate, because the Crown later arrested Eulate for illegally transporting enslaved people out of New Mexico and for issuing *vales*, paper orders that allowed the bearers to seize Puebloan children, dubiously deemed "orphans," and forcibly enslave them.[52]

The bickering and constant power struggles that characterized the relationship between Spanish religious and secular officials in New Mexico reflected their competition to control the land, resources, and human inhabitants of the colony, including the Puebloans. Secular officials and Spanish settlers had two primary methods of extracting tribute and forced labor from the Puebloans, the *encomienda* and *repartimiento* systems. An encomienda was a grant from the Crown that gave an individual the right to communal labor from a specified number of individuals in a pueblo. Governors distributed pueblos as encomiendas to well-placed Spanish officials and settlers who offered the governors political support. *Encomenderos* collected tribute payments from the pueblo, and although they were not authorized to demand personal service or labor from the Puebloans, they often did.[53] As an additional burden, under the *repartimiento de indios* ("allocation of Indians," i.e., a forced labor system), Spanish officials could legally assign Puebloans to public works projects. Theoretically, the duration of the work was to be limited and they were to be paid for their labor. In reality, officials in New Mexico often ignored these regulations.[54] There was truth to the governors' accusations that the friars exploited Puebloan labor, just as there was truth to the friars' claims that the governors levied unfairly heavy demands for tribute and forced the Puebloans to provide unpaid labor. The Puebloans understood the hostile relationship between church and state and often used it to their advantage. They waited, for example, until a governor had fallen into disfavor before requesting compensation for their labor.[55]

The Pecos could not avoid the legal and illegal demands of Spanish officials, which changed the environment and their relationship to it. Spanish officials put the Puebloans to work digging irrigation canals, planting crops, and transporting goods. While building the church for Fray Andrés Juárez, the Pecos had acquired an array of carpentry skills. Soon, Pecos workmanship and Pecos lumber became a coveted resource throughout the colony. Correspondence between Governor López de Mendizábal and Diego González Bernal, the *alcalde mayor*, or district officer for the region encompassing Pecos Pueblo, refers to the carpenters of the pueblo. In 1660 the governor mentioned the "boards I ordered made and ready at Pecos this week."[56] Cutting timber for the church as well as for construction projects throughout the colony may have extended the cleared area around Pecos Pueblo or depleted some species, such as ponderosa pine, in the vicinity. Logging and building homes for the Spaniards kept the Pecos from tending their own fields and repairing their own pueblo.

Even more burdensome than physical labor were the Spanish demands for tribute of food stores. For many generations, Puebloan communities had survived frequent drought cycles by storing crop surpluses. The colonial tribute system threatened their resilience by redistributing the surpluses to colonists, who were dependent on Puebloan assistance to survive in the remote, arid region. Each Puebloan household owed a yearly tribute to the Spaniards consisting of a fanega of corn (1.6 bushels, about half of what would feed one person for an entire year) and a woven cotton blanket or deer or bison hide. The governor raised tribute levels in 1643 to one fanega and one blanket or hide each quarter, owed by each eligible individual, not household. Pueblos like Pecos also collected piñon nuts to satisfy tribute payments. In 1660, Governor Mendizábal wrote to Diego Bernal, complaining that "they have brought only twenty-three fanegas of piñon nuts" from Pecos, reminding Bernal that fifteen had yet to be delivered.[57] As the population declined at Pecos, meeting these demands became increasingly onerous. In an environment where the climate and growing season too often conspired against a successful harvest, the obligation to surrender part of their food in tribute payments created a precarious situation for the Pecos.

Probably the first Spaniard to receive Pecos Pueblo as an encomienda was Francisco Gómez, a soldier and colonist who arrived in New Mexico during Oñate's brief rule as governor. By the 1660s, his son, Francisco Gómez Robledo, had inherited the encomienda. Robledo also held shares in three other pueblo encomiendas—Taos, Shongopovi, and Acoma—but he amassed the most tribute from the Pecos. In the 1660s Robledo received "170 units per collection, or 340 per year, 'in buckskins, mantas, buffalo hides, and light and heavy buffalo or elkskins'" from Pecos.[58] In contrast, he received only fifty units from a half share in Acoma per year. Pedro Lucero de Godoy received tribute from twenty-four households at Pecos Pueblo, and the friars at the Pecos mission had access to tribute from ten households.[59] Caravans from Mexico, arriving around once every three years, brought needed supplies to the Franciscans and took back the livestock, hides, and piñon nuts that had been collected from the Puebloans.[60]

Puebloan cultural systems made Spanish efforts to dominate the Puebloans somewhat easier. Unlike the nomads on the nearby plains, the Puebloans' concentrated populations in settled farming communities enabled the Spanish governors to exert control and for the Franciscans to indoctrinate them. The Puebloans also faced more dire consequences if they attempted to resist. It was much easier to destroy the resources of a sedentary people—their fields and homes and stored foods—than those of a constantly moving population. Although the Spaniards attempted to convert the nomadic Apaches, it was not until the Apaches needed Spanish aid against the Comanches that the Spaniards enjoyed any sort of success.[61]

The Pecos could not avoid the Spaniards. The location of Pecos Pueblo—at the gateway to the plains, whence, the Spaniards quickly learned, came valuable bison hides, tallow, and meat—made it an irresistible target. It provided a starting point for exploration to the east and, once the capital moved to Santa Fe in 1610, stood between the capital and potential threats from the plains. Its large population and prosperous situation made it appealing to both Franciscans and secular officials. The Franciscans could save many souls at Pecos, and whoever received Pecos as an encomienda enjoyed substantial profits.

"There Is Not a Fanega of Maize or Wheat in All the Kingdom": *The Ravages of Famine and Raiding*

Each autumn, Fray Andrés Juárez watched from the doors of the church as a cavalcade of Plains Apaches arrived at Pecos with trains of dog sleds loaded with supplies and goods, setting up their tepees in the meadows east and south of the pueblo, preparing to trade. Amid the barking dogs and heaps of bison hides, Juárez saw the potential for gaining further converts. He wrote to the viceroy that "many times when [the Apaches] come they will enter the church and when they see there the *retablo* [painting] and the rest there is, the Lord will enlighten them so that they want to be baptized and converted to Our Holy Catholic Faith." Juárez seized the initiative and traveled onto the plains himself to meet the Apaches in their own territory.[62]

During Juárez's (mostly futile) attempts to bring Christianity to the Apaches, they remained on friendly terms as trading partners with the Pecos. As the seventeenth century progressed, however, their relationship changed. Accounts of Apache raiding in the colony appear in the first decade of the 1600s.[63] At Pecos, raiding became a frequent occurrence by the 1640s and 1650s and intensified in the 1670s.[64] The shift in the Apaches' relationship with the Pecos arose from the environmental and cultural changes sweeping the region. The resources brought by the Spaniards, such as sheep, cattle, and metal tools, proved powerful inducements to increase raiding. The Apaches could easily steal unguarded cattle, in particular. The Apaches' acquisition of the horse by the late 1600s also changed their relationship with the Pecos. The horse allowed the Apaches to expand their raiding capabilities. They could travel faster and take more with them. Pecos Pueblo was a tempting target, particularly with the increasing amounts of Spanish livestock and manufactured goods at the pueblo.[65] Mounted on horses, the Apaches struck quickly and then disappeared with their captured goods. In the year of 1640 alone, Apaches stole 20,000 fanegas of corn from the Puebloans and Spaniards of New Mexico.[66] As Spanish demands depleted surplus stores of corn that could be exchanged for other goods, some traditional trading partners resorted to raiding to maintain the expected supply. The Apaches were not united—some bands continued to trade peacefully while others raided—but those who did attack kept the colony in a constant state of fear. In addition, Spanish demand for deer, elk, and bison products meant the Pecos now had more at stake during the annual trade fairs with those Apaches who remained at peace. Tribute payments had depleted their trade stores of corn, yet the Spaniards still wanted bison hides and meat as well. Obtaining those may have reduced food supplies at Pecos Pueblo to an even greater extent.[67]

As the 1660s and 1670s progressed, Pecos and the other pueblos bowed under the combined pressure of Spanish tribute demands, forced labor, and Apache raiding. Drought during these decades worsened their plight. Fray Juan Bernal, agent of the Inquisition in New Mexico, sent a saturnine letter to his superiors in Mexico explaining why he could not send a prisoner to them:

> The whole land is at war with the very numerous nation of the heathen Apache Indians. . . . No road is safe. One travels them all at risk of life for the heathen are everywhere. They are a brave and bold people. They hurl themselves at danger like people who know not God, nor that there is a hell.
>
> The second calamity is that for three years no crop has been harvested. Last year, 1668, a great many Indians perished of hunger, lying dead along the roads, in the ravines, and in their hovels. . . . The same calamity still prevails, for, because there is no money, there is not a fanega of maize or wheat in all the kingdom.

Forced to subsist on cowhides, the Spaniards were suffering as well, Bernal stated.[68]

The famine that Bernal spoke of began in 1667 and, in some areas, lasted through 1672. As with most shortages, the famine did not affect everyone equally. Poorer Puebloans and Spanish settlers suffered to a greater extent than those who had managed to achieve some success in farming. The Franciscans, who had always maintained they hoarded grain and livestock precisely for times such as these and not for their own profit, initiated an extensive supply system.

They sent supplies from mission stores by heavily guarded wagon trains to Spanish settlements and pueblos in need of aid throughout the region. Pecos, the only pueblo that still had supplies to spare, sent "twenty fanegas of wheat" to the general food supply of the colony.[69]

Despite the aid of the Franciscans, the diets of the Puebloans, including the Pecos, declined in quality both during famines and when harvests improved. The demands of tribute and trade, increasing numbers of livestock that often trampled the fields of corn, and the loss of control of arable land depleted the Pecos's traditional food supply. Bone chemistry data from burials at Pecos Pueblo shows how these new stresses affected their diet. By 1675 the amounts of corn consumed had decreased. Wild plants such as nuts, berries, herbs, edible bark, and roots probably made up the difference, supplying perhaps 20 percent of the Pecos diet. Apache and Spanish demands for corn compelled the Pecos to turn to other food sources, while Spanish demands for hides required the Pecos to overhunt local herds of mule deer, perhaps decreasing populations to the point where venison no longer figured extensively in the Pecos diet.[70]

Although perhaps an exaggeration, Fray Juan Bernal's dismal description reveals how the imposition of Spanish rule combined with environmental conditions to disrupt the Puebloans' world. Pecos, for example, had weathered many droughts before without facing starvation because they maintained adequate surplus stores of corn and delegated men and women to seek wild plants and hunt animals at greater distances if necessary. Disease, which had disrupted labor networks and depleted the population, undermined the Puebloans' ability to obtain enough food. The Spanish horse gave their Apache enemies new speed and strength, and it increased the quantity of food and goods raiders could carry away. The Spaniards' demands for tribute and forced labor, which rose sharply in the mid-seventeenth century, also reduced the Puebloans' ability to provide for themselves. Some Puebloans may have found conversion an acceptable price in exchange for Spanish promises of protection against Apache raiders, but for most the conditions created widespread resentment. The Franciscans and their God were suppressing the natural religious order, rituals, and lifeways of the Puebloans and destabilizing their environment and their trade relationships with the nomadic people of the plains. The kachinas, forsaken by the Puebloans, were angry, vengeful, and required tribute in order to bring back rainfall and abundant crops. In 1680, the cumulative effect of these interdependent stressors reached the breaking point, and the Puebloans revolted, driving the Spaniards out of New Mexico.[71]

The success of the revolt depended on coordinated action between previously independent Puebloan communities united by the Tewa ceremonial leader El Popé at the San Juan Pueblo and other religious leaders and war captains. But despite the fact that many Puebloans joined together to oust the Spaniards, internal divisions remained. Among the Pecos, some warned Fray Fernando de Velasco, one of the friars at the Pecos mission, of the impending revolt several days in advance. The district governor of the Pecos carried the news from Fray

Fernando to Antonio de Otermín, the royal governor in Santa Fe, but he took no immediate action. The uprising unfolded in the eastern pueblos without opposition. Members of the Pecos who were determined to drive away the Spaniards killed Fray Juan de la Pedrosa, another friar at the pueblo, as well as a Spanish family of five. With the aid of members of the sympathetic faction at Pecos, Velasco fled in hopes of finding refuge at Galisteo, but Tanos rebels murdered him en route. A few days later, Pecos rebels joined with warriors from San Cristóbal, Galisteo, and other pueblos in an attack on Santa Fe, where they suffered heavy casualties. The terrified Spaniards who survived the attacks fled south to safety, leaving the Puebloans once more in sole possession of the territory.

El Popé and the other leaders of the rebellion arrived from the north and ordered the rebels to reject and destroy all trappings of the Spanish world. Those Puebloans who sympathized with the Spaniards and remained loyal Christians were silenced, driven away, or murdered. At Pecos, either the pueblo inhabitants themselves or El Popé's contingent set fire to the roof of the mission church. The wooden beams burned in the conflagration, bringing the roof crashing to the ground. When the ashes had cooled, the Pecos tore down portions of the high walls and the western side of the convento. The church that had stood for eighty years as a symbol of Spanish domination was now a burned ruin, tumbled onto the stones of the mesilla. In the coming weeks, the Pecos constructed a new kiva in the nearby corral with adobe salvaged from the church and repurposed in service to the revival of the ancient ways.[72]

As they clambered around the fallen adobe walls, the Pecos surveyed a landscape that no longer harbored Spanish interlopers, but that bore the unmistakable marks of almost a century of Spanish influence. Wagon tracks led to Santa Fe. Soil erosion along the banks of Glorieta Creek marked where cattle and sheep trampled and grazed, and the animals themselves clustered in large corrals to the south of the pueblo. European plants grew in the fields and gardens. Many resources—piñon nuts, deer hides, timber—had declined in the valley to satisfy Spanish demand. Despite resource depletion and the effects of livestock grazing, however, ecological damage in the valley and environs had not approached a critical level, as it would in the nineteenth century. The Pecos population had declined dramatically and no Spanish colonists had attempted to settle in the valley. Still, the Pecos environment had changed. Although some Puebloans wanted to completely erase all signs of the Spaniards from the land, there was no going back. Bleating *Churro* sheep, stalks of wheat, the desolating effects of smallpox—these had become familiar to the Pecos. They had not become Spaniards, and much of their surroundings remained familiar, but neither their culture nor their environment could revert to the days before Fray Andrés Juárez stood before them and offered them bread while speaking strange words to his God.

THREE | # Strife and Settlement on the Borderlands
1680–1821

CAÑON DE PECOS, 1815—Juan de Dios Peña straightened from his work, resting his shovel on the mound of dirt. The beginnings of a new acequia connecting his fields to the Pecos River lay before him, the result of his labors that morning. He and the other settlers on the Cañon de Pecos grant had possessed their new lands for only a few months, but they were preparing to plant crops and had started constructing homes. Shielding his eyes against the sun glare on the water, Peña stared down the river to the south. The Pecos Pueblo still stood on its mesilla, but by 1815, the year Peña moved to the Upper Pecos valley, only a few inhabitants remained in residence. Peña frowned as he contemplated the fertile lands in the ciénega by the Pecos River. A priest no longer presided over the Pecos church to direct farming for the mission, and with so few residents living in the pueblo, the Pecos hardly planted any crops there now. The ciénega was far superior to his own lands, and yet it was going to waste. Scuffing the toe of his boot in the dirt, Peña contemplated the possibility of appropriating some of the land. It would benefit the Crown, after all. With better land, he and the other settlers could raise more crops and help make New Mexico a prosperous colony. Pushing the matter to the back of his mind, Peña returned to his task. He wanted to finish the acequia that afternoon as tomorrow he planned to ride southeast to San Miguel del Vado, a trip of some twenty miles, to do some trading.

Much had changed in the Upper Pecos valley in the 135 years since the Puebloans rose in revolt in 1680. In the revolt's immediate aftermath, the Pecos destroyed some signs of Spanish control, but the Puebloans did not completely reject all Spanish influences. El Popé, the leader of the revolt, urged the Puebloans to give up everything introduced by the Spaniards, but they kept the livestock, the crops, and doubtless many of the implements the Spaniards had brought.[1] In the absence of Spanish control, the Pecos could use the livestock and food for their own benefit. Although they chose to keep some of the new resources brought by the Spaniards, many of them did not want to see the Spaniards ever again. In the triumphant days after the successful revolt, the Pecos probably never envisioned a time when Hispanic settlers would move into the valley and begin taking their land.[2]

Yet despite the revolt's success, many of the Pecos may have feared the Spaniards' return to the region, and events proved their apprehensions correct. The Puebloans succeeded in forcing the Spaniards out of New Mexico, but the Spaniards had no intention of permanently giving up the colony and its value as a military buffer zone against the threat of encroachment from French and British expansion in North America. Maintaining a precarious foothold in El Paso, the Spaniards prepared to reconquer the province. Don Diego de Vargas, described by historian John Kessell as "a strutting aristocrat hungry to perform glorious deeds in an inglorious age," brought the pueblos back under Spanish control in 1692 and suppressed another revolt in 1696.[3] Relations between the Spaniards and the Puebloans did not revert to their pre-revolt status, however. To avoid the discord and discontent that had led to their ouster in 1680, the mission friars adopted policies more tolerant of Puebloan religious ceremonies, and Spanish settlers did not resume the encomienda system or require tribute payments from the Puebloans. The resistance of the Apaches and Navajos to Spanish control and their strengthened trade alliances with the Puebloans tempered Spanish ambitions. Despite easier relations with Spanish settlers and missionaries, the Pecos failed to regain their earlier prosperity in the eighteenth century. Disease epidemics continued to reduce the pueblo's population, and a new people invaded the region—the Comanches.

Comanche raiders began terrorizing Pecos Pueblo in the early 1700s, attacking people working in the fields by the Pecos River and driving away the pueblo's cattle and horses. The Spanish governor sent some troops to the pueblo's aid, but the Comanches maintained a powerful influence over New Mexican affairs throughout the eighteenth century. The Comanche raids delayed Hispanic settlements in the Upper Pecos valley and forced the Pecos to remain close to their pueblo, reducing their impact on the surrounding environment. Not until Spanish officials finalized peace accords with the Comanches in 1786 did the situation change. Freed from the threat of Comanche raids, Hispanos such as Peña petitioned the Crown for lands in the northern reaches of the colony. By that time, few Pecos remained in their ancient pueblo. As more Hispanos came to the area, land use in the valley intensified once more, but it assumed a different form from the Pecos's earlier practices. Peña and the other settlers expected to turn the valley into a prosperous settlement with many individual homes, gardens, and fields. He wanted to provide for his family, but he also desired to acquire capital through trade—with Mexico, the Comanches, and even the forbidden Americans to the east. The Pecos in the late seventeenth century lived in an environment that had been changed through Spanish contact but still bore many of the same patterns of land use that had persisted through several centuries—human population concentrated in the pueblo, dry and irrigated agricultural fields scattered throughout the valley, and camps of Apaches arriving to trade. The arrival of the Comanches disrupted these patterns. Later, peace with the Comanches allowed the establishment of a new Hispanic community in the Upper Pecos valley, created by Peña and other settlers.

"A Cross Was Left for Them, Placed as a Sign of Peace": *The Spanish Reconquest of New Mexico*

Under Vargas's leadership, the Spaniards who returned to New Mexico in 1692 were determined to avoid repeating the mistakes of their predecessors. They did not want resentful, bitter subjects who plotted their overthrow. They wanted peace in the colony, now formally termed the *Nuevo México* province—peace that would allow them to reestablish their livestock industry and farming enterprises and encourage settlers to move north to the region. Vargas still contemplated using force to achieve this peace, but when he reached Pecos, the pueblo residents fled, remembering previous violent encounters with the Spanish. Unable to attack or lay siege to an empty pueblo, Vargas captured several Pecos, including an elderly woman named Hobe-wagi. Hobe-wagi told Vargas that many of the older residents of Pecos Pueblo wanted to meet peacefully with the Spaniards, but younger members of the pueblo insisted that abandoning their home was better than acquiescing to Spanish control once again. Vargas stayed at the pueblo for several days, hoping the Pecos would return, and he kept Hobe-wagi with the twenty-seven other captives his soldiers had detained. Vargas eventually gave up waiting. He set his captives free and departed for Santa Fe without destroying or damaging the Pecos's home or the plentiful crops and stores of vegetables and corn, a calculated decision to bring the Pecos to his side. "A cross was left for them, placed as a sign of peace," Vargas recorded. Although Vargas had been willing to force the Pecos to comply, the lack of opposition required him to consider other strategies.[4]

After receiving the submission of several other pueblos, Vargas returned to Pecos Pueblo. This time the Pecos welcomed Vargas and his men. The shift in the pueblo's position reflected the flexibility and factionalism of Puebloan politics, which differed dramatically from Spanish practices. For example, El Popé, the leader of the 1680 revolt, disparaged the Spaniards but attempted to consolidate his power in a Spanish manner. He tried to make himself the sole leader of the Puebloans, bringing them all into a unified conglomerate.[5] The Puebloans, though, had never operated in such a manner. Their slow decision-making process, in which many people discussed potential actions and one person's decision did not necessarily bind another, offered flexibility and adaptability but also limited the Puebloans to some extent. The centralized Spanish power network allowed them to make decisions faster, relying on one authority figure who, although he answered to others, could also act at their behest.[6] When the Spaniards vacated the colony in 1680, internal divisions returned among the Puebloans.

Hobe-wagi's explanation to Vargas of strife within Pecos Pueblo—of older members who wished to accommodate the Spanish versus younger members who wanted to resist—reflected these political and social divisions. Vargas attempted to exploit these differences at Pecos and gain firm control of the pueblo after receiving its capitulation. He installed a number of political figures, including Juan de Ye, a resident of Pecos, as the Pecos governor. Juan de Ye proved to be an invaluable ally of Vargas, warning him of potential rebellions and bringing 140 Pecos warriors to help the Spaniards retake Santa Fe. He lost his life in an attempt to negotiate a peaceful agreement between the Spaniards and the rebellious Taos Pueblo.[7] The Spaniards retained the persistent loyalty of many Pecos, especially traditional farmers, who included leaders such as Juan de Ye. But a faction of younger Pecos—traders and hunters with ties to the plains—continued to resist cooperation and joined ongoing plots of rebellion with like-minded people from other pueblos. Clashes between Pecos sympathetic to the Spaniards and those opposed approached civil war on multiple occasions in the closing years of the seventeenth century. But a failed revolt in 1696 was the last meaningful effort to turn back the tide of Spanish settlers and return the province to Puebloan control. Many Pecos participated in the revolt, and the rift in the community further weakened the Pecos's position and set the stage for further decline in the eighteenth century.[8] Indeed, the Pecos Pueblo's continued loss of population and power contributed to the willingness of some Pecos to allow the Spaniards to reestablish their presence in the valley.

The twelve years between the 1680 revolt and the reconquest had not been easy ones. Over the previous century, the Spaniards had severely disrupted the Puebloan way of life. Merely removing the Spaniards did not ensure a return to older ways, particularly during a time of violence and internal strife. The diseases the Spaniards had brought did not disappear either. The overall Puebloan population in New Mexico declined from 17,000 to 14,000 between 1680 and 1700.[9] The population continued to fall at Pecos Pueblo, too. The Spaniards also disrupted trade, which had always been important to Pecos. The Pecos did not find it easy to resume old trading patterns. The Spaniards left behind livestock and goods after the revolt, but also took with them the protections offered by their soldiers and their guns. Some evidence suggests that in the absence of the Spaniards, the easternmost pueblos of Pecos and Taos established a thriving livestock trade with the Apaches and other Plains Indian tribes, using the Spanish horses hastily abandoned in 1680.[10] But other evidence points to an increasingly violent relationship that disrupted potential trade. Juan de Ye apparently pleaded with Vargas to help Pecos reestablish their trade fairs with the Apaches. When several Apaches came to survey the situation, Vargas did everything he could to convince them of the Spaniards' honorable intentions. By the end of August 1694, trade fairs were held regularly in the summer and fall at Pecos Pueblo with

Apaches, Spaniards, and pueblo residents participating in the exchange of goods that supported the overall economic success and stability of the region.[11]

Whether or not the Puebloans did establish a livestock trade of their own, Vargas found too few livestock when he returned to satisfy Spanish ambitions. Many livestock may have been killed after the revolt or the Puebloans may simply have allowed the herds to decline to levels they could easily maintain. In any case, few animals remained at the pueblos, and Vargas distributed more than 6,000 head of livestock, including 4,000 sheep, to the settlers who came with him. Vargas also gave 200 head of sheep to the Franciscans to aid in rebuilding their missions at the pueblos, including the one at Pecos. These efforts did much to reestablish the population of domestic animals, but several decades passed before numbers were high enough to renew livestock exports to Mexico that were common before the revolt.[12]

Although the Spaniards did not reinstitute the encomienda and tribute system, they did pressure the Pecos to work for them. Often the tasks related to the Pecos's carpentry skills and the timber supplies in the area. In 1723 a judicial review of governor don Félix Martínez's administration revealed that he owed the Pecos payment for two thousand boards they had cut and hauled for him, as well as the physical labor that had taken the Pecos away from tending their own crops.[13] A 1776 account by Fray Francisco Atanasio Domínguez, a visiting Franciscan sent by the Crown to report on the spiritual and economic progress of the missions, recorded that "most of [the Pecos] are good carpenters" and that the "sierra provides them with timber."[14] The Spaniards also had not lost their desire for piñon nuts. A letter from Fray Manuel de San Juan Nepomuceno y Trigo in 1754 refers to the piñon trees in the mountains between Pecos and Santa Fe that "every three years affords delight to the taste with [their] crop of piñones."[15]

The return of a Franciscan friar also placed renewed labor demands on the Pecos. Fray Diego de la Casa Zeinos resumed the ministry at Pecos in 1694 and oversaw the construction of a new, temporary church that utilized the north wall of the old church, still standing over seven feet high. In 1705 Fray José de Arránegui compelled the Pecos to build a more permanent, but smaller, church structure on top of the original mission church ruins. The Pecos also repaired and improved the convento and corrals.[16] They constructed new corral complexes south of the church to hold livestock, perhaps adding onto corrals that survived the revolt. One set of rooms probably served as mangers for oxen and had a gate that opened onto the fields around the pueblo.[17] Archaeologists have located the remains of a stone corral on the west side of Glorieta Creek, and although it is not clear exactly when the corral was built, it is definitely of post-revolt construction.[18]

The Franciscans required the Pecos to once again plant crops for them in addition to their other labors. Fray Manuel de San Juan Nepomuceno y Trigo recorded that the Pecos "sow for the father four fanegas of wheat and one cuartilla of corn. . . . They pay no obventions, but they furnish for the assistance of the father and the convent four boys, a bell-ringer, a porter, a cook, three grinding-women and the wood needed for use."[19] The Pecos had not, of course, abandoned agriculture after the revolt. When Vargas came to Pecos Pueblo, he noted it was "well supplied with all sorts of vegetables and maize." Sending his men to search for the recalcitrant Pecos, Vargas recorded how the "squads spread over the mountain and range bordering the milpas [fields] across the river from the pueblo."[20] With the return of the friars, the Pecos either planted additional fields or dedicated existing fields to the friar's sustenance. Evidence of other agricultural pursuits surfaces occasionally. A report by Fray Juan Miguel Menchero in 1744 refers to Pecos Pueblo as having "one hundred and twenty-five families. . . . A river flows through the settlement, and on its banks there are plum trees of the kind called in Spain 'yolk of egg,' whose fruit is very savory and pleasant to the taste."[21] Apparently these were plum trees planted on either the banks of Glorieta Creek or the Pecos River. New food sources for the Pecos such as fruit, spring wheat, and produce from kitchen gardens provided additional variety and security for the community's ongoing viability in a time of change. Although some Pecos may have viewed the produce as unwelcome evidence of Spanish influence, the Pecos could not afford to reject it.[22]

For a brief period, the presence of the Franciscans at Pecos Pueblo resulted in an increase in the numbers of livestock at the pueblo and possibly a slight intensification in farming. The Franciscans of the eighteenth century, though, did not possess the same power as their predecessors. Conflict continued between the friars and the governors, but new attacks on Franciscan power appeared as well. The bishop in Durango took an interest in New Mexico and began arguing that the province would fare better under his control. He accused the friars of charging ridiculous prices for marriages and burials. They still had not learned the Puebloans' languages and had failed to truly instill Christianity in their charges. Many of the bishop's allegations bore a measure of truth. After a brief, intensified campaign against Puebloan religion, the Franciscans stopped attempting to eradicate traditional Puebloan lifestyles. By the 1720s, a policy of accommodation became the norm. The barriers separating Puebloans and Spaniards, which had been so important to Oñate a century before, eroded. Partly, the Spaniards feared inciting the Puebloans into mounting another rebellion. But the presence of a new enemy—one that targeted Spaniards and Puebloans alike—also brought them together. As the Comanches moved from the Great Plains proper into the southwestern plains, Spanish settlers, Franciscans, and Puebloans had to join in common defense or perish.[23]

"I Have Fortified These Two Pueblos of Pecos and Galisteo": The Growing Power of the Comanches

The consequences of Puebloan resistance in 1680 and 1696 did not end at the borders of New Mexico. Many Puebloans, disillusioned after the failure of the 1696 revolt, fled New Mexico and joined the Apaches on the plains. The influence of Puebloan culture had already affected the Apaches, who had adopted irrigated farming beginning in the 1500s. The addition of many Puebloans in the late 1600s accelerated the process. The Apaches expanded their territory, moving farther onto the central plains, where they encountered the Comanches, who were migrating south from present-day Wyoming. The Comanches were eastern Shoshones who had split from their parent tribe and were in the midst of transforming into a pastoral society, having acquired horses from the Utes around 1690. The Pueblo Revolt had hastened the dispersal of Spanish horses across the Southwest when fleeing colonists left many of their livestock behind. Apaches then obtained some of these horses through roundups of the remaining herds and trading with the Puebloans. The Utes, who successfully bred large herds from the horses they obtained from Spaniards in the mid-seventeenth century and the dispersal of livestock after the revolt, soon had enough to trade to their Shoshonean relatives, the Comanches. Horses gave the Comanches military power and mobility, allowing them to claim territory on the plains. The Comanches called horses "the God-dog." Less vulnerable to attacks and able to hunt and travel more easily, the Comanche population increased from around 7,000 in 1690 to around 20,000 by 1786—a dramatically different experience from the sharp population decline the Puebloans suffered following Spanish colonization.[24]

Soon, Comanche raiding became a dire threat to the New Mexican colony and the surrounding region and to Pecos and Galisteo in particular. The presence of large livestock herds in New Mexico, especially after the Spaniards' return, provided an incentive for the Comanches to extend their territory from their hunting grounds on the southern plains into Spanish-occupied lands. Accounts of Comanche raiding first appear in New Mexico around 1706.[25] The Apaches, who had kept up an alternating policy of raiding and trading with the Spaniards and the Puebloans, found themselves under a sustained attack. They began retreating from the plains and appealed to the Spaniards for aid. The Apaches promised to convert to Christianity and maintain settled villages if the Spaniards kept the Comanches away. The prospect of having a friendly Indian group as a buffer between their northern provinces and threats such as the Comanches or the French appealed to the Spaniards. In 1719, 1723, and 1724 expeditions of Spanish soldiers and native auxiliaries set out for the plains but failed to prevent Comanche attacks. Hesitant Spanish officials in Mexico City did not fully support the policy, and by the late 1720s the Comanches had driven the Apaches from the plains. Several Apache bands settled near Pecos, reflecting social ties stemming from years of trade with the pueblo.[26]

The Comanches soon dominated the southern plains. Their reliance on buffalo hunting meant they needed to supplement their diet with carbohydrates—food the Puebloans and Spanish settlers possessed. The Utes, living in the mountain valleys and plains to the north and west of New Mexico, allied with the Comanches in 1706 and joined them on their raiding expeditions.[27] The Comanches also developed a profitable trade to the east with such groups as the Wichitas and Taovayas, who in turn passed goods into French Louisiana. The Comanches needed livestock and enslaved people for this trade, which they could also obtain in New Mexico.[28]

Pecos Pueblo's position on the eastern border, as well as its close ties with the Apaches, made it a favorite target for the Comanches. By the mid-1730s, the pueblo faced endemic raiding. In 1746 a Comanche attack resulted in several people killed and horses stolen. In 1748, the same year an epidemic struck, the Comanches, Pecos, and Spaniards fought before the walls of the pueblo. Between 1744 and 1749, the Comanches killed 150 Pecos. The Spaniards recognized that losing Pecos would leave Santa Fe open to attacks from the plains, and in the 1740s, a Spanish squadron took up residence west of the convento, although they often had to leave the pueblo to defend other settlements.[29] In 1750, Governor Tomás Vélez Cachupín alerted the viceroy of the defensive measures he had installed at Pecos Pueblo and nearby Galisteo Pueblo. "I find it necessary to garrison them with thirty presidial soldiers," he wrote, adding that he had "fortified these two pueblos of Pecos and Galisteo with earthworks and towers at the gates capable of defending them against these enemies."[30] Archaeologists have found evidence of construction that could relate to the garrison and may have been the small presidio. Located between the church and Glorieta Creek, the evidence consists of a compound of Spanish construction with several small corrals.[31]

The escalation of violence in New Mexico in the eighteenth century altered not only relations between the Puebloans and the Spaniards but their relationship with the land as well. Deep canyons, the steep walls of mesas, dense concentrations of trees—these landforms now held the potential for both defense and sudden attack. Although raiding had been a component of inter-tribal relations in northern New Mexico for centuries, the constant pressure of Comanche and Ute raiding in the eighteenth century strengthened the associations between the environment, fear, and death. Historian Ned Blackhawk argues that "by the mid-eighteenth century the colony's relations of violence had become so normative that the physical and natural worlds were now imbued with violent meanings."[32] The piñon-juniper forests around Pecos, for example, not only offered wood and food to the pueblo's inhabitants but also offered cover for raiders sneaking up on the pueblo. Under Comanche pressure, the sphere of human influence on the surrounding environment near the pueblo diminished—fewer livestock grazed along the river banks, and fields farther away from the pueblo lay fallow.

Not all relations between the Comanches and the Puebloans consisted of violence, however. Like the Apaches, the Comanches also sought to trade with the Puebloans. Taos and Pecos became important trading centers for the Comanches when they were not attacking them. Puebloans and Spanish colonists developed a brisk trade of horses, knives, clothing, and manufactured goods for human captives and animal hides supplied by the Comanches. The Comanches also became a source of manufactured goods, including guns, for New Mexico. The Comanches obtained British and French guns through a variety of channels and soon possessed enough surplus to trade the guns in turn. These, along with horses, mules, and enslaved people, changed hands at seasonal trade fairs.[33]

The Comanches' ties to the French territory of Louisiana worried the Spaniards, who constantly feared an attempted French takeover of their northern colonies. To the colonists' frustration, any news of French incursions on the plains created greater excitement in Mexico City than the deaths of hundreds at the hands of the Comanches. Many Spanish officials recognized, however, that it was often French traders providing the Comanches with the weapons that made them so deadly.[34] During the 1700s, several Frenchmen made the long journey over the plains to New Mexico in pursuit of trade, not territory. In 1739 French traders arrived in Santa Fe via Taos. Others followed, including four who arrived at Pecos Pueblo in 1750. These Frenchmen probably traveled on a path similar to what later became the Santa Fe Trail. New Mexicans, hungry for manufactured goods, welcomed the French. Governor Gaspar Domingo de Mendoza entertained the first party of French traders who arrived in New Mexico in 1739, and he sent them off with a list of goods the province urgently required. When suspicious Spanish officials heard of the contact, they made it clear that Frenchmen who came in the future would be removed precipitously. Mendoza's successor, Tomás Vélez Cachupín, followed Spanish policy and arrested any French traders who arrived.[35]

Vélez Cachupín proved to be an able administrator and pursued peace with the Comanches. Spanish policy toward Comanche attacks had been inconsistent, depending on the governor in office at the time. Vélez Cachupín negotiated a treaty in 1752 that gave the Comanches open access to the trade fairs at Pecos Pueblo. The treaty also terminated Spanish aid to the Apaches, and the remaining bands retired from the Llano Estacado and resettled near Pecos. The Apaches and Pecos apparently grew quite close at this time, and when the Apaches "went for their brief hunting forays they often left their women and children behind in the town." The Utes also formed an alliance with the Spaniards after their accord with the Comanches fell apart. The 1752 peace was kept until Vélez Cachupín departed, whereupon relations with the Comanches degenerated into raiding and violence once more. Vélez Cachupín reestablished peace upon his return in 1762, but when he permanently left New Mexico in 1767 the peace broke once again and was not reestablished for twenty years.[36]

"This Pueblo Is Very Much Besieged by the Enemy":
The Effects of Comanche Raiding at Pecos Pueblo

The failure of the accords between the Comanches and the Spaniards had devastating consequences for New Mexican residents. Settlers abandoned villages and ranchos under the pressure of Comanche raids. The numbers of livestock in the province declined as the Comanches stole large herds. By the 1760s, accounts of the fall trade fairs at Pecos disappear from Spanish records.[37] Sporadic but continuous raiding kept the inhabitants of the pueblo in a constant state of terrified uncertainty. The Spaniards in Santa Fe tried to help Pecos Pueblo as their limited manpower permitted. On March 10, 1769, reports of a potential Comanche attack galvanized *alcalde mayor* Tomás de Sena, who hurried to Pecos Pueblo with a squad of soldiers. The Pecos, thinking the threat had disappeared, released the stock from the sheltering corrals near the pueblo. The Comanches struck immediately. Four Pecos died, and Sena recorded that the Comanches "did run off 42 horses and kill part of the cattle, while the cattle still in the corrals were unharmed."[38]

Besides stealing livestock from the pueblo, the Comanches also made it dangerous for the Pecos to farm in their fields by the Pecos River. In September 1771, when the wheat was ready for harvest, a squad of Spanish soldiers escorted the Pecos to their fields. The Comanches attacked, but the Pecos and their Spanish protectors managed to retreat to the pueblo with both the wheat and livestock. The Pecos were not always so lucky. In August 1774, one hundred Comanches attacked the Pecos working in their milpas. Nine died, and the Comanches captured seven others.[39]

The cumulative effects of raiding wrecked the Pecos's daily lives. Fray Francisco Atanasio Domínguez, touring New Mexico in 1776, recorded the sufferings of the people of the province. He included a lengthy account of conditions at Pecos Pueblo:

> The Indians have arable lands in all the four principal directions, but only those which lie to the north, partly east, enjoy irrigation. The rest are dependent on rain. These irrigated lands are of no use today because this pueblo is so very much besieged by the enemy, and even those dependent on rain which are at a distance cannot be used. Therefore, but a very small part remains for them. Since this is dependent on rain, it has been a failure because of the drought of the past years, and so they have nothing left. As a result, what few crops there usually are do not last even to the beginning of a new year from the previous October, and hence these miserable wretches are tossed about like a ball in the hands of fortune.
>
> On the other hand, Governor don Pedro Fermin de Mendinueta, Knight [of the Order of Santiago], has come to their aid with twelve cows, which, added to eight old ones they had before (which were all the enemies had left them), make twenty. As for horses, they have twelve sorry nags all together when they once had a very great number.[40]

Comanche depredations forced the Pecos to abandon their irrigated fields in the ciénega of the Pecos River northeast of the pueblo. The raids also completely demolished the livestock herds at the pueblo, which had once probably numbered in the hundreds.

Periodic disease epidemics continued to ravage the pueblo, compounding the effects of the Comanche hostilities. Spanish burial records from the Pecos mission record population losses correlating with ten epidemics in the period from Vargas's reconquest in the 1690s up to 1821. An epidemic struck in 1695, some type of fever that claimed older Pecos in particular. Nine years later, in 1704, another epidemic occurred, taking eighteen members of the pueblo. A 1728 measles epidemic claimed fifty-six lives. Scarcely over a year later, in 1730, another outbreak, possibly smallpox, took another fifteen. Smallpox epidemics followed at ten-year intervals, in 1738, 1748, and a possible outbreak in 1759. A 1780 epidemic of smallpox occurred throughout New Mexico, killing over 5,000 Puebloans, including some at Pecos.[41]

The cumulative effects of these epidemics were devastating. The loss of adults depleted the Pecos's ability to farm and hunt. The deaths of children, which increased in later epidemics, precluded population recovery. In 1692, the population was about 1,500. Two detailed censuses completed in the eighteenth century document the subsequent sharp decline. By 1750, only 449 people lived at Pecos Pueblo. In 1790, only 152 remained.[42] Although the Spaniards introduced a smallpox vaccine to New Mexico in 1804, by then it was already too late.[43]

The Pecos had few weapons against disease, but they often took up arms and joined the Spaniards in fighting the Comanches. Spanish forces always consisted of both soldiers and native auxiliaries and sometimes other allied warriors such as Apaches or Utes. Spanish policy prohibited providing guns to Puebloan subjects, but officials often ignored the regulations. Still, the expeditions could hardly mount a serious attack on the formidable Comanches. The Spaniards scored occasional victories, but frequent defeats or inaction negated their effect. As the continuing deaths and attacks at Pecos Pueblo attest, Spanish attempts at defending New Mexico failed miserably. Indeed, despite numerous efforts to fortify their frontier, the Spanish military never had a hope of defending the vast borders of the province with the inadequate forces allotted to them.[44]

The intensified Comanche raiding and depopulation at Pecos in the two decades following 1767 reduced the effects of humans and domesticated animals on the Pecos environment. The accounts of Comanche raiding reveal that in 1769 the Pecos had about 42 horses and an unidentified number of cattle.[45] All of these livestock concentrated in the area around the pueblo, extending down to Glorieta Creek and perhaps on the other side of the arroyo. As Comanche raids worsened, the Pecos probably kept the livestock close to the pueblo to avoid losing them during attacks. This action contributed to continuing erosion along Glorieta Creek and on the mesilla. The Pecos also abandoned numerous fields due to the persistent raiding, and invasive weed species grew in the disturbed soil. Obtaining sufficient water also became a problem. In his 1776 report to the Crown, Fray Francisco Atanasio Domínguez commented that "along the small plain between the sierra and the pueblo a very good river of good water and many delicious trout runs from north to south, but the water is not taken for use in the pueblo because it is about half a league away and there is very great danger from the Comanches. Therefore they have opened some wells of reasonably good water below the rock, and that is used for drinking and other purposes."[46]

The Pecos continued to farm closer to the pueblo, however. Domínguez provided a detailed description of the various milpas about a quarter of a league from the pueblo that he observed in 1776. He noted five plots of varying size: a non-irrigated kitchen garden for green vegetables below the cemetery to the west, a large, non-irrigated milpa north of the kitchen garden, and another beyond it that received irrigation from the creek. A fourth, large milpa dependent on rain lay beyond the kitchen garden to the west, and to the south, another non-irrigated milpa. He remarked, "I give no account of their crops because the Indians give me none. Indeed, they do say uproariously that wheat, maize, etc., are sown, except for chile, and that a sufficient amount is harvested. For the present the aforesaid plant them for themselves, and when there is a father, they do the work for him."[47]

Spanish settlement of the Upper Pecos valley, which later brought higher numbers of people and livestock to the area once again, remained out of the question. Men such as Juan Peña did not care to risk their lives by settling in an area preyed on by Comanches. Although some Apache bands came to live in the area, they concentrated on hunting and gathering and did not establish any permanent settlements. Overall, the second half of the eighteenth century witnessed a diminished human presence in the Upper Pecos valley. The remaining Pecos experienced a landscape that bore the evidence of decades of Comanche raiding—abandoned fields, only a few remaining cattle and horses, and the constant fear of wondering when Comanches might appear out of the trees or come galloping along the banks of the river.

"They Know Now More than Ever the Truth of Our Peace": The Comanche Peace of 1786

Just when it appeared that Pecos Pueblo might collapse entirely, the situation began to improve. Realizing they could not defeat the Comanches, the Spaniards attempted to build a strong trade relationship with them instead. Through trade, the Spaniards hoped to make the Comanches reliant on Spanish goods and thus unlikely to threaten their suppliers—a policy often employed by the French and British elsewhere in North America.[48] The victory of Juan Bautista de Anza in 1779 over Cuerno Verde, a Comanche war leader, gave the Spaniards a starting point for negotiations. Renewed war with tribes to the east and several smallpox epidemics had recently raged throughout the area inhabited by the Comanches, known as Comanchería, making them more amenable to peace. In addition, the American Revolutionary War drew French and British traders to the east and away from their trade with the Comanches. Although the process took almost a decade, in 1786 Ecueracapa, a prominent Comanche political figure, arrived in Santa Fe as the spokesperson for the Comanches, charged with negotiating a peace. Shortly before his arrival, Comanches had once again raided Pecos Pueblo. Ecueracapa executed the leaders of the raid to demonstrate Comanche goodwill.[49]

The Comanches entered the negotiations as the stronger party. Among a series of demands that gave the Comanches license to trade when and where they wanted in eastern New Mexico, Ecueracapa requested, once again, "the establishment of fairs and free trade with Pecos." He also required safe passage through Pecos to Santa Fe and the termination of the Spaniards' peaceful relations with the Apaches. After their first meeting, with conversation smoothed by the consumption of fine chocolate, Anza moved the treaty negotiations to Pecos Pueblo. For three days, while the leaders discussed the terms of the peace, Pecos, Comanches, and Spaniards mingled in the meadow east of the pueblo. Numerous Comanche bands arrived and camped in the vicinity. Anza formally opened a trade fair upon the conclusion of negotiations, admonishing all parties to behave themselves. After a successful afternoon of trading, Anza commented that the Comanches "proclaimed publicly that they know now more than ever the truth of our peace."[50]

The Comanche peace ushered in a brief period of prosperity for Pecos Pueblo. Seasonal trade fairs occurred once more. Along with Taos, Pecos served as the primary point of contact with the Comanches. Puebloan traders sought horses in particular. The Comanches "traded so many horses that Taos and Pecos were soon reported having 'a considerable number.'" Pecos Pueblo also served as a meeting place for Comanche and Spanish emissaries. Jupes and Yamparikas, two divisions of the Comanches, came to the pueblo in 1787, also seeking a treaty with the Spaniards, as the first had primarily been negotiated with the Kotsotekas. Various intermediaries who could translate for the Spaniards and Comanches took up residence at the pueblo, including José Mares, a plains explorer who appeared in the 1790 Pecos census.[51] Peace did bring an end to Pecos Pueblo's friendly relations with the Apaches, however. The Comanches demanded that the Spaniards join them in making war on the Apaches, who became the common enemy of Spaniards, Pueblos, Utes, and Comanches alike.[52]

Spanish officials deluded themselves into believing peace with the Comanches had given their empire a nation of subject Indians between its northern provinces and the encroaching United States. In 1803, the United States purchased the Louisiana Territory, and Spain regarded the expansionist ambitions of the new nation with alarm. The Americans believed the Louisiana Territory extended far to the west—much farther than the Spanish Crown was willing to concede. Spanish officials hoped the Comanches would serve as a buffer, preventing American expansion. It became apparent, however, that the Comanches did not consider themselves subjects of Spain. They accepted Spanish gifts—a heavy burden for the poor provinces of New Mexico and Texas—but did not deem themselves bound to Spanish politics. Instead, they cultivated trade relationships with the

Americans to obtain the manufactured goods that New Mexico and Texas could not provide.[53]

The 1786 peace brought some changes to Pecos Pueblo and the surrounding environment, but it did not inaugurate a long-lasting revival of the pueblo. Although the number of livestock increased due to trade fairs, the numbers never reached seventeenth- and early eighteenth-century numbers. A few Pecos families resumed farming in the ciénega, but much of the land remained fallow. The small number of inhabitants remaining in the pueblo—only 152 by 1790—no longer needed as many fields or livestock. The diminishing presence of Franciscans at Pecos also contributed to the decline in agricultural and livestock production. Despite the physical presence of the church, friars came to Pecos irregularly during the eighteenth century and never stayed long. Although they were supposed to live at the pueblo, the friars often stayed in the colonial population center of Santa Fe and visited the pueblo at infrequent intervals. After the peace, the growing Hispanic population in the area captured the majority of the friars' attention, and their presence at the Mission Nuestra Señora de los Ángeles at Pecos continued to wane. In 1782 the Franciscans formally declared Pecos Pueblo a *visita* of Santa Fe, meriting only the occasional services of a visiting friar.[54]

While the peace treaty did not intensify land use at the pueblo, it created an opening for Hispanic settlement. As historian Robert MacCameron argues, peace with nomadic tribes such as the Comanches ended a cyclical pattern of environmental change on the edges of the New Mexican frontier. Places like the Upper Pecos valley had long experienced fluctuating intensity of land use, reflecting periods of defense when people could not freely exploit resources and periods of decreased hostilities when land use could expand. The larger population centers of Santa Fe and Albuquerque, which did not suffer as much from Comanche raiding, experienced a more linear, dramatic pattern of environmental change during the colonial period. After the Comanche peace, environmental change in the Upper Pecos valley ceased fluctuating and intensified as Hispanic settlers began to claim the land for themselves.[55]

"We Have Registered a Place That Today Is Barren and Unsettled": *Hispanic Settlement in the Upper Pecos Valley*

With the Comanche threat removed, Hispanos moved beyond established Spanish towns and formed new communities on the northern and eastern borders of the province. Men like Juan de Dios Peña looked to these regions and envisioned the possibility of forming prosperous farming and ranching communities. The diminished power of the Franciscans also opened areas to settlers who no longer had to compete with the friars' monopoly on arable lands or their large livestock herds. Hispanic population expansion proved to have more lasting consequences for Pecos Pueblo and its environment than the brief resumption of trade with the Comanches. In the final years of the eighteenth century, a new system of land ownership and use arrived in the Upper Pecos valley.

Pecos and Spanish conceptions of land ownership bore little resemblance to each other when contact first occurred in the sixteenth century. Over the succeeding years, a system ascribing ownership to the Puebloans evolved based on a conglomeration of Spanish legal traditions that became locally accepted practice in New Mexico by the mid-1700s. Technically, the Spanish Crown never decreed that the Puebloans owned any land. However, as vassals of the Spanish Crown, they theoretically could possess land, and the Spaniards were obligated to protect their wards from disposing of that land to their own detriment. The initial Spanish policy of keeping settlers and Puebloans separated resulted in the notion that Spanish settlers could not occupy the four leagues surrounding a pueblo or use them for grazing livestock (a league equals 2.6 miles). By the 1700s everyone in New Mexico—including the Puebloans themselves—had come to believe that a pueblo actually owned these four leagues. Whether or not the Spanish Crown had ever intentionally granted the leagues, they became Puebloan property in the minds of everyone concerned. As historian G. Emlen Hall says, "Ironically, in Hispanic eyes New Mexico pueblos came to own only what non-Indians could not acquire."[56]

The concept of the pueblo league, or grant, introduced foreign ideas of land ownership to Puebloan society. Although certain people or families may have controlled land, and the pueblos probably occupied recognized territories, formal, legal measures of that land did not exist, nor the idea that the pueblo as a whole "owned" a piece of property. Hispanic land practice, however, did make such distinctions through a mix of communal and individual ownership. The Spanish Crown awarded grants to settlers and within each grant, officials parceled out individual pieces of property. The grants also included large pieces of communal land for grazing, hunting, and foraging activities. Some Spanish land grants were expressly for grazing purposes while others were community grants, meant for the establishment of a permanent village.[57]

Peña and the other settlers who began moving to the Upper Pecos valley expected to make full use of the land—in their own individual, irrigated fields and also by grazing their animals in the surrounding meadows and forests, which also provided ample timber and firewood. By the beginning of the nineteenth century, the Pecos no longer used all the arable land available to them, particularly the fertile fields by the Pecos River. In 1731, Hispanos began using the term *sobrantes*, meaning "extra" or "surplus" for these "unused Pueblo Indian lands." Because these lands often were the best in any given area, they tempted incoming settlers. Settlers argued that if a pueblo was not using the land it should be given to someone who would.[58]

The Pecos ciénega was not in immediate danger from the first Hispanic settlers who came to the valley. The San Miguel del Vado grant, awarded to a group of colonists in 1794 who quickly founded a village of the same name, was about twenty miles downriver, southeast of the pueblo. Although the settlers did not threaten Pecos lands, they did threaten its status as the gateway to the plains. Located slightly closer to the plains, the new village replaced Pecos Pueblo as the primary eastern point of call for Comanches and other traders. Not only its location, but the people who inhabited San Miguel made it attractive. Some of them were *genízaros*—freed enslaved people of mixed tribal derivation and their descendants. Members of the settlement understood the Comanche language and perhaps even possessed kinship ties with the Comanches. Residents of villages like San Miguel also ventured out onto the plains to trade with the Comanches rather than waiting for the Comanches to come to them. Known as *comancheros*, they met with the inhabitants of Comanche *rancherías* (small rural settlements) far from Spanish officials and their taxes and regulations. *Ciboleros*, Hispanic bison hunters, also took to the plains during the long peace with the Comanches. The cibolero became an important cultural figure in eastern New Mexico, where many Hispanic villages began to resemble their Comanche counterparts. The Comanche language became almost universal in eastern New Mexico.[59]

Hispanic settlers, then, encompassed a diverse mix of ethnicities and backgrounds. Colonial New Mexican legal records began identifying Hispanic settlers in the late eighteenth century as *vecinos* ("citizens"), and a common Hispanic identity took shape. In addition to their interactions with nomadic tribes, the vecinos often had strong cultural and social ties to the Puebloan communities of northern New Mexico. Both groups found themselves politically and economically marginalized by the colonial elites, who often boasted a purer Spanish heritage. Although the degree of influence the Puebloans had on Hispanic villagers is hard to quantify, it should not be underestimated. Particularly in more remote areas, many settlers intermarried into and joined Puebloan communities, absorbed Puebloan wild plant and agricultural knowledge, and had deep exposure to the religious activities connected to the Puebloan way of life.[60]

Although it attracted many traders and settlers, San Miguel remained a fairly primitive outpost. Fray Buenaventura Merino, the resident priest in 1801, described his district in a report, presumably encompassing both the remaining inhabitants of Pecos Pueblo and the residents of San Miguel. The friar depicted a settlement with a bare, subsistence economy. He reported that "Hispanos and Indians grew maize, wheat, and a few vegetables in fields irrigated by the Río Pecos, but only enough to subsist. They ran only a few head of cattle and no sheep or goats 'because the enemies do not let them increase.' . . . There were no industries or commerce worth mentioning, no bridges over the river, and no good timber for the royal navy."[61] The enemies mentioned by the friar were the Apaches, who, in the wake of the peace accords, had become the common adversary of Comanches and Hispanos alike.[62]

Although it was remote, San Miguel was in many ways a typical Spanish colonial settlement in a province characterized by deprivation and isolation. An 1803 report from Governor Fernando Chacón to Spanish officials tells a story, similar to Fray Buenaventura Merino's account, of "the natural decadence and backwardness" of colonial New Mexico. In addition to the persistence of subsistence-level farming and limited livestock operations, Chacón also noted that a barter economy continued to prevail. During his 1807 exploratory expedition to the region on behalf of the young American republic, Captain Zebulon Pike also noted the poor conditions of the Spanish colonial economy in northern New Mexico and its tenuous connections to supplies and trade outside its remote location. As Pike observed, the infrequent biannual caravans from Mexico were barely adequate to supply the populace with the goods required to maintain strong relationships with Indian trading partners. Opportunities to mine known deposits of copper, tin, and lead remained untapped. These limitations slowed or even prevented rapid change in the environment, however. Ecological transformation in New Mexico would have been significantly greater if large deposits of silver had been discovered. Without a mining boom's voracious demands for water, wood, livestock, human labor, and poisonous mercury and lead, the province escaped large-scale damage to the environment and human health.[63]

The small community of San Miguel del Vado may not have been prosperous, but it grew steadily, and its presence encouraged more settlers to come to the Upper Pecos valley. In 1813 three men, Francisco Trujillo, Diego Padilla, and Bartolomé Márquez, applied for a grant between San Miguel and Pecos Pueblo, which became known as the Los Trigos grant. The application gave vague boundaries for the grant, but the applicants claimed the grant did not overlap with the Pecos Pueblo league. However, the settlers eventually encroached on the league's southern border. To the north of the pueblo, in 1815, Juan de Dios Peña and several others petitioned for land. They submitted a statement to the governor, recording that "we have registered a place that today is barren and unsettled . . . outside of the property of [Pecos Pueblo]." Originally called the Cañon de Pecos grant, it became known as the Alejandro (or Alexander) Valle grant later in the nineteenth century. The Crown awarded both grants in 1815. Settlers at Los Trigos began building and planting. On the northern grant, settlers immediately started eyeing the Pecos ciénega and its abandoned fields a short distance downstream.[64]

A local official, Matías Ortiz, measured both grants when he formally placed the settlers in possession. Both measurements favored the Hispanos over the residents of Pecos Pueblo. Although the applicants claimed otherwise, both grants actually overlapped the northern and southern boundaries of the league. The Pecos understood that the new grants threatened their territory. In 1818 they lodged a formal protest with the alcalde mayor at San Miguel, Vicente Villanueva. They accused a settler, Juan de Aguilar, of going beyond the boundaries of the northern grant and building on pueblo land. Villanueva came upriver to the pueblo and conducted a survey himself. He found that indeed, Aguilar was on the Pecos grant. Aguilar protested in turn, claiming that Villanueva had used faulty survey methods.[65]

The process of surveying reveals both the desires of the Hispanos to claim the land legally and also the arbitrariness of their claims. Surveys of pueblo leagues were supposed to start at the church, which usually stood in the center of the pueblo. At Pecos Pueblo the church stood a distance to the south. Some surveyors started at the church anyway or in the cemetery adjacent to it. Villanueva altered the rule to fit the situation at Pecos by beginning at the north corner of the pueblo complex. Hispanos and Pecos also debated the proper length of a rope and whether the surveyor stretched it tightly. Villanueva argued the Pecos survey should go above depressions in the ground, such as arroyos, which would give the pueblo more land than if a surveyor did not stretch the rope over such features and instead descended into such depressions, considerably shortening the league measurement.[66]

Despite the protests of the Pecos, Hispanic settlement in the valley continued. It proceeded slowly at first. The three original families of the Los Trigos grant may have constructed temporary summer homes and had gardens and livestock on the grant by 1821. These were located approximately "ten miles below the Pecos ciénega."[67] An epidemic in 1800 struck not only Pecos Pueblo but also the Hispano community downriver at San Miguel del Vado and perhaps other settlers closer to the pueblo. Subsequent disease outbreaks appeared to strike Hispanos and pueblo inhabitants with varying force. An 1802 epidemic among the Hispanos did not seem to affect the Pecos. An 1816 outbreak also affected the Hispanos more severely, although it took the lives of at least eighteen Pecos adults as well.[68] Despite disease and the difficulties of establishing themselves in a new place, the Hispanic population continued to increase while the pueblo population declined. By 1821 only fifty-four people remained at the pueblo. In contrast, around 170 Hispanos lived in the area in 1800, and their numbers increased to 738 by 1821. Despite the increasing numbers of Hispanos, the decline in the Puebloan population was so drastic that there were more human beings living in the region at the beginning of the Spanish colonial period then by the end.[69]

As more settlers came to the region and peace allowed for easy movement between communities, traffic between Santa Fe, Pecos, and San Miguel del Vado intensified. In the late eighteenth century, Spanish officials awarded Hispanic settlers the Cañada de los Álamos grant near what later became Cañoncito, located between Pecos and Santa Fe. Settlers began grazing their livestock around Cañoncito. With settlers north of the Pecos grant as well, on the Cañon de Pecos grant, livestock grazed in far more areas than in any previous period, with the possible exception of the mid-1600s. Although livestock numbers grew steadily in New Mexico after 1786, their effects were localized.[70] Around Hispanic settlements, such as San Miguel, or pueblos like Pecos, and along trade routes, the environment probably became degraded to some extent. But because people usually kept livestock close to settlements, the herds did not impart extensive damage to the watersheds of the Pecos River and Glorieta Creek. Other activities, too, fostered only small-scale resource exploitation. Although Juan Peña no doubt hoped to prosper, he and the other settlers only managed to maintain a subsistence lifestyle. Tools remained primitive—wooden hoes and perhaps rudimentary plows for breaking the soil. Building techniques continued in the same vein as the Puebloan tradition of using materials from the earth—stones, soil, sand, and straw. Unlike the wooden structures common in other parts of colonial North America, these buildings did not contribute to deforestation.[71]

New economic policies pioneered by the Spanish Crown beginning in the late 1700s began to improve a stagnant frontier economy, but they also increased the human impact on the environment. Livestock remained the colony's biggest export, and the numbers of sheep in New Mexico continued growing. By the end of the eighteenth century, the colony exported more than 20,000 each year.[72] A more robust local political system also developed in the seventeenth century. Spain permitted the formation of *ayuntamientos*, or town councils, with an elected body of representatives termed the *diputación*. The majority of male Spanish subjects in New Mexico, including Puebloans, gained citizenship rights. In part due to increased political participation from settlers on the frontier, the Spanish *cortes* (representative assembly) at Cádiz, in Spain, passed a law in 1812 that allowed for the distribution of unused pueblo land. The local diputación ruled on all such cases.[73] Juan Peña could expect support from local officials if he decided to move into the Pecos ciénega.

The popularity of these reforms demonstrated the determination of settlers to obtain land in New Mexico and achieve a more autonomous government. Cultur-ally, the people grew further away from Spanish Mexico. Ties to the Comanches and the Puebloans, as well as the large population of formerly enslaved Indians who became incorporated into their society, helped to develop a distinct Hispanic identity. By the early nineteenth century, New Mexicans divided themselves into two groups—Pueblo Indians and Hispanos.[74] The Puebloans had few reasons to support the Spaniards, and the Hispanos had many reasons for wanting greater independence. When Mexico declared its independence from Spain in 1821, few in New Mexico actively supported the rebellion, but neither did they protest their new status as republican citizens.

"Consider the Extent of the Pain That We Suffer": *Pecos in the Mexican Republic*

Agustín de Iturbide led Mexico to declare its independence from Spain in 1821, and New Mexicans cautiously embraced the new government. They did not want to appear too enthusiastic in case Spain managed to reassert control. But as the weeks following independence stretched into months, some New Mexicans expressed hope for the future. Donaciano Vigil, a prominent New Mexican landholder and politician, who moved to the area around Pecos in 1854, remembered that "we expected to enter a new era of happiness and this word, and the word 'liberty,' were those that were most used and most repeated in those days."[75] However, it soon became apparent that, like Spain, Mexican officials left the citizens of its northern frontier—New Mexico, Texas, and California—to fend for themselves with only sporadic and limited aid from the central government. Some New Mexicans advocated provincial independence, culminating in a brief rebellion in 1837. Although the rebellion failed, New Mexicans continued to strive for greater autonomy.[76]

Some of the regulations passed by the new government did meet with the approval of Hispanic New Mexicans. The Mexican government condoned the efforts of the local governmental bodies of ayuntamientos and diputaciónes to distribute the unused land surrounding pueblos.[77] In February 1821, just before independence, a group of settlers petitioned Governor Facundo Melgares for the unused land of Pecos Pueblo in the ciénega, claiming the few families who still lived in the pueblo did not need all the land. The petitioners argued they would be able to cultivate the land instead, turning an economic liability into a profitable enterprise.[78] The grant application was never carried through, but in a report by a local official, Juan Rafael Ortiz, he questioned not whether the residents of Pecos Pueblo *owned* the land but whether they *needed* the land. A new group of petitioners used the same tactic when they applied for a grant of the Pecos sobrantes in 1823. The Pecos resisted these attempts to seize pueblo lands, firmly stating the land was theirs, and they needed it to raise irrigated crops. Probably reflecting years of intermarriage and social ties, the local government at San Miguel del Vado supported the Pecos. Vicente Villanueva, the alcalde mayor who had previously surveyed the Pecos Pueblo league to the benefit of the Pecos, declared the Pecos did indeed own the land. Accepting this conclusion, the diputación denied the petitioners.[79]

Undaunted by the ruling, many settlers began to move into the land around the ciénega through a variety of illegal means. Diego Padilla, who already had been awarded land in the Los Trigos grant, finagled a promise of farmland from the diputación secretary and supposedly bribed the Pecos with a few cattle. The Hispanic settlers quickly began improving the land. By 1826, around five miles of irrigation ditches supported their cultivated acres.[80] Others continued to apply for land grants. In 1825 the diputación granted more of the ciénega to Miguel Rivera, Domingo Fernández, Luis Benavídez, and a variety of co-applicants.[81] More petitions followed, and soon the diputación had granted the majority of the communal pueblo lands to Hispanic settlers.

The Pecos tried to reverse the continuing usurpation of their lands. In 1826 and 1829, they petitioned the governor directly, asking for the removal of the settlers. "Consider the extent of the pain that we suffer when we see ourselves violently despoiled of our lawful possessions," the Pecos pleaded.[82] The diputación had no right to allot a pueblo's land, they claimed. The diputación waffled back and forth on the issue. No matter what the government ruled, no one forced the settlers to relinquish their claims. The settlers claimed a Pecos sold them the rights to the ciénega in 1830. Although they still retained the legal rights to the rest of the grant, the Pecos had lost the most valuable land along the Pecos River. They maintained that the settlers harassed them, preventing them from growing crops and herding livestock. The inability to support themselves also inhibited population growth, which would have strengthened the Pecos's claims to the ciénega. More than a century of stressors—disease epidemics, Comanche and Apache raiding, internal factionalism, land disputes, and the growth of San Miguel del Vado as an important trade center—had diminished the size and influence of the Pecos population to the point that it was no longer a viable community able to assert a strong claim to the land.

In 1838, the remaining twenty-one Pecos chose to move to Jemez Pueblo. Their names, as translated, reveal how their identity remained interwoven with the natural world they inhabited. There were nine men in the group: the Pecos governor, Se-h-ng-pae ("eagle tail mountain," aka Juan Antonio Toya); Shi-to-ne; Wayu; Wa-kin ("eagle down," aka Francisco Kota); K'ela ("Navajo"); Hopeh ("Hopi," aka Miguel Pecos); Toon-kanu ("fox"); Tabu-taa ("clown tea"); and Zer-wakin ("snow-white eagle down," aka Jose Miguel Vigil). The group also included nine women: Pove ("blossom"); Tyi-koon wachu ("flint society rainbow"); Shynj-dyu-kinu ("mountain lion young corn," aka Simona Toya or Toribio); Sntyu-wagi ("turquoise altar"); Hobe-wagi ("kick-stick altar," aka Rosa Vigil Pecos); Toh-wagi (aka Juanita Kota Fragua); Ma-ta; Haiashi; and the anonymous wife of Toon-kanu. Three children also accompanied the adults to Jemez: Tsa-aku ("piñon boy"); Daloh; and Sesa-whi-ya (aka Agustin Kota Pecos).[83] Although the Pecos had to abandon their pueblo and its mission church, they removed the painting of their patron saint, Nuestra Señora de los Ángeles de Porciúncula (Our Lady of the Angels) and placed it in the care of the Hispanic residents of Pecos village, who promised to continue observing the feast-day mass of the saint at the mission church each year. Yet with the Pecos gone, the pueblo and church on the mesilla began slowly crumbling, the natural effects of wind and rain hastened by settlers scavenging the structures for usable timber and stone.[84]

In the wake of the last remaining Pecos's departure, the Hispanic settlers rapidly cultivated fields and grazed their livestock on the lands in the area—the most intense land use since the seventeenth century. The majority of the settlers lived around the ciénega in what became the center of the village of Pecos. Some scattered further down the river on land that is now part of Pecos National Historical Park. These settlers included José Mariano Ruiz, who purchased his land in 1839 from Gregorio Calabaza, a Pecos Indian. Benigo Quintana also settled along the Pecos River, purchasing a plot of land in the 1850s, although Quintana's family did not begin living there until the 1870s.[85]

If Mexican independence did not bring all the changes New Mexicans initially hoped for, it did offer local governments the opportunity to assert greater control over land distribution. The Hispanic settlers of Pecos seized the moment and took over the fertile lands along the Pecos River. Despite the protests of the Pecos, Mexican officials never tried to force the settlers off the land. The

Pecos did not forget their homeland, but the Hispanic settlers now governed the uses of that land. Although the numbers of settlers remained small, and their effects localized, their presence heralded the beginning of a new period in the region's history. Juan Peña, planting his first crops along the Pecos River, believed the new settlements would prosper. The peace with the Comanches continued to hold, and the new republican government in Mexico promised to consider the province's needs and desires more carefully than the distant Spanish Crown had ever done. But although the Upper Pecos valley's future may have appeared secure, it would continue to be at the crossroads of change in the coming decades.

FOUR | Claiming the Land and
Contesting Its Future
1821–1916

KOZLOWSKI'S TRADING POST, 1858—Helen Kozlowski dismounted from the wagon, tired and dusty, and surveyed the adobe house in front of her. Six thick posts buried in the ground supported the roof of a porch, but otherwise the structure was simple and plain. Inside, she found three rooms—enough space to house her family and also accommodate travelers passing by on the Santa Fe Trail, which had been an important trade route since 1821. Her husband, Martin Kozlowski, recently retired from the 1st Dragoons stationed at nearby Fort Union, had purchased the ranch and hostelry from its previous owner, James Gray. Martin fetched his wife and young sons, four-year-old Joseph and two-year-old Thomas, from Missouri to their new home in the Upper Pecos valley.[1]

Helen probably had heard tales of New Mexico from the merchants who embarked on the Santa Fe Trail from Franklin or Independence, Missouri, both popular jumping-off places. But the dry air, piñons, and rocky mesas must have seemed exotic to someone accustomed to the verdant, humid valleys of Missouri. In Missouri most of her neighbors had been other Euro-Americans like herself. Helen was born in Ireland, and her blonde-haired, blue-eyed husband was from Poland. Here, Hispanic settlers composed the majority of the population, and they had been citizens of Mexico a mere ten years before. But in 1848 the Mexican-American War transferred their fortunes into the hands of the United States and brought increasing numbers of settlers like Helen and her family to New Mexico.[2]

Although Pecos was an alien environment to Helen in many respects, she found comfortingly familiar elements as well. Many of the traders and travelers who passed by on the Santa Fe Trail and stopped at the house were English-speaking American merchants or immigrants on their way to California. They

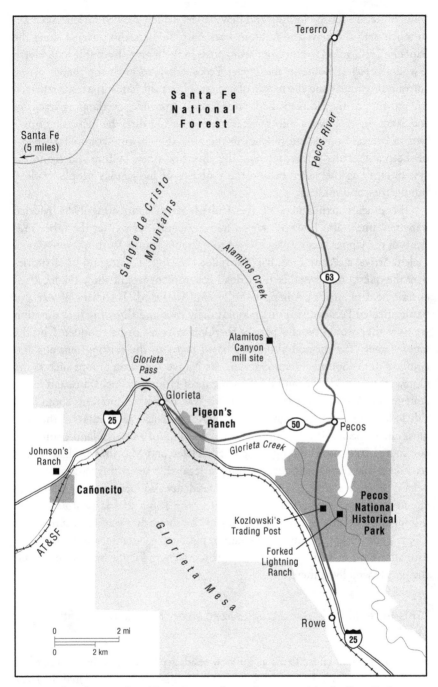

Sites noted in chapters 4–7, Upper Pecos valley and environs. Map by Erin Greb.

brought items such as clothing and newspapers, which allowed Helen to remain in touch with the news and fashions back East. Soldiers also traveled along the Santa Fe Trail, going to and from army posts in the region. Even if it took Helen a while to feel at home in the Upper Pecos valley, to learn the shapes of the surrounding mesas and the names of her neighbors, the landscape itself reflected the growing connections to the United States. The wide, overlapping tracks of the Santa Fe Trail, worn into the trampled grass and dirt; the increasing numbers of private homes and ranches in the area; the growing commercial herds of sheep and cattle—all represented the effects of a new culture and economic system entering the valley behind the footsteps of indigenous people, traders, immigrants, and soldiers.

The exact consequences of the United States conquering New Mexico remained uncertain, however. Helen and her family, as well as the other residents of the Upper Pecos valley, faced a tumultuous future. Within three years of Helen's arrival at Pecos, the Civil War roiled the United States and its territories over the question of whether the federal government would allow the legalized enslavement of African Americans to expand westward. The chaos of war and battle affected Pecos, disrupting people's daily lives and throwing into question whether they would remain part of the United States or be conquered by the Confederacy. The turmoil also exacerbated many of the existing tensions and conflicts in the Southwest among nomadic Native American groups such as the Comanches and Apaches and the settlements of Hispanos, Puebloans, and Euro-Americans. Even after the end of the Civil War, persistent questions about legal title to land and property rights bedeviled New Mexican inhabitants as the U.S. government dealt with determining the ownership of Mexican land grants and communal lands surrounding villages. For Helen and Martin, who had simply settled on their land without obtaining a legal title to it, this issue may have been a constant source of anxiety. Pecos residents also faced shifting economic circumstances when the railroads arrived in the 1880s and large-scale timber, mining, and grazing operations developed. By the early twentieth century, the Upper Pecos valley had undergone radical political, economic, and social transformations, all of which had extensive consequences for the environment and the people who lived there.

"This Intrepid Little Band . . . Realized a Very Handsome Profit": The Santa Fe Trail

Martin Kozlowski chose Pecos as the new residence for his family because of its location on the Santa Fe Trail and the financial opportunities it offered. In 1821 the Mexican government lifted the restrictions on commerce with the United States previously imposed by Spanish officials and opened the province to foreign trade.[3] American traders, who had known about the potential for market expansion in the region since the publication of Zebulon Pike's journals in 1810, immediately took advantage of the new political circumstances. In November 1821, William Becknell and four others arrived in Santa Fe with a load of goods from Missouri. Josiah Gregg, who later traded and traveled on the trail, recorded that "this intrepid little band . . . notwithstanding the trifling amount of merchandise they were possessed of, realized a very handsome profit."[4] The arrival of Becknell's party officially opened the Santa Fe Trail.[5] The trail not only served as a passageway for goods but also encouraged other Americans to come to New Mexico. Enterprising settlers arrived—willing to become Mexican citizens if it allowed them to profit off the growing trade and start their own farms and ranches. Fur trappers also arrived in New Mexico seeking beaver pelts to supply the insatiable international fur market. Although the influx of traders, trappers, and settlers did improve the provincial economy, many newcomers had no qualms about pursuing their fortunes at the expense of New Mexicans. Local elites who profited from the influx of capital often did so to the detriment of the Hispanic villagers and Puebloans. Subsistence agriculture remained the norm for most New Mexicans.[6]

All travelers on the trail passed through the Pecos area. Unlike in earlier times, Pecos Pueblo did not play a substantial role in the trade. The pueblo ruins became a curiosity instead, a landmark on the trail, and travelers concocted fantastical stories about its previous inhabitants.[7]

But Pecos remained a crossroads, a gateway at the eastern plains, and entre-preneurs took advantage of that fact. In or near the Pecos area, three business-men started hostelries alongside the trail offering lodging and meals for travelers. A man named Alexander Valle owned the largest of the hostelries, known as Pigeon's Ranch. Valle came to Pecos in 1851.[8] He had been born in St. Louis and possessed both American and French ancestry. Alexander's original last name was probably Valle, but when his mother married a man named Hyacinth Pigeon, Alexander began using the name as well. Valle did not own the land where he built his ranch but chose it as a conducive location for a business. Located between the Pecos Pueblo ruins and Glorieta Pass, Pigeon's Ranch stood a short distance from the Santa Fe Trail in a grove of cottonwood trees along Glorieta Creek. The complex Valle constructed included numerous buildings, stables, corrals, sheds, bake ovens, a well and cistern, and an inn large enough to house and feed forty people. Merchants traveling to and from Santa Fe and other sundry visitors found accommodations and food for themselves and their animals at the ranch. Valle himself owned stock, including a herd of sheep.[9]

In the 1850s, James Gray established a second hostelry, "Roseville," in close proximity to the Pecos Pueblo ruins.[10] The pueblo provided an attraction for interested travelers to explore while resting their caravan and making camp for the night before proceeding on to Santa Fe. By 1858 Gray had sold the prop-erty to Martin Kozlowski. Kozlowski came to America in 1853 from Warsaw, Poland, and served briefly with the United States cavalry in military campaigns against Indians.[11] The hostelry property stood well within the Pecos Pueblo grant. Like Valle, neither Gray nor Kozlowski possessed legal title to the land. Gray simply chose a promising and apparently unoccupied location, as many settlers did, and Kozlowski purchased the ranch from Gray without obtaining a legal title. Unlike Pigeon's Ranch, Kozlowski's was not a large operation—in the 1860 census he reported owning one horse, four oxen, and eight pigs. Kozlowski had fifty improved acres by the banks of Glorieta Creek from which he harvested around eighty bushels of corn annually.[12]

A third ranch/hostelry complex stood at the southern egress of Glorieta Pass. Anthony P. Johnson, also from St. Louis, bought an established ranch here in 1858, probably from a Hispanic settler. Johnson's Ranch, as it was known, was modest in scale like Kozlowski's.[13] Although neither Kozlowski nor Johnson owned many animals, their ranches hosted the large livestock herds that hauled wagon caravans over the Santa Fe Trail. A trade caravan could include over two dozen freight wagons and hundreds of oxen, horses, and mules. Oxen, weighing 1,800 to 2,000 pounds each, were the most popular choice for hauling wagons, with twelve to sixteen oxen per wagon. Every wagon train also had a herd of extra animals following it to take the place of any oxen or horses that became lame or sick. The passage of these caravans had severe environmental consequences for the land on either side of the trail. The livestock trampled and overgrazed vegetation, both the animals and the wagons contributed to erosion and soil compaction, and many watercourses became polluted and barren.[14] Wagoners created overlapping sets of tracks on the trail over the years. In the Pecos area, numerous remnants of Santa Fe Trail ruts still exist from Kozlowski's to the far bank of Glorieta Creek west of the pueblo. Large numbers of livestock and the heavy travel on the Santa Fe Trail denuded vegetation around Pigeon's, Kozlowski's, and Johnson's ranches and increased erosion along creek beds, arroyos, and the trail itself during the fifty years it remained the primary travel and trade route through the area.

Other environmental effects followed the opening of the Santa Fe Trail. The Sangre de Cristo Mountains, directly to the north of Pecos, drew fur trappers to the region. The trappers hunted beavers, a keystone species that provides many benefits to riparian ecosystems. By 1825 the southern Sangres, including the Pecos River, had been trapped out, and the beaver exterminated from the region. Riparian diversity decreased, and as beaver dams disintegrated, floods became increasingly hazardous to the human settlements along the river.[15]

"The Sounds of Thousands of Animals":
Hispanic Land Use Patterns

While the Santa Fe Trail created many changes in the environment around Pecos, the area had already been transformed as a result of the new agricultural practices introduced by Hispanic settlers. Helen Kozlowski and her family arrived to find dozens of Hispanic families who had been in the Upper Pecos valley for several generations, working the land and grazing their livestock. The nineteenth-century Hispanic settlers carried out a distinctive set of subsistence practices on their land. During the years under Spanish rule, when the alcalde mayor formally granted settlers their land, "the alcalde took the grantee by the hand and walked him over the land, while the grantee plucked up grass, threw stones to signify his dominion over the land, and shouted 'Long live the King!'" Under Mexican rule the president took the place of the monarch. Beginning their occupation in this way signaled the settlers' right and intention to utilize the resources of their land.[16]

The land use system employed by Hispanos had its roots in Spain and had evolved over the centuries. The system worked well in New Mexico, where settlers needed access to limited resources spread over a large expanse of territory in order to make a living. Upon the settlement of a land grant, each settler received several separate pieces of land. The division of a land grant in Mexico, for example, awarded each family distinct parcels for building their home, planting a garden, and planting field crops. Each family also had access to the communal land that constituted the rest of the grant and allowed for grazing, firewood and timber harvesting, and other subsistence activities.[17]

The community also cooperated to irrigate their agricultural fields. The *acequia madre*, or main irrigation ditch, received water from the river and distributed it by gravity throughout the settlement. Together, the community cleaned and maintained the ditches every spring. Secondary ditches, called *sangrias* ("bleeders"), diverged from the main acequias to water individual fields, with hollowed log flumes serving as channels across ravines. Watering occurred on a rotating basis, ensuring all users received water. In an arid environment, this system made the most of a limited resource for the benefit of the community.[18] In the marshy ciénega of the Pecos River, almost entirely under non-Indian control by 1825, Hispanos probably refurbished and expanded irrigation ditches that had been created by the Pecos. Settlers also constructed a new ditch on the west side of the river.[19]

Until the late nineteenth century, when the American population in the region grew and brought with it more sophisticated agriculture tools, the type of farming carried out by Puebloans and Hispanos remained primitive and scarcely changed from that of their ancestors. Tools, including plows, were often wood. The scratch plow, used throughout the Spanish and Mexican periods, cut a shallow six-inch furrow rather than turning over the soil, which greatly reduced soil loss. Antonio Barreiro, a Mexican official serving as the legal advisor to the territories in the 1830s, and an advocate for the economic development of those territories, recorded that "in New Mexico, agriculture is completely neglected. The inhabitants of this country do not engage in large scale farming, from which they would doubtless derive much profit." Although traders on the Santa Fe Trail brought iron tools, including two-handled steel plows, many could not afford such luxuries, so they continued to be of limited use and were difficult to replace when broken. Only those with draft animals could utilize plows, and only the wealthy owned livestock in great numbers. Even the communal grazing lands were typically used most extensively by the richest members of a community, who owned large herds of sheep and cattle.[20]

The consolidation of resources within the hands of a few became increasingly common during the early nineteenth century. A stratified society developed in which the merchant and landowning class grew rich off the opportunities presented by the distribution of land grants and the Santa Fe Trail trade.[21] Sheep ranching proved to be especially beneficial for a small number of Hispanos. Beginning in the 1700s, the *partido* system became common practice in New Mexico. Under this system, *partidarios* entered into three- to five-year contracts with owners of large herds. The owner gave ewes to the partidario, who gave annual payments of lambs and wool in return. At the end of the contract, the original number of ewes had to be returned to the owner.[22]

This system put much of the risk on the partidario. For example, Agustín Armijo, who lived in or near Pecos village, and another settler from Alameda entered into a contract in 1833 with Juan Estevan Pino, one of the wealthy landholders of the area. Armijo agreed to take care of around 1,100 ewes, paying 20 percent of the profits to Pino each year. Moreover, Armijo agreed to forfeit not only his possessions but his personal freedom if he reneged on these terms, and thus risked falling into peonage.[23] The system was not entirely disadvantageous to the partidario, however, and could be used in a variety of ways in an economy where hard currency was scarce. For example, later in the nineteenth century, the Charles Ilfeld Company in Las Vegas, New Mexico, used the partido system to finance its customers' debt. Instead of seizing the herd of an indebted customer, the Ilfeld Company bought the sheep, crediting the purchase to the customer's account while leaving the sheep with the customer. The company required a certain number of lambs or pounds of wool each year and benefited from the unpaid labor. The company also retained their customer, while the debtor could repay the debt without losing his assets. An analysis of fifty-one partido accounts with the Ilfeld Company in the period from 1888 to 1900 showed that thirty-three of the partidarios terminated their accounts successfully, fourteen were unable to pay their debts, and the remainder continued to keep their accounts open.[24]

In whatever way the sheep were kept, there were a great deal of them in the Upper Pecos valley in the nineteenth century. The herds of Juan Estevan Pino serve as a good example. As the account of the partido contract shows, Pino owned large sheep herds. He lived in Santa Fe but owned interests in several land grants in the area on which he pastured his livestock. By 1835 Pino and his sons, Manuel Doroteo and Justo Pastor, owned 900 cattle and 18,000 sheep. At first, Pino pastured these animals on another tract of land that he owned on the Juan Bautista Valdez grant in northeastern New Mexico. However, after 1837 his livestock on that grant became the favored target of Indian, perhaps Comanche, raids. Pino moved both herds to Pecos.[25] During the summer, herders may have pastured the animals in the higher mountains, but the animals also grazed close to villages. Unsurprisingly, the large herds consumed all the appetizing vegetation in the vicinity. Baldwin Mollhausen, acting as topographer on an army expedition to chart a wagon road through the Southwest in 1852, left a description of a herd of sheep near Anton Chico pastured about twelve miles from the village and numbering around 5,000 to 6,000 that was probably similar to the herds by Pecos. Mollhausen recorded that "the closely cropped grass now told us, almost as plainly as the sight of the flocks and herds at a distance that we were approaching a settlement. . . . The air seemed filled with a confused murmur, that became louder as we advanced and the sounds of thousands of animals [*sic*] voices was mingled with the tinkling of many bells from an enormous flock grazing in the valley."[26] Pino probably moved his herds throughout the Pecos area, but in the winter most of the animals returned to Pino's land by the Pecos River, taking advantage of the custom that allowed for grazing on stubble fields. Other wealthy ranchers in Pecos followed the same practice. As in most Hispanic settlements, lots in Pecos consisted of narrow "long lot" fields stretching down to the river. During the summer, fences enclosed the lots, but settlers removed the fences after harvest to allow for livestock passage and grazing.[27]

As the Pecos village grew, land use intensified. Allowing cows and sheep to graze fields in the winter gave the land no respite. The large herds probably wandered throughout the area, including further downriver. Livestock compacted the soil and reduced both the extent of ground cover and the height of grasses, which in turn reduced the ground's ability to retain water. Flooding became more severe, and erosion increased.[28] As historian David Hornbeck says, the system of land use was "based on satisfying current needs."[29] To prosper in New Mexico, people had to make use of every available resource. The addition of large livestock herds, however, taxed the long-term viability of those resources.

Martin and Helen Kozlowski readily adopted local practices when they arrived in Pecos. Although Martin did not own large herds of cattle or sheep, he probably allowed the animals he did own to wander freely, grazing on the communal lands surrounding the valley. He did not own any land by the Pecos River, but he may have built a small acequia to utilize water from Glorieta Creek. Helen doubtless gathered piñon nuts each fall with her neighbors. The Kozlowskis also adopted Hispanic ideas of land ownership, which centered on use and occupation as opposed to legal title. Martin did not have a legal claim to his ranch property, but he built on it and farmed on it, which was enough for his neighbors, many of whom rested their own claims to land ownership on the same principles.

"Under the 'Star-Spangled Banner'":
New Mexico Becomes a United States Territory

The Kozlowskis not only moved to Pecos because of the Santa Fe Trail but also because by 1858 New Mexico was a U.S. territory. Under the expansionist policies of President James K. Polk, the U.S. decided to push its territorial claims west and south, and in August of 1846, Stephen Watts Kearny arrived in New Mexico at the head of a detachment of the United States Army. The U.S. Army moved on to invade Mexico, and by 1848, Mexico had surrendered and agreed to sell its territory north of the Rio Grande to the U.S.[30] After only twenty-seven years as part of the Mexican Republic, Pecos was now in U.S. territory. Like most political boundaries, the new border that placed half of Mexico into the United States reflected only human interests. As historian Patricia Limerick notes, "The resulting division did not ratify any plan of nature. The borderlands were an ecological whole; northeastern Mexican desert blended into southwestern American desert with no prefigurings of nationalism. The one line that nature did provide—the Rio Grande—was a river that ran through but did not really divide the continuous terrain."[31]

Some New Mexicans resisted the American invasion, but New Mexico had long been oriented eastward. The Comanches, not Mexico, had been the most important force in the region for decades, and New Mexico's ties to the U.S. had strengthened since 1821.[32] Many New Mexicans might have preferred to form their own independent republic, but pragmatism won, and the U.S. Army swiftly quelled rebellious elements in the populace. Donaciano Vigil, who owned extensive land around Pecos, became an important liaison between the new territorial government and Hispanic residents, acting first as territorial secretary and then as a member of the territorial legislature.[33] In particular, Vigil advised on matters relating to land claims, a pressing question to residents who wanted the new government to recognize their rights of ownership.

To gain control of its new western lands, the United States government did not stop at suppressing dissidents and funding surveys. The government wanted residents to prove land titles legally, in accordance with decades of American land practices. After the Treaty of Guadalupe Hidalgo, signed in 1848, government officials began determining exactly what sorts of lands they had acquired, who owned them, and how they could be put into the hands of American citizens. In the negotiations over the treaty, Nicolas Trist, the U.S. ambassador to Mexico, originally inserted an article that would have automatically validated under U.S. law all existing Mexican land grants. During ratification, Congress removed the article. As historian Malcolm Elbright describes Congress's intent, "The United States looked at the treaty as an enormous real estate deal; it expected to get clear title to most of the land it was paying for regardless of the property rights of Mexicans." Instead of starting with legal validation from the U.S. government, Hispanic settlers who lived on land grants would have to prove their claims to the land in U.S. courts. For many Hispanos, who lacked any knowledge of the American legal system and often did not possess a clear paper trail proving their ownership, this was a heavy burden indeed.[34] As the territorial government began adjudicating land claims, Hispanos lost more and more land to Anglos who controlled the government and legal systems. Anglos who had moved to the area when it was still under Spanish or Mexican rule also faced the possibility of losing their land.[35]

Although the federal government posed a threat to land claims, the sustained presence of the U.S. Army in the region also brought economic opportunities. The army built a string of forts in New Mexico, including Fort Union, northeast of Pecos, and Fort Marcy, in Santa Fe, and took up the task of protecting merchants and settlers from Comanches, Apaches, and other Indians who contested American control. The army required prodigious amounts of supplies—food for the soldiers, fodder for animals, and timber for construction. At first, the army tried to transport needed items over the plains from Fort Leavenworth in Kansas—thousands of cattle arrived with Kearny in 1846, for example. But transport over the plains was expensive and time-consuming. Almost immediately, the army began buying goods from local New Mexicans.[36]

The army often contracted with one individual who supplied them with corn, wheat, and other items purchased from farmers in the area and consolidated into one shipment. Alexander Valle, the operator of Pigeon's Ranch, acted in this capacity. Valle may have cultivated fields himself, and many other farmers around Pecos were producing crops to meet the military demand as well.[37] In 1860, there were 374 soldiers in San Miguel County, which included Pecos village. The army's needs only increased once the Civil War began. In August 1862, Valle sold "6,000 pounds of corn and 11,072 pounds of fodder" to the army, paid for by Captain J. C. McFerran, Assistant Quartermaster. In December 1862, Valle "was paid for 15,496 pounds of corn and 29,015 pounds of fodder," and in March of the following year the army bought "35,536 pounds of corn and . . . 50,477 pounds of fodder to be fed to the public animals."[38] The market provided by the U.S. Army afforded valuable opportunities to the inhabitants of the Upper Pecos valley, while increasing the intensity of agricultural activity.

The U.S. Army not only bought supplies from farmers and ranchers but also improved local infrastructure. The army needed to move between its forts quickly and easily. In 1857 alone, Congress provided $32,000 to improve roads in New Mexico. In the vicinity of Pecos village, Captain John N. Macomb of the Topographical Engineers widened the Santa Fe Trail from Santa Fe to Fort Union and reduced steep grades. Enjoying the benefits of improved roads, immigrants to New Mexico increased after 1848. Newcomers such as Kozlowski, Valle, and Johnson came to Pecos to profit off the Santa Fe Trail trade, but the safety and economic opportunities afforded by the military presence also factored into their decision. New Mexico grew from a population of 61,547 in 1850 to 93,516 in 1860 (although the numbers did not accurately reflect the population of Puebloans). The Anglo population alone went from 1,600 to 6,300—3,100 of whom were in the military.[39] At the Kozlowskis' ranch and hostelry, Helen led a busy life. She cooked meals for guests and washed clothes and made beds for those who spent the night. Her duties attached to her husband's business came in addition to her family responsibilities—caring for her children, sewing, and cleaning. The Kozlowskis eventually had six children, who married local Hispanic men and women and integrated into the Pecos community.[40]

That community included many inhabitants who labored in a system of debt peonage and forced captivity. In 1849, New Mexicans seeking to gain statehood had developed a constitution that prohibited slavery, but despite the words written on paper, slaves remained a key facet of the economy in New Mexico. Apaches, Navajos, Utes, and Comanches continued to raid each other and New Mexican settlements. Captives from these raids were sold in New Mexico or taken south to Mexico. Comancheros often brokered these trades or ransomed captives for high prices. Although the captives were referred to as "peons," the system was akin to chattel slavery. Peons could obtain their freedom only by paying a certain sum to their owners. Peonage was also common among the landless sheepherders who were a major source of labor in the remote, provincial economy.[41] The seasonal subsistence economy established in northern New Mexico required high inputs of human labor, and the barter-driven economy also created a major incentive for maintaining a regular supply of human captives who could be exchanged for needed goods.[42] The baptismal records of Pecos Pueblo and San Miguel del Vado reveal the presence of these individuals at Pecos or in the surrounding area. For example, an entry on March 14, 1811, recorded the baptism of José Miguel, a two-year-old Comanche boy, who had probably been captured in a raid and then sold to a Hispanic family. An entry for May 25, 1827, recorded the baptism of José María de la Asención, the illegitimate child of María Guadalupe, who had been purchased as a *criada* (female domestic servant) from the Navajos. The baptism records also record the presence of many mixed-race individuals.[43]

The hypocrisy in New Mexico's constitution was ultimately a moot point, for Congress chose not to ratify the document. But inevitably, upon becoming part of the United States, New Mexico became embroiled in the long-standing conflict over whether the federal government would allow slavery as practiced in the southern states to expand. When the Civil War broke out in 1861, many Confederates looked to New Mexico and other western territories as land filled not only with useful resources, including gold, but also as a place where they could garner additional proslavery representation because "the peculiar institution," in a different form, already existed there. Some antislavery members of Congress argued that the arid, high deserts of New Mexico would never support an agricultural system reliant upon chattel slavery, and that slave labor had no practical place in agriculture requiring irrigation. In doing so they perpetuated a misconception that New Mexico was free from slavery, ignoring the thousands of individuals subjected to forced labor.[44] Regardless of whether Confederates possessed a clearer understanding of New Mexican society, the region remained a strategic component of their territorial and economic ambitions. The United States had invested significant military resources in New Mexico because it was an essential component for building a coast-to-coast empire, and the Confederacy had the same ambition.[45] First, though, the Confederates would have to defeat the U.S. Army garrisoning the numerous forts in the region. Pecos, located close to Santa Fe and on a key transportation route, was about to find itself at the center of the coming conflict.

"Our Boys Were All Anxious for a Fight": The Battle of Glorieta Pass

Perhaps U.S. Army officers occasionally stayed at Kozlowski's Trading Post as they traveled between the garrison at Santa Fe and Fort Union, located approximately seventy miles northeast of Pecos. But on the morning of March 28, 1862, Helen looked out her door to find an entire army camped around the trading post. Commanded by Colonel John P. Slough, the force consisted of both regular army soldiers and volunteers from Colorado and New Mexico. The First Colorado Volunteers, known as the "Pike's Peakers," were miners and frontiersmen accustomed to winter in the Rocky Mountains. They had marched swiftly in harsh conditions from Denver to Fort Union upon receiving word of an incipient Confederate invasion. At Fort Union they resupplied and joined other troops, including New Mexican volunteers, before moving on to Pecos.[46] Captain Rafael Chacón, who served in numerous military campaigns in the Southwest, led Companies I and K of the First Regiment New Mexican Foot Volunteers. San Miguel County, including Pecos, was well represented on the muster rolls of New Mexican volunteers as well.[47]

Major John M. Chivington, leading an advance force of 418 men, chose Kozlowski's as a camping site for the same reasons it had been attractive to people for hundreds of years: the convenient water supply of Glorieta Creek, available wood for fires, and grazing land for livestock. The camp itself became known as Camp Lewis after Captain William H. Lewis, who commanded a detachment of regulars. John Miller, a volunteer from Pueblo, Colorado, sent a letter to his father describing the terrain he had just marched through. "The face of the country is very rough and rocky and covered with stunted pines and cedars," he wrote, adding, "What soil there is, is very light and easily washed, and consequently full of deep washed ravines and gullies."[48] Some of these gullies may have been the result of overgrazing and soil erosion.

While the federal troops settled in at Kozlowski's, the invading Confederates drew ever closer. The Confederate invasion of the southwestern territories began in July 1861. Henry Hopkins Sibley, a former U.S. Army officer, led the invasion. Sibley hoped to capture the rich gold mines of Colorado for the Confederacy once the conquest of New Mexico was complete and then continue to the coast to seize California's gold mines too, as well as capture coastal ports to subvert the eastern Union blockades. At first, the Confederates achieved success—they subdued federal troops in Arizona and declared it a Confederate territory. In Arizona, closer to Texas cotton culture and with many business connections to Texas merchants, the Confederates encountered sympathizers to their cause. Sibley assumed many New Mexicans and Coloradoans would also support the Confederacy. But Confederate sympathies diminished rapidly as one went north. Although we do not know Helen and Martin Kozlowski's opinions on the conflict, they may well have been glad to see the Federals arrive. By this point, the Confederates' immediate goal was capturing Fort Union and seizing its supplies. The Kozlowskis may have feared for the safety of their property, not to mention their lives, as the Confederates drew closer to Pecos. In any case, with Union troops camped around their home, the war was now on their very doorstep.

Although Pecos residents had escaped immediate involvement in the Civil War up to that point, the conflict had created ripples of violence throughout the New Mexico Territory. When the U.S. Army withdrew much of its manpower from the Southwest at the beginning of the war in 1860, it left a power vacuum. The number of federal troops in the Southwest had been small to begin with, but an uneasy peace prevailed in the 1850s with the Apaches and Navajos. In April 1860, the largest band of Navajo warriors ever assembled attacked the U.S. outpost of Fort Defiance in their territory. The Navajos mounted this attack for various reasons, but one of the most important involved the increase in Navajos captured and sold into slavery during the period from 1820 to 1860. During this time, the Navajos became "the most heavily enslaved Indian nation in New Mexico." In response to the Navajos' attack on Fort Defiance, communities formed local militias. In Santa Fe, five hundred men under the command of Manuel Antonio Chaves de Noriega, a Mexican Army veteran known as "the Little Lion of the Southwest," set out to attack the Navajos. Pueblo Indians often joined these forces as scouts and auxiliaries, including from the pueblo of Jemez, where the Pecos descendants had recently settled, having left Pecos Pueblo in 1838. The U.S. Army also entered the fray, but then in 1861, the outbreak of war in the east drew away federal troops and supplies.[49]

The unrest was not confined to the Navajos. Troubles with Apaches in Arizona broke out in early 1861. But again, in the midst of a series of retaliatory attacks, many of the federal troops left for the east. In their absence, Apaches, Utes, and Comanches all increased their raiding activities. In New Mexico, the fighting with the Navajos continued as well. Long-standing tensions in the region, held partially in abeyance by the presence of federal soldiers, reawakened.[50] Navajo and Apache raids on Puebloan, Hispanic, and Anglo settlers and traders increased sharply in the 1860s.[51] In the midst of this turmoil, the Confederacy mounted its invasion of New Mexico. The U.S. volunteers and regulars gathering at Kozlowski's on March 25 under Colonel Slough included Manuel Chaves, who had recently led attacks against the Navajos. As a native of New Mexico who was familiar with the surrounding country, Chaves and the thirty *nuevomexicanos* under his command would prove a valuable asset in the coming days.

Meanwhile, the combined Confederate troops of the Second Texas Mounted Rifles and the Fifth Texas Regiment gathered in Santa Fe had heard of Slough's advance. Led by Major Charles L. Pyron, the Texans left Santa Fe to meet other Confederates and fight their way to Fort Union. They were low on food, as U.S. troops had removed or destroyed much of the supplies in Santa Fe. Civilians had driven their horses out of reach of the coming Confederate troops and hidden their corn and wheat. Approaching Pecos, the hungry Confederates chose another of the Santa Fe Trail hostelries for their camp, settling down at Johnson's Ranch in Apache Canyon at the southern end of Glorieta Pass on March 25, the same day the Federals arrived at Kozlowski's. Johnson and his family had fled the area, probably heading north toward Las Vegas and Fort Union, along with many other Santa Fe residents. The weather was cold and snowy. One of the Confederates, William Lott Davidson, recalled spending a chilly night at Johnson's Ranch. Davidson later wrote "the weather was so cold and our covering so light that we could not sleep much at night."[52]

On the night of March 25 neither the Confederates, camped at Johnson's Ranch, nor the Federals at Kozlowski's realized they were within eleven miles of each other. They did not remain ignorant for long, however. Both commanders—Pyron and Chivington—sent out pickets to scout ahead. John Miller was one of the Union scouts and recalled arriving at Pigeon's Ranch early in the morning of the twenty-sixth. "Here we searched the premises," Miller remembered, "and after old Pigeon [Alexander Valle] found out who we were, after we told him we were Pike's Peakers or Colorado boys, he fairly danced, he was so delighted." Valle informed the Federals that four Texans had been at his ranch the night before. Now aware that their enemy was close at hand, Miller and the other scouts continued more cautiously. Suddenly, they came upon the four Texan scouts, who mistook them for fellow Confederates. Miller recalled that "they asked us if we came to relieve them. . . . Our lieutenant told them yes, we came to relieve you of your arms." The Confederates surrendered, and Miller helped bring them back to Chivington at Kozlowski's ranch. Chivington's forces immediately set out for the enemy camp, following the Santa Fe Trail. He passed Pigeon's Ranch and entered Apache Canyon.[53]

Despite—or perhaps because of—the failure of his scouts to report back, Major Pyron's forces also started off along the Santa Fe Trail, heading for the Federals he suspected were somewhere ahead. In the early afternoon, in the winding, steep, and rocky corridor of Apache Canyon, the two forces met among the trees. "Our boys were all anxious for a fight," Miller remembered.[54] The following battle, which lasted several hours, involved a series of retreats and holding actions by the Confederates. Finally, Chivington organized a cavalry charge. The cavalry attacked the Texans from the front while others went up the canyon sides to engage the enemy. Confusion and disorder reigned among the Confederates. Many fled down the canyon to their camp at Johnson's Ranch and set up defensive lines at the egress of the canyon. The Union soldiers took forty to fifty Texans prisoner—a substantial victory. By then it was around five o'clock and Chivington, worried about meeting a larger enemy force further ahead as the sun went down, chose to withdraw.

Chivington's force returned through the darkness across Glorieta Pass to Pigeon's Ranch, where they left the most critically wounded men in a makeshift field hospital, took several hours of rest, and buried the dead nearby. When they ran out of water, they had to retreat another five miles back to their campsite just south of Kozlowski's ranch. The next day, March 27, the nervous Confederates fully expected another attack. They fortified their position at Johnson's Ranch and waited anxiously through the long day. No attack materialized, however. Chivington had chosen to wait at Kozlowski's for the rest of the troops under Colonel Slough. Slough arrived after an eighteen-hour march with three hundred men at two in the morning on March 28 and immediately made plans to move forward and attack the Confederates again. Meanwhile, Colonel William R. "Dirty Shirt" Scurry arrived at Johnson's Ranch after a twelve-mile march with six hundred nearly frozen men and a supply train of eighty wagons to relieve Major Pyron of the Confederate command. Scurry also quickly became impatient and decided to advance.

Now that he knew the general territory, Slough sent Chivington's command of 480 men up the slopes of Glorieta Mesa on a road that led to the small village of Galisteo. Manuel Chaves guided Chivington and his men, along with several other nuevomexicanos, including Major Luis Baca and Indian superintendent James Collins. A wealthy rancher, Chaves knew the terrain of Glorieta Mesa well because of his sheep ranching operations in the area.[55] Slough instructed Chivington to swing around and hit the Texans on the flank while his command engaged them in a frontal assault. While Chivington and his men headed up the snowy slopes of Glorieta Mesa, Slough continued to Pigeon's Ranch, where he discovered his pickets eating breakfast. Sent forth once more, the scouts had gone only a short distance before they met Scurry's pickets.

The following battle repeated the previous day's events in reverse. This time the Federals formed successive lines of defense, dropping back under the determined advance of the Confederates. Two hills west of Pigeon's Ranch, which became known as Windmill Hill and Artillery Hill, offered attractive positions for artillery. A rocky ridge leading northwest of the ranch, although too steep for cannon to easily surmount, served as a roost for sharpshooters who could use the mountainous terrain and tree cover to their advantage. These initial lines held only briefly. In the second phase of the battle, the Federals repaired to Windmill Hill, with the artillery concentrated on the Santa Fe Trail. The Confederates attacked on all sides. "The firing now became very brisk," Union captain Herbert M. Enos later reported.[56] With the absence of Chivington's men, Slough was outnumbered. As the danger of the Confederates flanking his men on Windmill Hill increased, Slough withdrew to Pigeon's Ranch. Here a long adobe wall, which stretched from the ranch buildings across to the lower slopes of Artillery Hill, provided cover. The Union artillery took up position on Artillery Hill, following a logging road to the upper slopes. Other soldiers climbed the ridge to the northeast of the ranch, which quickly earned the sobriquet "Sharpshooter's Ridge."

Scurry charged the men at Pigeon's Ranch multiple times, but the line held. Confederate artillery fired down the Santa Fe Trail at the Federals. Once again, the Texans pressured the right and left flanks of the Union line. The wooded terrain obscured everyone's vision, but Lieutenant Tappan, in charge of the Union cannons, realized his position was untenable. When Slough withdrew from Pigeon's Ranch after a concerted attack on his right and center, Tappan's men were left stranded. A precarious retreat succeeded, and the Federals regrouped further down the road. The final Union position offered a rocky and wooded slope to the north, a position for the artillery in the center, and the ravine of Glorieta Creek on the left for shelter. Although the Texans attacked once more, by this time both sides were exhausted. After failing to break the Union line, the Confederates withdrew to Pigeon's Ranch.

There, Scurry received word of the disaster that had befallen the Confederates' camp in his absence. Led by Chaves over Glorieta Mesa and unable to hear the ongoing fighting due to an acoustic shadow, Chivington and his troops emerged from the woods on the slopes above the Confederate camp. Scurry, who apparently believed the surrounding mesas to be more impregnable than they actually were, had left only a few soldiers behind with the wounded. Descending down the steep, seven-hundred-foot slope aided by ropes and halters from their horses, Chivington's force quickly overpowered the small Texan rearguard. As the afternoon wore on, and aware that Scurry's force could return at any time, Chivington ordered the Confederates' supplies destroyed, including ammunition, clothing, and food. The loss of the supplies was crippling in the remote New Mexican conditions. Most of the hundreds of mules were either shot or driven away, and local residents later appropriated the wandering survivors. Chivington's men also took seventeen Confederate prisoners and captured about thirty horses and mules, and then retreated back up Glorieta Mesa.

As they struggled up the slope, they encountered Father Alexander Grzelachowski (Padre Polaco, "the Polish Priest"), chaplain of the Second New Mexico Infantry. Since his arrival in New Mexico with Bishop Lamy, Grzelachowski had been assigned to posts at San Felipe Pueblo, San Miguel del Vado, and Las Vegas. Chaves willingly surrendered his position as guide to Grzelachowski, who knew the area even better than Chaves did. On his white horse, the priest led the Federals through a shortcut off the northeast face of the mesa. Chivington and his men stumbled through a snowstorm to the road near Pecos Pueblo and along the Santa Fe Trail to Kozlowski's, bringing word to Slough of their triumphant raid. Upon arrival at the camp, Grzelachowski's horse fell dead from exhaustion.[57] The assistance of locals like Grzelachowski and Chaves was key to Chivington's successful raid.

The Battle of Glorieta Pass, although bloody and protracted, had brought victory to neither side. Scurry had taken a few miles of ground, advancing to Pigeon's Ranch, but Slough was not defeated. He could easily retreat back to Fort Union if necessary—an imposing obstacle for the Confederates. It was the destruction of Scurry's supplies that tipped the balance in the Union's favor. Sibley had relied on obtaining supplies from captured U.S. forts or from New Mexican inhabitants. But U.S. troops had burned their supplies, and the locals either fled, taking their food and livestock with them, or possessed little themselves. Already suffering from low provisions, now Scurry had no means of keeping his men alive in the remote region. Although Slough did return to Fort Union, as his orders had been to harass the enemy and nothing more, Scurry could not follow. Cold and exhausted, the Confederates left Glorieta Pass on March 30, walked twenty-two miles back to Santa Fe, and by summer had straggled more than 2,000 miles back to San Antonio, losing 30 percent of the soldiers along the way to heatstroke. In addition to facing each other on the battlefields around Glorieta, both the Union and Confederate troops had been forced to reckon with the harsh and remote New Mexican landscape. In all Civil War battles, "as weapon, shield, and prize, the terrain was never neutral."[58] At Glorieta Pass, the extremes of weather and terrain provided strategic advantages for the Union forces, who were prepared for the conditions and who relied on the knowledge of friendly local inhabitants. While the weather and the terrain were not the only reason the Federals won, the soldiers' varying abilities to endure the conditions, as well as access to basic resources and supplies, proved as important as military prowess, munitions, and battle tactics. The mountainous, late-winter conditions in the Upper Pecos valley shaped the events that unfolded in the spring of 1862.[59]

Helen Kozlowski may have heard the distant cannon fire during the battle, and she was surely relieved when the Confederates retreated and her home was no longer so close to the battlefield. Those residents who fled returned, and everyone took stock of the destruction. Both Alexander Valle and Anthony Johnson submitted claims to the federal government after the war for damages sustained during the fighting and also for the looting carried out by the Confederates as they retreated. Valle complained he had suffered "wear, breakage and destruction of inclosures [*sic*], fences, walls, doors, gates, water tanks, cisterns or wells, timbers, furniture, clothing, relics, Jewelry, money, carriages, etc."[60] He also requested reimbursement for 31,000 pounds of shelled corn, 14,200 pounds of fodder and hay, and 120 dozen bundles of sheaf oats.[61] Johnson requested reimbursement for "a stolen horse and two oxen, twenty bushels of corn, forty gallons of molasses, miscellaneous clothing, and one barrel of whiskey."[62] The supplies at Kozlowski's ranch were probably also depleted, although presumably the Federals paid for what they requisitioned, as no evidence of complaints from the Kozlowskis exist. Martin Kozlowski later noted, "When they camped on my place, and while they made my tavern their hospital for over two months after their battles in the canyon, they never robbed me of anything, not even a chicken."[63]

The Civil War dragged on for three more years, but the Confederates never returned to Pecos. Meanwhile, General James Carleton led a campaign against the Navajos from 1863 to 1864 that resulted in "the Long Walk" to the Navajos' confinement on the Bosque Redondo reservation on the Pecos River, about 150 miles southeast of Pecos Pueblo. There the treeless desert, infertile soil, and alkaline water offered none of the sustenance found at the river's headwaters. During the fighting, Ute and Mexican war parties and raiders capitalized on the situation to capture and sell Navajos. Historian Andrés Reséndez estimates that one to three thousand Navajos were enslaved and that "wealthy New Mexicans each possessed four, five, or more Navajo slaves." Ironically, the war that came to embrace the cause of emancipation in the east led to further enslavement in the Southwest. By 1867, the Apaches' resistance had also been quelled, and the United States became and remained the dominant force in the Southwest. The unofficial enslavement of Indians continued, as neither the Civil Rights Act of 1866 nor the Fourteenth Amendment applied to "Indians not taxed," and forms of debt peonage persisted into the twentieth century.[64]

The end of the Civil War did not bring relief to those living in forced-labor conditions in Pecos. They did not find much reason to cheer the United States' new hegemony. But for other residents of Pecos, including Helen and Martin Kozlowski, the cessation of war must have been cause for celebration after the tumultuous first half of the 1860s. They must have hoped for a return to peaceful, prosperous times, and in 1866, their operation became a stop on the Barlow and Sanders stage line.[65] But new transformations and changes were on the horizon—most significantly the arrival of the railroads. In 1869, the two halves of the first transcontinental railroad met in Promontory, Utah. It was only a matter of time before railroad barons, seeking new routes, laid tracks near Pecos. The Kozlowskis, Valle, and Johnson all depended on the existence of the Santa Fe Trail passing by their doorsteps to bring travelers and customers to their hostelries. If the railroad came, they might lose that business. There was also the question of their claims to their land, a question faced by all of those occupying the Pecos Pueblo grant. Under Spanish and Mexican law, use of the land had been enough to prove ownership. But the U.S. territorial government expected a legal chain of title, with documentary evidence as proof. Helen and Martin, for one, possessed no such documents, and they must have wondered, as the dust from the Civil War settled, whether they could continue to make their home in Pecos.

"I Do Some Buying of Wheat and Corn": Land Ownership and a Changing Economy

When several railroads converged in the region in the late 1870s, the New Mexican economy and environment underwent a tremendous transition. The Atchison, Topeka & Santa Fe (AT&SF) Railroad and the Denver and Rio Grande (D&RG) Railroad approached northeastern New Mexico from southern

Colorado, both laying tracks toward Raton Pass. In February 1878, the AT&SF won the race and became the first to extend its tracks into New Mexico. A year later, the railroad reached Las Vegas, north of Pecos, which became a center for shipping and commerce in the region. The AT&SF chose to follow roughly the same route as the old Santa Fe Trail—through Glorieta Pass and the Pecos vicinity—because of the valuable timber in the area, the presence of Santa Fe, and the natural pass afforded at Glorieta that people had used for centuries to cross into the Rio Grande drainage.[66] Although the route was similar to the Santa Fe Trail, the tracks did not pass directly by Kozlowski's Trading Post, Pigeon's Ranch, or Johnson's Ranch. While there were stops in nearby towns and settlements, the train, its cargo, and its passengers steamed past these hostelries, carrying away a large percentage of the trade and traffic.

In the Upper Pecos valley, the railroad changed demographics, settlement patterns, and the economy. New communities—many of them short-lived—proliferated along the railroad tracks. Rowe, first called Kingman Station but renamed by 1889, appeared west of the Los Trigos village. Los Trigos itself disintegrated as its inhabitants moved to Rowe.[67] Across Glorieta Creek, north and west of the pueblo ruins, two clusters of buildings formed in the 1880s, large enough to be marked as separate villages in the 1880 census. These were Baughl's Siding, also called Baughl's Switch or Bowll's Switch, and La Joya. Baughl's Siding lasted only two years and La Joya probably not much longer.[68] Indeed, all of these communities were temporary affairs—constructed to accommodate the needs of the railroad and abandoned when railroad construction moved to other parts of the region.

A diverse population called these settlements home while they lasted, and some people probably stayed in the Pecos area permanently. Pecos had always possessed connections to other landscapes and other people, but distance and time had tempered those connections. The railroad erased such inhibitors and brought Pecos into sudden and immediate contact with outside influences. The 1880 Pecos census recorded people who hailed from Ireland, France, England, and other areas of Europe. The influx of new immigrants pushed the population of the "precinct of Pecos" upward from 536 in 1900 to 667 in 1910. In 1910 forty-two local men worked for the railroad. New industries thrived in Pecos village, providing services for the railroad workers. The 1880 census showed a restaurant keeper and a saloon keeper in Pecos. Three blacksmiths worked "within five miles of each other." By 1900, a "whiskey salesman, jewelry salesman, grocery salesman, and others" plied their trade. A simple division of Pecos residents into "farmer, laborer, and farm laborer" no longer accurately described the area.[69] Whereas the popular perception of western towns and frontier settlements in this period is one of many men and few women, the Pecos area, as well as other places that had a long history of Puebloan and Hispanic settlement, was quite different. Many women, children, and family units populated these towns.

The arrival of the railroad brought other changes to Pecos. Wooden railroad ties, railroad cars, telegraph poles—all required timber for construction. A mile of narrow-gauge track consumed 104,000 board feet of lumber, which translated into roughly ten to fifteen acres of New Mexican forest.[70] The AT&SF, a standard-gauge track, used even more. In just two years following the arrival of the railroad, about thirty sawmills churned out lumber in the southern Sangre de Cristos.[71] The Pecos Pueblo grant also had attractive stands of timber, particularly on Glorieta Mesa and in the northern sections of the grant where ponderosa pine, Douglas fir, and other coniferous species were more prevalent. Some Pecos residents quickly capitalized on the new demand for timber. Adolph Bandelier, an archaeologist who investigated the ruins of Pecos Pueblo in 1880, climbed Glorieta Mesa and noted passing the "tie-camp of Mr. Keno." As he ascended, Bandelier took advantage of what he termed a "tie-shoot," the cleared path Keno used to roll or drag ties for the railroad down the mesa.[72] Another Pecos resident, Donaciano Vigil, allowed a sawmill in an adjacent arroyo to use the water from his irrigation ditch.[73] A map from a government survey in 1877 shows a sawmill on the east side of the Pecos River, directly across from the ruins of the pueblo, perhaps the one mentioned by Vigil.[74]

Piñon and juniper, although not suited to railroad construction, were valuable as firewood and also for making charcoal. Mining smelters used charcoal for fuel, and as mining operations expanded in New Mexico in the late 1800s, so did extensive timber use. Although pine and fir could also be turned into charcoal, green piñon trees were preferred. Charcoal was produced in airtight kilns, where the wood was partially burned through the gradual exclusion of oxygen. Charcoal kilns located at Lamy, southwest of Glorieta, were probably the closest to Pecos and may have used piñon harvested in the Pecos area.[75]

The railroad, the valuable timber, and the grazing land on the Pecos Pueblo grant—all drew the attention of speculators and investors interested in profiting from the resources of the Upper Pecos valley through land purchases and subsequent timber cutting or resale. The arrival of the railroads drew the attention of not only investors from the East, but from Europe as well, and foreign capital bankrolled unprecedented economic development in New Mexico.[76] The interests of these investors directly conflicted with those of the Kozlowskis, Valle, Donaciano Vigil, and the other settlers in the area who had been living on the grant for decades, claiming the land through right of use. But these were not the only people who possessed competing interests and claims to the land in the Upper Pecos valley. The Pecos Indians, although they now lived in Jemez Pueblo, still thought of Pecos as their homeland and felt they had been driven off the land involuntarily. They had never received payment for the grant, and in the 1850s and 1860s the Pecos sought to obtain a patent to the grant from the U.S. government so they could sell the land. Congress confirmed the Pecos grant in 1858, before the legal standing of Puebloan leagues and land grants grew increasingly confused.[77] Recognition of the Pecos league as a valid land grant did not mean that the Pecos and their descendants possessed clear title to the land, could demand the land back, or sell the land themselves. Previous legislation prohibited the distribution or sale of Indian land except under a treaty, and Congress became mired in debate over the question of whether the Puebloans could be called "Indian tribes." John P. Slough, the leader of the Union troops at the Battle of Glorieta, who later became a territorial judge, issued a decision in 1867. Slough ruled that because the Puebloans were "civilized," they could not be called "Indian tribes" and thus the Hispanic and Anglo settlers who had taken their land had done so legally.[78]

The Puebloans did not intend to allow this decision to stand, however, and they planned legal challenges. In the meantime, land speculators pursued purchasing grants from the Puebloans, hoping the courts would invalidate the claims of any settlers on the land, such as the Kozlowskis. Anglo-American men most well-placed to profit off these endeavors included those who worked for the Office of Indian Affairs and had connections among the Puebloans. One of these men was John N. Ward, who had served as an interpreter, clerk, and agent for the Office of Indian Affairs since 1850. Ward had worked with the Pecos at Jemez Pueblo and knew about the valuable tracts of land in the Upper Pecos valley. In 1868 Ward purchased a northern quarter of the Pecos Pueblo grant from the Pecos and also obtained the power of attorney to sell the rest of the grant. By 1872 the remaining portion of the grant became consolidated under the ownership of Frank Chapman, who purchased Ward's quarter. Chapman, a Las Vegas merchant and land speculator, also bought the remaining 14,000 acres from the Pecos for $4,000—Ward's quarter cost Chapman significantly more. Chapman posted signs around the grant warning against trespassing, but the fact remained that the entire Pecos village as well as Kozlowski's ranch were located on the land Chapman had just purchased.[79]

Although Chapman did nothing to try and evict the settlers, his purchase of the land halted further expansion of the town of Pecos downriver. The precise survey of the Pecos grant and the creation of a paper title under the federal government allowed for the land to be sold and bought by people who might never have set foot in Pecos. Despite the physical absence of men like Ward or Chapman, the absorption of Pecos into an Anglo system of ownership changed the landscape. As historian G. Emlen Hall describes it, after Chapman purchased the land, "the northern seven thousand acres of the Pecos Pueblo grant belonged to the Hispanos and the southern eleven thousand acres belonged to the succession of speculators who followed Frank Chapman."[80] The Kozlowskis were not alone on this southern portion—other homesteaders also occupied small plots of land. A homestead owned by Anicieto Rivera was probably occupied through the late 1800s, and around 1890 Pedro Ruíz began occupying a site that belonged to his father along the southern border of the Pecos Pueblo grant. Anicieto Rivera may also have owned another homestead, which showed signs of occupation in the early 1890s.[81] The Kozlowskis and their Hispanic neighbors could do little as surveyors, lawyers, and government officials divvied up the land in the valley with little or no regard as to how the local inhabitants had occupied the land and made use of the area's resources as individual families and as a community.

The story took a new turn when in 1873 the Commissioner of Indian Affairs ordered Thomas B. Catron, a U.S. attorney in Santa Fe, to bring suit against settlers who had encroached on Puebloan lands. For reasons that remain obscure, Catron chose the Pecos Pueblo grant as his first test case and filed suit against Martin Kozlowski. The threat of losing their land, which had loomed over the Kozlowskis for years, now became quite real. The case made its way to the Supreme Court, although by that time Martin had been dropped and other defendants were put in his place. Now known as *United States v. Joseph,* the case resulted in a decision similar to John Slough's several decades earlier. As with Slough, the Supreme Court ruled the Puebloans were not tribes and thus the settlement of their lands by Hispanos and Anglos was legal. The court did not consider whether the Puebloans were United States citizens.[82]

This decision at least temporarily prevented the Pecos Indians from trying to reclaim the land, but the Kozlowskis and their neighbors could not rest easily as the legal title to the Pecos Pueblo grant remained in the hands of investors who might one day decide to take a more personal interest in Pecos. Chapman's title to the land had transferred to his partner Andres Dold upon his death. Dold managed a mercantile store in Las Vegas, and he received rent and stumpage fees from itinerant businessmen who were operating tie camps on the grant.[83] Dold sold the land to J. Whitaker Wright of Philadelphia in 1881, and for the next seventeen years the title passed around the stock markets of the east, particularly New York. The men who bought the title had never been to Pecos and most had no intention of going there. They were able to trade the paper title to land thousands of miles away thanks to American surveying practices. Spanish surveys had usually recorded only the main boundary markers of a grant, leaving the rest of the grant vaguely defined with irregular outlines that conformed to the available resources of the land and the needs of settlers. But American surveying methods used precise, standardized measurements and strove to create an orderly system of grids on the land. For example, when an American surveyor, John Garretson, surveyed the Pecos Pueblo grant in 1859, the result was a perfectly formed square plopped down upon the landscape. Precise measurements allowed land to be treated as a standardized commodity. It could be sold and traded by people who never visited the actual place because they owned a piece of paper giving the exact location and measurements of the property.[84]

While these transactions were taking place in far-off New York, the inhabitants of Pecos went on selling and trading the land locally. The Pecos descendants at Jemez had sold the title to Frank Chapman in 1872, but they also sold portions of the grant again in the late 1870s and 1880s to Hispanic inhabitants of the Upper Pecos valley. Two separate paths of ownership of the Pecos grant developed—a virtual one in the hands of Anglo businessmen and one in the hands of Pecos residents tied to occupation of the land.[85] These local transactions also affected land outside of the Pecos Pueblo grant that is part of Pecos National Historical Park today.

The Kozlowskis hung on to their property, but Alexander Valle sold his ranch to a George Hebert in 1865. Hebert, who continued to operate the ranch as a stage stop and also added a post office, gave up the business in 1887 and sold the ranch to Walter and Sarah Taber. The Tabers built a house on the property and operated a store and the post office for a time, but they did not use many of the older ranch buildings. The structures suffered from disuse and neglect, and by 1920 only a corral, a three-room building, and the remnants of an adobe wall remained.[86] Although photographs from the 1880s still show wagons and live-stock at Pigeon's, they depict an emptier landscape, absent the bustling of people and animals that must have characterized the ranch in earlier decades when the Santa Fe Trail and not the railroad served as the main transportation route.[87]

In 1869 Anthony Johnson also sold his ranch.[88] Johnson's Ranch continued to function as a stop on the Southern Overland Mail route through 1880, but following the arrival of the railroad and the cessation of the mail route, Johnson's Ranch probably began falling into ruin. Photos from the early twentieth century show a decrepit structure, perhaps abandoned.[89] Certainly, people continued to live in the area, by then known as Cañoncito. A post office was located there briefly, from 1879 to 1880. Between 1880 and 1891 the parishioners of Cañoncito built a church, called the Nuestra Señora de Luz, which remains in use today.[90] These people probably owned some livestock and carried out small-scale farming.

The Kozlowskis persisted with their ranch and stage stop, even as the railroad and legal battles threatened both their livelihoods and their property rights. Travelers continued to stay there through the 1870s and exclaimed over the excellent trout obtained from the Pecos River.[91] When the railroad arrived in 1880, the stage stop ceased functioning as a waypoint, yet it remained a working ranch. The Kozlowskis faced more turmoil when, in 1878, Martin Kozlowski shot and killed a man who was in a confrontation with his sons. Martin pleaded not guilty to the crime of murder and served a two-year sentence in Las Vegas. After his release, the Kozlowskis continued to operate the ranch for more than a decade and eventually moved to join family in Albuquerque, where Helen died in 1895 and Martin in 1905.[92]

Although the Kozlowskis were gone, the land remained in their family. But the ultimate ownership of the land was still an open question. In 1896, John L. Laub of Las Vegas acquired the title to the Pecos Pueblo grant through the New York connections, bringing control of the title back to the region. Laub was a timber cutter and railroad tie contractor based in Las Vegas and had been cutting timber on the grant for several years before acquiring ownership. Laub "went on using the property for the next year and a half, cutting more timber and hauling more ties."[93] But Laub did not retain possession for long, and in

1898 he sold the title to the operators of Gross, Kelly, & Company, based in Las Vegas. The Gross Kelly Company operated wholesale and retail stores throughout the region, including one in Pecos. They also dealt in timber cutting and shipping wool, sheep, and cattle. They purchased the Pecos Pueblo grant for its timber and continued to carry out tie cutting operations on the grant.[94] Jerome Kunkle, who owned a section of land located north of Glorieta Creek, sold the timber on his tract to the Gross Kelly Company even though, as part of the grant purchased by the company, the timber technically already belonged to them.[95]

The Gross Kelly Company recognized the contradiction in having to buy timber for which it had already paid. Unlike previous owners, the company decided to do something about the situation and initiated a suit to gain clear title to the grant. They confronted a confused situation, as locals had continued selling and purchasing land on their own, ignoring the title rights of Dold, Laub, and the various New York investors. After 1910 a few local landowners began selling their property to D. C. Collier and Company. Collier lived in California and served as president of the Panama-California Exposition Company and as an officer in the San Diego branch of the American Institute of Archaeology. Collier was interested in Pecos for its archaeological potential, and also entertained schemes for a summer resort and irrigation development. Collier's ownership of the land conflicted with that of the Gross Kelly Company. Francis C. Wilson, who acted as attorney for both Collier and the Gross Kelly Company, filed a quiet title suit on behalf of Gross Kelly in 1914.[96]

Once again, Pecos residents faced the possibility of losing the claims to their land. The year before, Thomas Kozlowski, one of Martin's sons, either returned to the old trading post and rebuilt some of the structures or leased the land to someone who tried to revive the ranch. A 1913 survey shows two plots of "cultivated land" by the Kozlowskis' former residence. Other residents living near the pueblo ruins included Archibald D. Catanach, who operated a grain mill along the Pecos River. The mill had been built at some point after the Civil War. Constructed of wood with two to three stories, the mill received its water from a quarter-mile-long acequia that extended from the Pecos River to a reservoir on a small hill west of the mill. A wooden flume then carried the water from the reservoir to the mill. The acequia joined the Pecos at a bend in the river—a dam was probably constructed at this site to force water down the acequia. Catanach's mill used more modern machinery than other mills in the vicinity, such as one originally operated by Donaciano Vigil and later by his sons. Vigil's mill used a large grinding stone of lava, three-and-a-half feet in diameter, acquired from La Bajada Hill, southwest of Santa Fe, the same location where many Puebloans found metates for grinding. Vigil's mill, however, could only produce whole-ground flour, whereas Catanach's had the machinery for separating the bran and germ and producing refined flour.[97]

As the Gross Kelly Company initiated their quiet title suit, D. C. Collier quickly sold the tracts he had bought to the company, hoping to avoid costly legal battles. Pecos residents, however, prepared themselves for a fight, determined to prove their rights to the land. Realizing that attempting to evict the entire population of Pecos from the grant would be impossible, Gross Kelly settled for the 10,870 acres in the southern portion of the grant. The case made no mention of any possible claims the Pecos Indians may yet have possessed. To the newly arrived tie cutters and railroad workers, the only evidence of the former powerful and populous pueblo community was the pueblo ruin itself.[98]

Gross Kelly's quiet title suit solidified the borders around the land in the Upper Pecos valley. Land that had once been controlled through use and occupancy now belonged to people through a legal title. Allowing one's livestock to wander freely through the valley brought the risk of legal action. If a land owner such as Gross Kelly protested, the offender could be taken to court on trespassing charges. Although much of the land outside the town of Pecos remained unfenced, and cattle still grazed along the Pecos River, by the pueblo ruins, or on Glorieta Mesa, the legal mechanisms were now in place to halt free grazing if a land owner so desired.

The usurpation of lands once held in common aroused resentment in many Hispanic citizens whose families had lived on the land for decades. In 1889 in San Miguel County, a group calling themselves the *Gorras Blancas* (White Caps) formed in opposition to the growing privatization of communal lands and water rights. The Gorras Blancas cut fences—both of Anglos and other Hispanos—and destroyed railroad tracks. They also undertook more conventional forms of protest by attempting to force companies to set standard prices for hauling and cutting railroad ties and encouraging railroad teamsters to strike. The Gorras Blancas enjoyed a great deal of local support, but their activities lasted little more than two years. Upon the formation of an area chapter of the People's Party, which also championed the rights of farmers against wealthy interests, many of the members of the group joined, and their more subversive activities ceased.[99]

Most people simply tried to find a means to survive in an economy driven by the railroad and encompassed by an environment of rigid legal and physical boundaries. As Hispanos lost land to Anglos, they also lost grazing territory. Some Hispanos in turn encroached on Puebloan lands, but many men, instead of owning their own herds, found employment as ranch hands with large livestock operations. By the 1910 Pecos census, more men worked on stock ranches than those who herded their own sheep and cattle. The number of farmers in the valley also began to drop. In 1910 ninety-seven men worked as farmers, farm laborers, or herders. By 1920 more men reported a second source of income—freighting or stock raising—in addition to farming.[100] People continued to raise crops for profit, though. For example, newspaper accounts from 1925 refer to the early crop of head lettuce at Pecos and mention B. A. Ruter (also spelled Reuter), who was planting sixty acres of head lettuce, two acres of peas, and three acres of cauliflower on lands he owned south of Pecos village.[101]

But increasingly, men found employment outside the Upper Pecos valley, sending money home to family members and returning themselves for only short periods. The sugar beet fields in northern Colorado attracted thousands of workers during the planting and harvesting seasons. The Colorado Fuel and Iron Company also employed large numbers of northern New Mexicans in the coal fields of southern Colorado. Indeed, these industries relied on the low-paid labor of Hispanos and Mexicans. Men were not the only ones to leave home looking for work. The sugar beet industry, in particular, drew entire families to work in the fields.[102]

At Pecos, many found it impossible to maintain a livelihood solely from the immediate environment. Archibald Catanach's mill, for example, remained a small-scale enterprise. In a 1918 letter requesting a license for his mill he described it as "a small mill about 60 bushel capacity a day and I grind the most on toll for the people and I do not run regular. And I do some buying of wheat and corn on a small scale."[103] Although the Catanach mill was the largest mill between Las Vegas and Santa Fe, it still could not survive. Catanach sold it to E. R. Crews in 1918, and the mill probably ceased operation shortly thereafter.[104] Thomas Kozlowski's attempts at reviving his family's old ranch also failed. In the 1920s Thomas lost the land due to a failure to pay taxes.[105]

The changes in the economy and land ownership that upended the lives of many in Pecos also wrought havoc on the Pecos environment. Of course, Hispanic ranchers and farmers, and the Pecos before them, had not always regulated their use of resources. Timber depletion and overgrazing had been a problem on a local scale before the late 1800s. But by the turn of the twentieth century, large ranches spread across northern and eastern New Mexico, the numbers of cattle and sheep had increased, and timber demand had skyrocketed. The forests of the Pecos watershed bore the impacts of such intensive resource use.

Overgrazing and upstream erosion had particularly severe impacts on riparian areas. Photos taken in 1915 of Glorieta Creek reveal a landscape with no willows or cottonwoods. The entire floodplain around the creek appears bare, and stands of piñon and juniper on the surrounding slopes are thin.[106] Similar conditions probably existed along the Pecos River.

A twenty-year drought in the late nineteenth century compounded the problems of overgrazing. When a wetter period began in the early twentieth century, the increase in runoff velocity and volume created trenching, deepening existing arroyos or creating new ones.[107] In the Upper Pecos valley, the first severe flood of the new century occurred in 1904. Heavy rains arrived late in the month of September, swelling the headwaters of the Pecos River. On the morning of September 30, the river overwhelmed its banks, sending floodwaters hurtling downstream. Communities all along the Sangre de Cristo range suffered, including Pecos and Las Vegas.[108]

As creek beds eroded and weeds replaced native species, environmental changes affected many species of mammals and birds as well. The increase in human population in the Pecos area, many of whom sought to supplement their diets by hunting and also enjoyed hunting as a sport, caused the local extinction of elk by 1888. The need to provide food for railroad workers, in particular, hastened the destruction of elk herds. Bighorn sheep were gone by 1903, and the mule deer population, which had probably declined in the fifteenth century when the population peaked at Pecos Pueblo, also fell in the twentieth century. This time, the population decline occurred over a much greater area. On the Carson National Forest in northern New Mexico only eight deer survived in 1915.[109] Species that depended on riparian vegetation also declined as river banks became denuded and eroded.

The Pecos landscape reflected the transitions in the regional economy. Livestock still roamed the mesas and forests, and people still planted crops in the Pecos ciénega, but by the 1920s these land uses had become less economically important. Upper Pecos valley residents, particularly men, left the area to find seasonal wage work. The agricultural landscape became the domain of the women who cared for farms and ranches in their absence. Local residents formed connections to other landscapes in Colorado where the presence of certain resources—coal and sugar beets—drew workers from northern New Mexico. The grain mill along the Pecos River testified to the continuing importance of local production; yet by the 1920s its grinding stones stood idle and its wheels had fallen silent.

The Pecos River to the east of the Pecos Pueblo ruins in 2009. Photo by authors.

View of Glorieta Mesa from the Pecos Pueblo ruins in 2009. Photo by authors.

View from Sharpshooter's Ridge of Pigeon's Ranch in June 1880. There is little vegetation along Glorieta Creek, and an open meadow beyond the ranch buildings. The man sitting on the rock in the foreground is holding an axe. Photo by Ben Wittick and courtesy of the Palace of the Governors Photo Archives (NMHM/DCA), negative no. 015782.

Photo of the mission ruins circa 1919 showing the denuded landscape. Photo by William H. Roberts and courtesy of the Palace of the Governors Photo Archives (NMHM/DCA), negative no. 149877.

An Indian Detours tourist bus stuck in the mud near Pecos in 1928. Photo courtesy of the Palace of the Governors Photo Archives (NMHM/DCA), negative no. 134659.

An aerial photo of the Pecos Pueblo and mission ruins taken by Charles Lindbergh in 1929 that shows the lack of vegetation around the mesilla and the Glorieta Creek drainage. Photo courtesy of the Palace of the Governors Photo Archives (NMHM/DCA), negative no. 130365.

Tom Greer's tourist attraction at Pigeon's Ranch circa 1935. Photo by T. Harmon Parkhurst and courtesy of the Palace of the Governors Photo Archives (NMHM/DCA), negative no. 009689.

Greer Garson standing by her truck on the Forked Lightning Ranch, wearing a cowboy hat and holding one of her poodles. Photo courtesy of the Hamon Arts Library, Southern Methodist University.

Annual feast day procession from Pecos village to the mission ruins with the painting of the patron saint of Pecos Pueblo, Our Lady of the Angels of Porciúncula (Nuestra Señora de los Ángeles de Porciúncula), circa 1988. Photo by Sydney Brink and courtesy of the Palace of the Governors Photo Archives (NMHM/DCA), negative no. HP.2014.14.1098.

A spray-painted message on a fencepost, "Don't Mess with Pecos," protests the proposed sale of the Forked Lightning Ranch to a developer in 1989. Photo by Edward Vidinghoff and courtesy of the Palace of the Governors Photo Archives (NMHM/DCA), negative no. HP.2014.14.1094.

Looking southeast from the Pecos Pueblo ruins in 2009, with a partially restored kiva in the foreground. The Park Service has maintained the view of the open meadows from the mesilla by mechanically clearing piñon-juniper ingrowth. Photo by authors.

Looking northwest at the Glorieta Creek drainage from the Pecos Pueblo ruins in 2009. The riparian vegetation in the creek bed is thick, and the slopes are heavily wooded with piñon-juniper. Photo by authors.

Pecos dancers at the August 2, 2018, Feast of Nuestra Señora de los Ángeles de Porciúncula at Pecos National Historical Park. Photo courtesy of the *Santa Fe New Mexican.*

FIVE | # Making a Living in
the Land of Enchantment
1916–1941

The Forked Lightning Ranch, 1927—Tex Austin urged his horse into the Pecos River, the stones in the shallows rimmed with frost. They splashed across, and Tex glanced back over his shoulder to make sure the party of tourists, astride their mounts from his stable, made it over safely as well. The tourists were in good spirits despite the chill in the autumn air, looking forward to a day of hunting and riding through the forests and across the mesas. In the evening they would return to Tex's Forked Lightning Ranch and enjoy a hearty meal, happily following the encouragement printed in the dude ranch's brochures to eat their fill as "no one keeps track of the helpings." Tex relished the chance to get out for a ride. He had spent much of his time during 1927 organizing a rodeo in Chicago, held at the end of August.[1]

Tex regarded New Mexico, and Las Vegas in particular, as his adopted homeland. When he traveled to Chicago or New York or London with his rodeos, he always touted the virtues of New Mexico as the perfect country to visit on a vacation. Just a few days before, the Las Vegas Chamber of Commerce had designated October 21 "Tex Austin Day" in recognition of his efforts to promote the state, and they held a celebratory banquet in his honor. During the evening, a letter by the author Clement Yore, an acquaintance of Tex, was read aloud. "He shaved, first, when he was nearly four," Yore wrote. "He was chewing Climax then, and they called him Panatella."[2] Yore went on to describe Tex's early career:

> Sometimes, he was so broke he rattled like an old Missouri Democrat wagon, coming to town, after it had wintered in a fence corner, and had been used for a harness rack all summer. Then I was told that he had spilled a lotta jack around Paso, San Antone, Roswell, Tucumcari, and other

seaport towns; had stole the Civil War guns out of the post office's front yard in El Paso to help Villa romp into the back-alley of Juarez. Soon somebody asked me if I ever heard of a cow-impresario by the name of Austin. When I said no that bird withered me with a glance![3]

Yore reminisced about when Tex organized a rodeo at Madison Square Garden in New York in 1922. "Then he blowed into New York and I see his pee-rade coming down Fifth Avenue," Yore elaborated. After relating how several of the show's "broncs" had gotten loose and ridden wild through the city, ending up in "night clubs and actresses' dressing rooms," Yore concluded that Tex "set little old Noo Yawk wild with the heaves! Yes sir, they heaved all the things like good luck tokens they could at Tex and said to him, 'Cowboy, we've seen 'em all, but you've give us a bronc show!'" Tex went on to take his rodeo to London, Boston, and Hollywood. "If there's anything in that glass around where this is being read," Yore wrote, "anything of a fluid nature, except buttermilk, coca cola, or hair tonic, then one of you rannihans raise it and gulp it, as my toast to Tex Austin." Yore concluded, "He's a first class showman, a whale of a friend. Lord, how he loves New Mexico and how he's always boosting the state, and if you asks me what my wish for him is I'll sure give it to you in this sentence: "Stay a long time, cowboy, stay a long, long time!"[4]

Tex chose not to comment on the accuracy of Yore's letter. Stories such as Tex riding with Pancho Villa served a man who made his living off people's fascination with the Old West far better than a more mundane reality. The success of Tex's rodeos, and also the dude ranch he started in the Upper Pecos valley in 1925, depended on the image of a mythic West inhabited by brave and daring cowboys, fiery horses, and American Indians who were either helpful sidekicks or villains depending on the needs of the story. At his Forked Lightning Ranch along the Pecos River, tourists expected to find horses, cattle, and cowboys—all of which Tex provided. If he could not manage to introduce them to real Indians, the ruins of Pecos Pueblo at least provided an appropriate setting for the myths and tall tales eagerly consumed by guests.

Tourists came to the Forked Lightning Ranch to have outdoor adventures with an "Old West" flair. Guests wanted to hunt deer and turkey, fish for trout in the Pecos River, and eat chuck wagon dinners on pack trips into the high country. Although Tex owned a sizable herd of cattle and horses, his uses of the land differed from those who had lived there before him. The cattle were not there just to grow fat and be shipped off to market—they also played a necessary role in the cowboy drama. The deer were not hunted to supplement a diet of corn or wheat—the ranch guests hunted them for pleasure. Whether or not the soil along the Pecos River could produce crops was immaterial—Tex bought supplies for the ranch in Pecos or Santa Fe that had been shipped to the region by railroad. From the porch of his ranch house, Tex looked out on a landscape he valued for its enticing scenery as much as its grazing capacity.

"The Night Stars Glow like Headlights":
The Upper Pecos Valley as a Tourist Destination

The ruins of Pecos Pueblo had attracted curious travelers on the Santa Fe Trail as early as the 1820s, but it wasn't until the railroad came through Pecos in 1880 that tourism began to play a larger and larger role in the economy of Pecos. The railroad capitalized on the growing fascination with ancient American Indian cultures, pueblo ruins, and quaint Hispanic villages to draw many tourists to the Southwest beginning in the late 1800s. Many of those tourists visited Pecos, and their presence brought a new meaning to the Pecos landscape. Under the "tourist gaze," Pecos became romanticized, mythologized, and deemed worthy of preservation.[5]

Railroad companies realized tourism could be a profitable business, that railroad cars could be filled with people just as easily as timber and coal. By the early 1900s, railroad companies, including the Atchison, Topeka & Santa Fe, embarked on a promotional campaign that presented the Southwest as the ideal tourist destination. Many promoters lauded the climate—dry, sunny, and warm with unique landforms, thick forests, and snow-capped mountains. Not only could tourists find a healthful climate but an enchanting history as well. One depiction of Santa Fe described it as possessing "something of that intangible air of mystery that the Moors brought from the Far East to Granada . . . transplanted to American soil by the conquistadores." Tourist narratives depicted New Mexico as a place that modern life had bypassed, where Puebloans, Navajos, and Hispanos carried out their ancient ways of life unchanged.[6]

The tourism industry combined ideas about race, the landscape, and traditional architecture into a romanticized image that could be marketed to tourists. Tourism relies heavily on visual imagery, and the landscape of New Mexico with its adobe homes, pueblo ruins, mesas, and piñon trees became as essential to the tourism industry as the people tourists encountered. As historian Sylvia Rodriguez argues, ideas about race became integrated into the landscape. Tourism in New Mexico "is striking for its extraordinarily successful mystification of race. It is successful because of the enduring and pervasive power of the iconic triad of Indian-Mexican-Anglo." Puebloans assumed the role of exotic "others" close to nature and spiritual powers. Such depictions stereotyped them as ideal stewards of nature and ignored the more complex history of resource exploitation in the Southwest. Although Hispanos often were saddled with the negative racist assumptions that came with the term "Mexican," the tourism industry usually depicted Hispanos as rustic villagers who lived simple, authentic lives. White tourists who came to New Mexico sought to experience such authenticity and exoticism through viewing pueblo ruins, attending American Indian dances, and purchasing hand-woven rugs or pottery.[7]

The growth of the tourism industry had implications for the New Mexican environment and the people who lived there. In order to perpetuate a romantic historical narrative, the tourism industry both preserved and created landscape features that tourists expected to see. Suddenly, New Mexicans had an economic incentive to preserve pueblo ruins, provide money for archaeological digs, and maintain the pristine, "enchanting" environment that attracted visitors and new residents. In doing so, the tourism industry provided economic opportunities for New Mexican inhabitants, including Hispanos and Puebloans. But tourism also maintained the ethnic boundaries that restricted Hispanos' and Puebloans' access to power, including control of land and resources.[8]

Archaeologists were intimately connected to the tourism industry, as they fed the public appetite for relics and stories of American Indian cultures. Pecos Pueblo, a substantial yet easily accessible ruin, attracted many archaeologists— both amateur and professional. In 1880, Adolph Bandelier, the pioneering scholar of indigenous Southwest cultures, was the first to conduct measurements of the ruins and gather a small quantity of artifacts for study. The first extensive archaeological excavation occurred under the direction of Alfred Kidder, who worked at Pecos from 1915 to 1929. Kidder used the newly popular technique of stratigraphic excavation, and his work at Pecos was the foundation for Rio Grande archaeology, including the southwestern classification periods still in use today. Kidder excavated both within the actual pueblo and church complexes as well as the midden heap on the east side of the mesilla, which contained the waste products of day-to-day life. The midden heap revealed a wealth of ceramics layered sequentially from earliest to latest. This discovery enabled Kidder and his colleague, Anna Shepherd, to formulate a ceramic typology that became the standard dating method for southwestern archaeology. Kidder's excavations "started a new era in American archaeology," not only through the development of stratigraphy and ceramic chronologies, but through Kidder's emphasis on data collection and analysis over simply recovering interesting artifacts.[9] Although archaeology encouraged preservation, it also endangered artifacts by disturbing or removing them and by raising their market value. Ruins and graves became tempting targets for relic hunters.

Casual tourists, too, often removed artifacts from unguarded archaeological sites. While tourists initially traveled by railroad, soon a new mode of transportation, the automobile, carried visitors down bumpy dirt roads to pueblos and mountain villages. The Fred Harvey Company, in partnership with the AT&SF, started its Indian Detours business in 1925. The three-day auto tour took tourists on a circuit between Santa Fe, Las Vegas, and Albuquerque. One of the stops was at Pecos. The ruins were visible only from the windows of a train car as it rushed past, but in an automobile, tourists could drive directly up to the pueblo and clamber about, searching for souvenir artifacts.[10]

With an automobile, people could travel to far-off destinations quickly and cheaply. Automobile ownership opened the United States to leisure travel. As urban populations grew, many people desired travel to destinations that afforded them the opportunity to experience a more rustic, "natural" lifestyle. Concern about the effects of industrialization and urbanization had led to the development of a "back to nature" ethic in the late nineteenth century, an ethic that promoted outdoor recreational pursuits as a way to combat the perceived problems of modern urban life. People also began participating in nature tourism—going to specific destinations to enjoy spectacular vistas, hike, mountain climb, and horseback ride. The growth of the National Park Service in the 1920s reflected the popularity of nature tourism. During the 1920s and 1930s, automobile ownership allowed growing numbers of Americans to spend their vacations in the outdoors.[11]

Rather than a relationship with the natural environment based on everyday activities related to producing crops and livestock for market and feeding families, this new relationship emphasized different aspects of the environment. Historian Paul Sutter describes the characteristics of a "leisure-based attachment to nature" that, for tourists, is "separate, distant, and exotic—a nature that one goes to see." Outdoor recreation also fosters a separation between leisure and everyday life. Hunting, fishing, or camping for pleasure attracts people because such activities are an escape from workday routines. Tourism affects "destination" locales like the Upper Pecos valley because it motivates local land holders to manage places to produce a specific experience of entertainment and escape for visitors.[12]

In the 1920s and 1930s, Tex Austin's Forked Lightning Ranch exemplified the growing importance of tourism to the Pecos environment and economy. Located "way out west an' a little bit south," as one tourist brochure put it, the Forked Lightning Ranch capitalized on the public's infatuation with the mythic Southwest and its ancient American Indian ruins, with a healthy dose of cowboy culture mixed in. The landscape was essential to the myth. Sparkling rivers rushing down from the mountains, mesas covered with piñon and juniper, cattle grazing and horses galloping by—these elements provided a well-recognized background to the tales of the Western frontier. For the tourists staying at the Forked Lightning, the right setting complemented the outdoor activities they enjoyed.[13]

Tex Austin's entire career and adult identity was based on the romance and myth of the West. Born Clarence Van Norstrand in 1885, he later changed his name to John Van "Tex" Austin, a name he considered more suitable for a rugged American cowboy. As an adult, Tex headed to California, where he worked in a few early western movies. By 1910 Tex was producing rodeos, including the Rough Riders Reunion in Las Vegas, New Mexico. His rodeos went to Wrigley Field in Chicago, and also to Boston, New York, and, in 1924, London. His involvement in the Las Vegas rodeo probably served as his introduction to the Pecos region, and his career in the entertainment industry provided ample proof of the profits to be made off people's fascination with the American West. Rodeos, like people's desire to "get back to nature," reflected the anxieties of an urbanizing America as more people moved to cities and left their rural roots behind. The dramatized shows also capitalized on the racial and ethnic myths evident in the tourism industry's depiction of New Mexico. In rodeos and on the silver screen, cowboys were always white, despite the fact that real cowboys came from a variety of racial and ethnic backgrounds, including African-American and Hispanic. Historian Louis Warren describes the romanticized Anglo cowboys showcased in rodeos as "racially distilled men, hardened by frontier combat. . . . [C]owboys were bulwarks against the modern age and all its miscegenated, manufactured, and artificial blandishments." Rodeos reassured audiences that white American masculinity had not perished in urban effeteness, although the rough handling of steers and other animals shocked some audience members who had never witnessed the daily practices of livestock handling on Western cattle ranches.[14]

Tex did not limit his entrepreneurial skills to traveling rodeo shows. In 1925 he purchased 6,000 acres of the Pecos Pueblo grant, including the Kozlowskis' old homestead, usually referred to as the Trading Post, with the intention of setting up a dude ranch with accommodations and diversions for tourists.[15] He purchased the land from the Continental Life Insurance company of St. Louis, which had obtained the land through a foreclosed mortgage.[16] It is unclear whether the Gross Kelly Company had mortgaged the land or if there was another owner between Gross Kelly and Tex. Tex also purchased a variety of small tracts scattered around the river. These included a homestead owned by Benigo Quintana and the one owned by Pedro Ruíz.[17] A 1934 Bureau of Land Management survey showed that Tex and his wife, Mary Lou, owned 6,229 acres and the Continental Life Insurance company owned about 4,000 acres west of the AT&SF railroad tracks—the majority of Glorieta Mesa within the Pecos grant.[18] The Gross Kelly Company had donated the pueblo and church ruins to the Archbishop in Santa Fe in 1920, who transferred it to the state in 1935.[19] Although Tex did not own the property, the ruins remained unfenced and unmanaged, and visitors to his adjacent ranch could wander freely about the site.

Tex named his ranch the Forked Lightning and hired the Santa Fe architect John Gaw Meem to design an attractive ranch house with twelve bedrooms on a plot of land with the Pecos River on the east and Glorieta Creek to the southwest. Meem designed the ranch in the Spanish-Pueblo Revival style, which reflected a romanticized, artificial view of New Mexican history. Architects in Santa Fe at the turn of the century, seeking a design that would reflect the city's unique history, selectively chose elements from various historic buildings to form the Pueblo Revival style. The style was calculated to appeal to tourists and fit within the mythic historical narrative developed by the tourism industry. The Spanish-Pueblo Revival style Meem used for the Forked Lightning Ranch house resembled an idealized Southwestern home with its long porch, protruding roof beams, and stucco walls. Elements of the Pueblo Revival style also created natural climate control for residents. The long, narrow *portal* (covered porch) provided shelter from the desert sun. The thick walls retained heat in the winter and maintained a cooler temperature in summer. In these respects, the revival style was more than just a superficial imitation of traditional Puebloan architecture. Tex incorporated Kozlowski's Trading Post into the ranch as the foreman's quarters. The Trading Post may also have provided extra beds for guests when necessary.[20] Tex removed the remains of the grist mill by the Pecos River and may also have demolished any structures associated with Hispanic homesteads on his land.[21] The Forked Lightning hosted a number of distinguished visitors over the years. Archaeologist Alfred Kidder held the first Pecos Conference on Southwestern Archaeology at the ranch in 1926. Charles and Anne Lindbergh also visited the Forked Lightning in 1929, and under Kidder's direction Charles Lindbergh took several aerial photos of the area around the Pecos ruins that contributed to Kidder's study of the site and captured the environmental conditions and land use patterns of the area at that time.[22]

Brochures produced by Tex detailed the numerous activities visitors could enjoy at his ranch. They could "stroll through an old orchard by the murmuring river" or "pull a few trout from the clear, cool waters of the old Rio Pecos."[23] One brochure claimed the river was "practically infested with trout."[24] Hunting parties occasionally sought out the deer and wild turkey when in season. Mealtimes were an important aspect of the visit. "Dinner and supper are served ranch style, placed on the large family table in big heaping dishes."[25] Visitors could choose from a variety of offerings. One menu included a "Special Mexican Plate" of chili con carne or posole and pork with tamales and frijoles. Other choices were Hungarian Goulash, Dinty Moore's Corned Beef and Cabbage, broiled sirloin steak, fresh mountain trout, "imported Italian spaghetti," oysters, and a "Cowboy Steak Sandwich on Toast."[26] Guests also enjoyed "fresh vegetables grown on Austin's ranch."[27] Other activities included "pack and chuck wagon trips to the high peaks" and riding parties. Tex Austin built a polo field adjoining the ranch house.[28] One brochure admiringly stated that at the ranch, visitors could find a landscape of unmatched beauty, where "the night stars glow like headlights," an idiom of mechanization that reflected how technology mediated people's experiences of nature.[29]

The Forked Lightning also operated as a working ranch with sizeable herds. These animals provided the appropriate scenery for tourists but also supported Tex's rodeo business. Tourist brochures boasted the cattle herd numbered in the thousands, but actual numbers were much lower. In a history of the ranch written in 2001, historian Andrew Young gives the number as "several hundred" cattle, citing an interview with a local resident and ranch manager. Tex leased another ranch near Santa Rosa, known as the Moon Ranch, as well as more land in the Pecos area, and he spread his cattle herd throughout these locations. Tex also owned a large horse herd.[30] Photos from tourist brochures show both the cattle herd and the horse herd, called the "remuda," watering in and crossing the Pecos River. The herds grazed on Tex's land in the valley and also on Glorieta Mesa. One brochure said the mesa "assures excellent summer feed for Tex Austin's cattle . . . . Dropping by sloping grades from this elevation, the cattle are worked through spring to winter feed at the lower pasturage, 3,000 feet nearer sea level, beside the Pecos."[31] These were probably the largest herds that had grazed in the area for a while—perhaps since the mid-1800s when the substantial herds of the Pinos and Vigils roamed the banks of the Pecos. The effects of the animals on riparian vegetation can be seen in a photo of Tex's ranch house. Taken from the banks of Glorieta Creek, looking north up to the house, the photo shows a bank practically bare of vegetation—no willows or cottonwoods grow along the creek.[32] Grazing similarly affected riparian vegetation along the Pecos River on the Forked Lightning Ranch.

Tex Austin was only one of many dude ranchers and proprietors in the Upper Pecos valley to profit from the tourist trade. A man named Tom Greer purchased Pigeon's Ranch in 1926 and turned it into a tourist attraction. Born in 1881 in Woodruff, Arizona, Thomas Lacey Greer moved to New Mexico in 1914, but before then he lived in El Paso, Texas, where he may have known Tex Austin. Perhaps his acquaintance with Tex led him to purchase land in the Pecos area and follow Tex's footsteps in capitalizing on people's interest in the history of the Southwest. Greer developed Pigeon's Ranch specifically to target tourists passing through the valley in their automobiles. Highways now crisscrossed New Mexico, including Route 66. Although the post-WWII years saw the transformation of Route 66 into a tourist icon, many tourists ventured to the Southwest in their cars in the prior decades as well.[33]

Greer utilized both the Hispanic and the American Indian history of the area as well as the Civil War Battle of Glorieta Pass to lure tourists into the old adobe building at Pigeon's Ranch. Photos of the ranch, as well as the reminiscences of Bill Greer, Tom's son, suggest Greer merged several attractions related to the Old West into a kitschy conglomeration. In the main building, decorated with animal skins, Greer opened a museum and sold a selection of curios and souvenirs. He advertised an adjacent building as the hospital used by Civil War troops, erroneously claiming that "parts of these old walls" had been constructed 200 years prior to his ownership of the property. Greer billed the old well across the road from the main building as "Coronado's Well," although it was probably constructed in the mid-1800s. Like Tex Austin, Greer had no interest in historical accuracy when myth served his purposes. In one photo, a sign mentions the "entrance to the cave" by Sharpshooter's Ridge, probably referencing some rock formation. Photos also show a man dressed in an Indian costume complete with headband and beaded necklaces as he talked to tourists. Bill Greer remembered his father keeping at least two pet bears, another element of the frontier atmosphere Greer imagined. According to his son, Tom Greer owned livestock as well—about eight to ten horses and 110 cattle. Besides offering extra income, the cattle and horses also contributed to the Western scene, just as they did at the Forked Lightning Ranch. Greer probably held a permit to graze the cattle in the surrounding forests, which were now owned and managed by the federal government. The animals also grazed around Pigeon's Ranch, and riparian vegetation along Glorieta Creek may have remained sparse. Greer also operated a gas station and garage at the ranch, and a plethora of hand-painted signs vied for tourists' attention as they drove past.[34]

Tourism introduced new ways of conceiving of and experiencing the Pecos environment. In economic terms, tourists valued the environment not for what was extracted—timber, grass, crops—but for what stayed in place. These values provided new rationales for landscape protection. Tourism was still a form of land use, but one that depended on preservation-oriented land management. Through tourism, new borders could be placed around landscapes—borders that separated landscapes that were "worthy of preservation" and conveyed romantic, idealized values. But although preserving a landscape such as a pueblo ruin afforded the illusion of timelessness, it required very active management to create that illusion in the first place.

"Herds of Wild Horses Scamper through the Piñon": Forest Management in the Upper Pecos Valley

By the 1920s, the U.S. Forest Service was the primary land manager in the Upper Pecos region, and the agency's policies affected both the environment and the community. Although the Forest Service managed the land for productive purposes—particularly grazing and timber extraction—recreation became an ever-growing emphasis as the twentieth century progressed. Like the National Park Service, the Forest Service represented a national manifestation of preservationist and conservationist ideologies. In 1892, President Benjamin Harrison had approved the creation of the Pecos River Forest Reserve.[35] The Pecos Reserve became the Santa Fe National Forest in 1915. A variety of administrative shifts and name changes occurred over the years, but the boundaries of the forest remained basically the same. In the Pecos area, as in most of New Mexico, the national forest consisted of the old communal lands—the land that people had used for grazing, firewood gathering, and piñon nut harvesting for centuries. The Santa Fe National Forest surrounded the Pecos Pueblo grant and the area around Glorieta and Cañoncito on almost all sides.[36]

The Forest Service operated with the assumption that trained professionals were better land managers than local residents, who wasted resources and destroyed the forests' sustainability. Professional foresters investigated the woodlands of the nation and often returned appalled by what they saw as wasteful and harmful practices, particularly in the large tracts of forests in the West. Justifying their reforms with science, the Forest Service put a halt to unrestrained timber cutting and grazing. Although the Forest Service never intended to stop these practices altogether—the agency stood by the principle that their lands were for public use—it instituted reform policies and regulations to improve the health of forests.[37]

In many cases the Forest Service correctly determined that local residents had abused forest resources. But foresters and other land management professionals often held views that, although in line with the prevailing science of the day, later proved to be ill-founded. For example, eliminating "bad" species, such as coyotes and wolves, to boost populations of "good" species, such as deer, was common practice. Wolves killed livestock whereas deer provided game for hunters. Forest rangers poorly understood the ecological role of predators. Aldo Leopold, working as a ranger on the Carson National Forest in the early 1900s, later criticized the Forest Service's predator policy, but at that time he was just beginning to develop his ecological land ethic. The function of fire in ecosystems also eluded many early land managers. The Forest Service approached fire from the perspective that all fires wasted valuable timber. Backed by the aura of professional authority and economic pressures to manage for maximum yield, the Forest Service suppressed fires whenever possible. The agency brought these management policies to the Upper Pecos region, with unforeseen consequences for the environment.[38]

One of the agency's main responsibilities concerned regulating the numbers of livestock allowed in national forests. Rangers in New Mexico realized that stock numbers would have to be cut drastically in order to improve the health of the range. Beginning in 1905, Forest Service officials instituted a permit system. Ranchers applied for a permit, and the Forest Service allotted them a certain number of cattle or sheep that did not exceed the number determined by managers as the carrying capacity of the range. Officials also felt grazing methods needed to be changed. Graziers drove their herds to the high country as soon as the snows began clearing, usually in early May. Because the animals arrived so early and stayed through the entire summer, grasses received no rest period.[39] Ranger John W. Johnson described the state of the range when he arrived at the Pecos District in 1918: "Removal of the excess [livestock] was necessary. Most of the climax-type forage was gone from the higher elevations and less valuable plants were taking its place. Some of the high open land around the head of the streams had nothing but skunk cabbage and sneezeweed. Erosion was active because summer rains are almost all of the flood type, and every heavy rain filled the streams with silt."[40]

The tourist industry also contributed to the problem. The tourist brochures for Tex Austin's dude ranch, for example, liked to portray livestock in a romantic light, explaining that "herds of wild horses scamper through the piñon."[41] To the Forest Service, however, these horses, as well as herds of cattle and sheep, represented an often uncontrolled, wasteful use of a threatened resource.

Grazing permits became an additional regulatory and economic point of controversy. In 1906, the Forest Service began charging fees for grazing permits. Fees began at thirty-five to fifty cents per head for cattle grazing year-round and five to eight cents per head of sheep for the summer only. The fees did not represent the true cost of grazing on the range—they were a "token payment" only. Still, stock owners protested having to pay for a formerly free common resource. And although the fees were relatively low, they were another burden for cash-poor families.[42]

The rangers quickly discovered the difficulty of determining exactly how many livestock permittees actively grazed in the forest. Ranchers were reluctant to reveal the true numbers of their herds because the government also counted animals for tax purposes. Ranchers also slipped greater numbers of livestock into the forest than their permits allowed—an easy matter in mountainous country—and kept stock on the range after the grazing season ended.[43] Many residents whose families had farmed and ranched in the area for years felt the old system worked and, moreover, was their birthright. The new rules and regulations on their former common lands threatened their livelihoods and identities.[44] It was often difficult for Forest Service rangers to balance the needs of local ranchers with their quest to improve the health of the range. Rangers lived in local communities, and many of their decisions angered the residents of those communities.[45] The rangers also often held conscious or unconscious biases concerning whose needs should receive priority. For example, in response to protests surrounding Forest Service orders to remove excess livestock from the range around Pecos, Ranger Johnson stated, "I knew that the larger stockmen were all for the cleanup. . . . the petition was not instigated by the responsible stockmen."[46] In Johnson's mind, "responsible" stockmen were the wealthier, often Anglo owners, not the poorer, often Hispanic residents who supplemented their income with small numbers of livestock.

The Forest Service was not only concerned with managing grazing but with other land uses as well. As game managers, both the Forest Service and the state of New Mexico lamented the significant loss of game species in the region in the nineteenth century. Under the supervision of the state game warden, a herd of Rocky Mountain elk from Wyoming was reintroduced on the Upper Pecos in 1915. First kept at the Valley Ranch, a dude ranch that opened in 1907 on the Alexander Valle grant two miles north of Pecos village, the elk eventually dispersed into the mountains.[47] The Forest Service gave no such consideration to replenishing "useless" predator species that, according to ranchers and many land managers, did more harm than good. In the 1920s, a trapper from the Biological Survey working around Pecos killed forty coyotes and ten bobcats in a month.[48] Timber wolves, whose numbers in the Pecos area had always been small, were completely gone by the early 1900s. The last grizzly bear in the area was killed in 1923.[49]

In addition to manipulating game species to please hunters, land management agencies also stocked fish species and reintroduced beaver in order to enhance fishing for recreational anglers. A 1912 report from the New Mexico state game and fish warden, Thomas Gable, documented the release of 3,200 brook trout into the Pecos River at Glorieta—a component of a statewide effort to meet the demand from anglers. In 1921 the state of New Mexico escalated its efforts with the construction of the Lisboa Springs Fish Hatchery a mile north of Pecos village. The state used funds from a gasoline tax to build the hatchery. The operation raised native black-spotted trout and non-native rainbow trout for release into the Pecos River and other streams around the state. Hatchery employees fed the fish horsemeat, kept in cold storage on site. The decrease in native species, particularly the Rio Grande cutthroat trout, probably began—or at least accelerated—in the 1920s, as the introduced and highly adaptable rainbow trout out-competed native fish for food and habitat.[50] A few decades later exotic species had almost entirely replaced the native fish species. But wildlife management practices and policies also supported the recovery of some native species when they served economic and recreational uses such as hunting and fishing. Gable's 1912 report highlighted the economic value of beaver dams that formed ponds at the head of streams because they provided trout habitat as well as stored water that could be tapped for irrigation. While acknowledging that the aftermath of extensive fur trapping meant beaver no longer existed in commercially significant numbers, Gable noted the presence of large numbers of beavers in San Miguel County, although he provided no estimates of quantity or specific locations. By the 1930s, naturalists had convinced the U.S. government of the value of beaver activity for flood protection and erosion prevention, and recovery efforts began. In New Mexico, Elliott Barker, director of the Game and Fish Department of New Mexico, worked to reestablish beaver in the Pecos River watershed. Barker and others carried captured beaver by horseback and released them in the tributary streams and main channel of the Pecos River.[51]

The Forest Service's fire-suppression practices had some of the most far-reaching consequences for western forests. In 1910, after a cluster of non-suppressed fires grew into enormous conflagrations that swept many western forests, destroying seven towns and taking eighty-seven human lives, the Forest Service instituted a policy of complete fire suppression. A study of fire regimes in several locations near Albuquerque showed a general lack of spreading fires at every site in the period from 1906 to 1992.[52] This sharp decrease in fire intervals probably occurred in the Pecos area as well. If a fire did start, the Forest Service made every attempt to stop it from spreading. The steam locomotives chugging through the Upper Pecos valley constantly threw off sparks, starting small fires along the tracks, but Forest Service rangers tried to extinguish each blaze. They also did their best to stop lightning-caused fires as well. Fire suppression caused a buildup of fuels in forests, interfered with cycles of plant regeneration, and may have contributed to piñon and juniper infill into former grassland areas.

"There Was a Feeling of Fellowship among All the People in Tererro": The Tererro Mine in the Pecos River Canyon

Forest Service rangers, hunters, and livestock owners were not the only ones affecting environmental quality in this period. The Tererro mine, located in the Pecos River Canyon thirteen miles north of Pecos village, became one of the most intensive resource-extraction operations in the area's history while also offering local residents employment, particularly during the Depression. The original claim, the "Evangeline," dated to prospector J. J. Case's discovery of a

1,000-foot long outcrop of complex ore in 1882. The outcrop contained copper, lead, zinc, and trace amounts of silver and gold. Case formed the Pecos River Mining Company, then sold it a few years later to A. H. Cowles. Cowles and his partners failed to develop it immediately and left the mine idle for years. In 1903, they experimented in copper ore production using a laborious hand-sorting method and transported the ore by mule train to Glorieta, an arduous journey. The venture quickly proved impractical, but in 1916 the Goodrich-Lockhart Company took an option to purchase if the mine could be shown to turn a profit. In the next five years, with the exception of a short wartime hiatus from 1917 to 1918, Goodrich-Lockhart mined and stockpiled about 150 tons of ore produced from the Evangeline and Katy Did ore bodies. The ore was tested for concentration and potential cost of milling. When a new process was developed for refining the ore in 1925, the American Metal Company purchased a 51 percent interest the same year and began intensive mining of lead, zinc, copper, and much smaller quantities of gold and silver.[53]

The American Metal Company needed to construct an entire infrastructure to support their operation. They handled land purchases necessary for the mine, a mill, a railway spur between the mill and the Santa Fe Railroad, and an aerial tramline built to transport the ore to the refinery. The whole operation was channeled through a dummy corporation in order to keep their plans secret until American Metal had purchased all of the necessary water rights and land parcels. The rugged mountain terrain made construction challenging, and mule trains packed in the materials to remote sites. During the first year, the company cut more than 250,000 feet of ponderosa pine from the national forest near Willow Creek and Indian Creek, both tributaries of the Pecos River.[54] As the company depleted timber, it moved through sequential locations to find more, starting with the eastern slope of the Willow Creek watershed, moving to the slopes of upper Davis Creek, and then to Indian Creek Canyon.[55]

Given the mine's remote location, miners did not commute from Pecos village but rather lived in company towns that grew up around the mine and near the mill. The mining camp of Tererro boasted a peak population of 3,000 residents and included a grade school, a post office, and a hospital. One miner, Wes Darden, recalled years later that the doctor at the hospital owned "several herds of sheep that were pastured over the mountains to the east. If one of his herders arrived at the office during hours, the patients would have to wait a little longer than usual while the good doctor inquired about his sheep."[56] The mine itself employed several hundred men. Darden stated the company's mineral rights lease required it to hire local men—at least 75 percent of its workforce. Darden remembered the many Hispanic families who lived in Tererro and also a number of men from lead and zinc mines in Oklahoma, Missouri, and Kansas who "worked hard and played hard." Although Darden claimed "there was a feeling of fellowship among all the people in Tererro," conflicts arising from ethnic tensions and general seg-regation of Anglo and Hispanic residents also occurred.[57]

Every day during the mine's peak years of operation, heavy buckets of rocks traveled the fourteen-mile aerial tramline to the Alamitos Canyon mill, located two-and-a-half miles northwest of Pecos village. Inspectors rode the ore buckets, too, making sure the cables were sound. At the mill, engineers used a differential flotation process to extract the valuable minerals. The mill utilized water from a small tributary of the Pecos River. Tailings ponds located downstream from the mill collected detritus on the outskirts of Pecos village. As ore production continued, the Tererro mine grew into an extensive complex. Two vertical shafts extended downward. While drilling them, miners hit an underground water source. The lower depths of the mine were always wet, despite pumps that operated constantly to keep the mines open. The mine was the largest lead and zinc mine in New Mexico, and the American Metal Company extracted 2.3 million tons of ore worth more than forty million dollars. Despite such returns, the company was forced to close the mine in 1939 when the ore body had been worked out.[58]

As an intensive resource-extraction operation, the Tererro mine had both short- and long-term impacts on the Upper Pecos environment. The logging, excavation, and construction associated with the mine increased erosion and runoff into the Pecos River. More detrimental to water quality was the influx of minerals, particularly lead, into the water of Willow Creek, the Pecos River, and Alamitos Creek as well as into the surrounding soil. At the Alamitos mill, heavy metals saturated the tailings ponds and leached into the creek. Some residents who lived near or downstream from the mill became concerned about the effects of these metals in downstream runoff or in the piles of tailings that people appropriated to use as fill in construction projects. Howard Lowe, who worked at the mill in the 1930s, recalled that to mollify locals worried about the possibility of contaminated water, Lowe and other mill employees would drink the water runoff in front of the doubters. But when the 1931 chili crop in Anton Chico failed, the farmers blamed it on the mill water. At a public meeting, representatives for the mine introduced a San Miguel County farmer who lived twenty miles closer to the mill and had harvested successful chili crops every year since the mine had opened. But to ease concerns, mining executives constructed a new tailings dam further downstream to prevent the possibility of contamination of the Pecos River during a heavy rainstorm.[59] It would not be until later decades that evidence of contamination and public health concerns led to large-scale remediation efforts.

"It Does Not Seem That the Indians Have Any Prospect of Making Recovery of This Land": The Pueblo Lands Board and the Pecos Pueblo Grant

Decades after New Mexico became a United States territory, the legal status of Pueblo Indian land grants remained unclear. And so, like the Kozlowskis before him, Tex Austin encountered uncertainties regarding his title to the Forked

Lightning Ranch. In 1928, Tex wrote to Herbert Hagerman, a member of the Pueblo Lands Board, regarding the title to his Pecos ranch. Tex addressed Hagerman as "Dear Gov," and inquired into the board's proceedings.[60] The board had just begun considering the claims of non-Puebloans to land within the Pecos Pueblo grant in preparation for awarding a monetary compensation to the Pecos who lived at Jemez. Tex enjoyed having the ruins of Pecos Pueblo nearby, a convenient excursion for ranch guests, but he wanted to make sure there was no chance the board would invalidate his title to the ranch.

Although the tourists who admired the ruins viewed the Pecos as a mythical people with no connections to living tribal members, the Pecos descendants had not forgotten their homeland. The Puebloans, including Pecos descendants, had long sought federal recognition of their loss of land to Hispanos and Anglos. Recognition of Puebloan losses first involved recognizing their rights to the land in the first place. Pablo Toya, a Pecos descendant at Jemez, wrote to the federal land office in Santa Fe in 1921 requesting a copy of the patent issued in 1868 for the Pecos Pueblo grant. Toya's request may have been in response to the actions of John Collier and other Anglo advocates for Puebloan rights and cultural pluralism who were agitating in Congress and the courts to have Puebloan lands restored. Local residents in Pecos village also remembered the Pecos people. They continued to keep their promise to observe the Feast of Nuestra Señora de los Ángeles de Porciúncula on August 2 each year. But that did not mean they supported returning the land where they had built their village and homes to the Pecos.[61]

As advocates mobilized to support Puebloan land rights, the issue quickly attracted controversy, as many Hispanos and Anglos besides those in the Upper Pecos valley faced the loss of their land if the courts decided that adverse possession—and even sales—of Puebloan lands were invalid. Opponents did not want the issue to go before the courts, where a decision would hinge on whether the Puebloans ever possessed the right to relinquish their lands in the first place. If the decision was no, all the Puebloans, including the Pecos, would regain their land. To the opponents' relief, the question ended up before the United States Congress instead. The Bursum bill, introduced in 1922, aimed to decide the question based on adverse possession. Under adverse possession, or squatting, an individual can acquire land based on continuous possession, which gave landholders at Pecos firmer ground to stand on and the Pecos themselves none at all. Collier and his allies rallied to oppose the bill. Nineteen pueblos, including a representative for the Pecos, also signed a letter objecting to the Bursum bill and stating that non-Indian settlers should receive money in compensation, and the Puebloans should receive their lands back—not the other way around. Collier hired an attorney who represented Indian interests: Francis C. Wilson—who, coincidentally, had helped the Gross Kelly Company assert its right to the Pecos Pueblo grant—would represent the case to Congress.

Unlike some Puebloans who remained in their ancient homes, the Pecos had left theirs long before. Ideally, Collier wanted to return all Puebloan land, no matter when that land had passed out of Puebloan control. Wilson adopted a more pragmatic view. He felt a statute of limitations should be imposed, which would leave no room for the Pecos's legal claim. Their opponents exploited the split between Collier and Wilson, and soon Pecos became an example of Puebloan land that would not be restored because it had been acquired by non-Indians many decades before. The Pueblo Lands Act, as finally passed in 1924, stated that title to Puebloan land could be proved based on a deed if acquired before 1902, ten years before New Mexican statehood, or could be proved based on adverse possession dating back to at least 1889. The Pecos would have no claim under either provision.[62]

The act also created the Pueblo Lands Board, which began considering each grant individually to determine the validity of claims and amounts of remuneration. At first, the board did not think it needed to deal with Pecos—the Pecos Pueblo had clearly been abandoned long before the 1889 date. By 1928 the board had changed its position and began an investigation of Pecos, which prompted Tex Austin to write them a letter. The board was not, as historian G. Emlen Hall concludes, determining "whether [the Pecos] had lost the tract, but rather how and to whom." The board chairman, Louis H. Warner, believed that no Puebloan claim to the land remained, as he noted in a memorandum to the Interior Department: "Under all the facts . . . it does not seem that the Indians have any prospect of making recovery of this land at this late date." The assistant secretary of the interior, Albert Finney, was not persuaded by this argument, although it would have allowed the federal government to abandon interest in the grant without determining ownership of individual parcels. Finney required the Pueblo Lands Board to proceed with the research, survey, and hearings procedure used on all other Puebloan grants.[63] Locals aided and abetted the surveys completed by the board. Because the board did not recognize communal lands, several Pecos residents extended their private land claims to include communal tracts, particularly to the east of the Pecos River.[64]

Upon concluding its surveys, the board issued deeds to the landholders. After making sure every portion of the Pecos Pueblo grant had an owner with a deed, the board considered how much the Pecos descendants at Jemez should receive for their lost lands. Typical of the narrow way in which the federal government construed the term "Indian," the board considered only those Pecos descendants who lived at Jemez, despite the fact that others had settled in closer communities, such as Glorieta. The board arbitrarily ignored the method it had used to determine the value of land for other grants and assigned the land at Pecos a flat rate of $1.50 per acre, taking no account of water rights. This resulted in the lowest remuneration paid to any pueblo—$28,144.95 for the entire grant.[65] When the Forked Lightning Ranch was sold in the 1930s, the buyer, W. C. Currier, paid $58,000 for just 6,000 acres.[66] The contentious legal disputes over Puebloan land grants showed how issues of land control still aroused deep emotions about the legitimacy of each community and their long-standing ties to the land. The arbitrary decisions of the Pueblo Lands Board in regard to the Pecos's claims demonstrate how issues of ethnicity, power, and inequality continued to dominate that conflict.

"When You Get to the End of Your Rope, Tie a Knot and Hang On": The Great Depression

In 1936 Tex Austin lost the Forked Lightning Ranch. The onset of the Great Depression had curtailed the tourist industry, and as reform-minded British audiences protested rodeo entertainment on the grounds of animal cruelty, Tex's comeback attempt in the traveling rodeo business failed as well. With the mortgages on his ranch and the sums he owed to creditors growing, Tex decided to try and find oil on his property. The well he drilled turned up nothing.[66] Despite his best efforts, he could not keep up with his debts and finally declared bankruptcy. Forced to leave the Forked Lightning, Tex and Mary Lou moved to Santa Fe and opened the El Ranchero restaurant. Although close to the Upper Pecos valley, the El Ranchero was a far cry from Tex's ranch and the cattle, horses, and cowboys he had spent so much of his life around. When his doctor told him he was going blind, Tex's despair was complete. He died by suicide in 1938.[68]

"When you get to the end of your rope, tie a knot and hang on," Franklin Delano Roosevelt told Americans suffering the effects of the Depression in the 1930s. Many residents of Pecos besides Tex Austin found themselves in dire straits during these years. Although the presence of the Tererro mine may have helped offset some of the Depression's effects in the Pecos area, in general the economic downtown hit northern New Mexico hard. The sugar beet industry in northern Colorado laid off workers as profits fell, as did southern Colorado coal mines and the railroads—all of which had become important sources of work for northern New Mexicans in the preceding decades. As opportunities for wage work became scarcer, families depended more on their gardens and livestock.[69] In an oral history project, conducted in 2002, elderly residents of Pecos reminisced about how their families survived the Depression. Almost all of them mentioned growing their own food, slaughtering livestock, or hunting[70] Residents could sell crops for cash as well, but the market quickly became glutted and prices collapsed.[71] Farming was never a sure enterprise. Heavy snowfalls in the winter of 1931 to 1932 in northern New Mexico killed livestock, and hailstorms and grasshoppers the following summer destroyed crops.[72] For those who had limited resources in the first place, such disasters could be devastating.

Other resources of the Upper Pecos valley continued to provide supplemental economic opportunities. John W. Johnson, the forest ranger, believed timber remained a crucial part of the local economy through the 1930s. "The economy of the area was based largely on timber products, mine ties and props, stulls, piling, railroad ties and sawtimber," Johnson remembered, adding that "Juniper posts were in great demand and a truckload of juniper posts could be sold anywhere at a good price." The demand for timber encouraged people to trespass on the national forest without permits in order to obtain it. Johnson recalled that "timber trespass had always been a problem and as the timber on private land was cut out, trespass on the forest increased."[73] Residents of Pecos also depended on the forest to provide cheap grazing land for their livestock. But the Forest Service, trying to remedy decades of overgrazing and unrestrained timber cutting, put restrictions on forest use and tempered the degree to which locals could rely on these opportunities. Historian John R. Van Ness argues that during the Depression "the consequences of grant land alienation, environmental degradation, and the drastic contraction of wage labor opportunities created a crisis of life-threatening proportions."[74]

The poverty conditions of many northern New Mexican villages attracted substantial federal government aid from New Deal programs designed to stimulate economic recovery. Federal programs such as the Works Progress Administration and the National Youth Administration, which emphasized the "traditional" aspects of village life such as crafts and farming, in many ways attempted to contain Hispanos within a static lifestyle—a lifestyle intimately connected to racial stereotypes. In other ways, though, federal aid did allow Hispanic villagers to maintain their cultural practices, if not always solely on their own terms. By 1935, 60 percent of Hispanos in northern New Mexico received some form of government aid.[75]

Another federal relief program, the Civilian Conservation Corps (CCC), provided employment and also affected the environment of the Upper Pecos valley. The CCC offered the chance of a steady job to unemployed men and gave several federal agencies, including the Forest Service and the Park Service, a sudden influx of workers. To the agencies, which usually faced the problem of an insufficient work force, the CCC crews represented an opportunity to catch up on neglected projects or to forge ahead with new ones. The CCC established a camp two and a half miles east of the Glorieta post office—just over a mile northeast of Pigeon's Ranch—in 1938. The CCC men built the La Cueva Road (County Road 63A) as well as access roads and a fire lookout tower north of Glorieta. This work helped the Forest Service with infrastructure needs and fire suppression. Ranger Johnson mentioned recruiting CCC men to help fight a 1938 fire in Hagus Canyon, a tributary of Glorieta Creek. After the camp closed in 1941, the army considered turning the remnant buildings into an internment camp for Japanese Americans during World War II. The plan did not mature, and Johnson helped remove the temporary buildings in the 1940s.[76]

As the residents of Pecos scrambled to turn resources into food and cash during the Depression, others also sought ways to profit from local resources. Although Tex Austin had failed to find any oil, interest in oil drilling on the Forked Lightning Ranch did not disappear. In August of 1934, officials of the Mexada Oil Company, based in Oklahoma, arrived at Francis C. Wilson's office seeking information about leasing the ranch. Wilson was serving as Tex's attorney in the bankruptcy proceedings. If oil was discovered, Wilson felt "everybody's troubles in this case would be over."[77] Nothing came of the Mexada Company's interests, either, and Tex surrendered the Forked Lightning to his creditors. In 1936, Wilson C. Currier purchased the majority of the ranch land for $58,000.[78] Currier was also involved in the oil business and probably hoped the rumors of oil would materialize into profits.[79]

Currier was not a stranger to the area—he owned a 3,000-acre ranch at the base of Glorieta Mesa and had vacationed with his family in the area for many years.[80] Ranger Johnson recalled that Currier had tried to increase the value of the Glorieta ranch by obtaining a "sizeable grazing preference" in the adjacent national forest, but the Forest Service rejected his request.[81] The Glorieta ranch may have been a more substantial operation than Currier's share of the Forked Lightning, which he bought based on its potential for oil. Currier's portion of the Forked Lightning Ranch did not include the ranch house and the 135 acres around it. Currier and his family moved into Kozlowski's Trading Post instead and remodeled the buildings and utilities. He kept only a few livestock at the Trading Post—two milk cows and some horses.[82]

Tex Austin's large horse and cattle herds disappeared from the Pecos landscape when Tex's western romantic retreat collapsed under the economic strains of the Great Depression. Under Tex's management, the Forked Lightning had offered tourists the chance to live out their fantasies of western life, complete with hunting, riding horses, and watching cowboys herd cattle. Locals also enjoyed recreational activities in the region and appreciated its rugged beauty. Although the Forest Service facilitated timber cutting and grazing, it also managed species specifically for hunters and fishermen, and it suppressed fires, helping create a landscape of dense forests that provided the setting for western adventures. Although the Depression curtailed tourism, people clung to the hope that better times would allow them to buy a car and travel westward themselves to experience all the "Land of Enchantment" had to offer.

SIX | Management and Mythology in a Postwar Landscape
1941–1980

THE FORKED LIGHTNING RANCH, 1964—On a warm June evening, a small group of Hollywood notables and wealthy Dallas oilmen mingled in the secluded courtyard of the Forked Lightning Ranch house. The Pecos River rushed by below them, gurgling over the rocks. The guests breathed in the scent of the dry desert air and walked across the bluegrass lawn in their shiny cowboy boots, warmed by margaritas and the flattering attention of their famous hostess, Greer Garson Fogelson. The day had been filled with activities befitting the guests of a gentleman rancher—a hearty "chuckwagon picnic" by the Pecos River at tables covered with denim cloths, an inspection of the ranch's picturesque stables and prize-winning herd of Santa Gertrudis cattle, and an afternoon horseback ride among the piñons. The evening would feature a mariachi band by lantern-light before the guests retired to their private bedrooms to listen for the haunting calls of coyotes in the darkness.

Greer Garson was a well-known movie star in 1949 when she married Texas oilman Elijah E. "Buddy" Fogelson, who had purchased the Forked Lightning Ranch before World War II. Like Helen Kozlowski, Garson stepped into an unfamiliar environment and culture the first time she visited the Pecos area. Unlike Helen Kozlowski and her family, she did not have to worry about making a living in Pecos. Garson came to the ranch for leisure and invited guests to enjoy the pleasures of the Forked Lightning as well. She often greeted her guests personally at the local train station wearing a colorful Western costume. "It was as if a great director had carefully arranged the scene and she was the cattle queen in some wild Technicolor movie," remembered one famous guest, radio and television personality Art Linkletter.[1] Indeed, the Fogelsons' life on the Forked Lightning Ranch relied as much on theater and mythology about the Wild West as had Tex Austin's tourist operation.

Garson's upbringing in England influenced her romanticized view of the American Southwest, and her experience as an actress working on Hollywood movie sets further affected the choices she made about managing the ranch during four decades of summer residence at the Forked Lightning. She developed a personal relationship with the ranch in those years, even as she perpetuated its mythology. The Fogelsons furnished their ranch with American Indian and Hispanic artwork and furniture and dabbled in local traditions such as baking bread in the *horno* oven they installed behind the ranch house. But they remained somewhat removed from the local community, arriving for annual four-month summer visits in their Fleetwood limousine but leaving the management of the ranch to staff in their absence when they were in Dallas and Los Angeles.

The Fogelsons' wealth and life of leisure inspired resentment in some local Pecos residents who continued to rely on the surrounding lands to graze their cattle, gather wood, and farm. Memories of a time when much of the Forked Lightning Ranch had been communal grazing land ran deep. The U.S. Forest Service's management techniques of the surrounding national forests also continued to cause friction with local residents. The Pecos descendants living in Jemez Pueblo had not forgotten their ancient home or the rights they believed they still possessed to the land either. At the same time, people who wanted to preserve the Pecos Pueblo ruins as a historic site and develop it to accommodate tourists began actively getting state officials and, later, the federal government involved in this project. Once again, as these various people interacted at Pecos with each other and the environment, change occurred, transforming the landscape and its future.

"Instead of Eight Cows to an Acre, It's More like Eight Acres to a Cow": The Fogelsons Buy the Forked Lightning Ranch

Greer Garson first visited the Forked Lightning Ranch in 1948. Buddy Fogelson had invited Greer and her mother to spend a week at the ranch after the premier of Garson's latest film, *Julia Misbehaves.* Buddy met Greer on the film set and was immediately taken with the red-haired actress. Only a few days later, at a dinner party at Garson's home, Buddy boldly told her "I'm going to marry you some day." Still smarting from two divorces, Garson resisted committing her heart to Buddy, but she immediately fell in love with Pecos. Expecting picket fences, duck ponds, and ponies, she wore high heels and an organdy dress the first time she visited the Forked Lightning Ranch. The rugged, arid environment of Pecos surprised, but also delighted, her. "I was immediately struck by the color of the earth, the sky, and the people," Greer remembered. She took particular note of the "Indian, Spanish, and pioneer American" history embedded in the landscape. "The wonderful thing is that they all get on well together. It's historic. Spacious. Thrilling. It's not like the lush pasturage of, say, Virginia. Instead of eight cows to an acre it's more like eight acres to a cow! I felt so fragile and uncomfortable in that vast, rugged land."[2] Garson's perceptions of Pecos reflected how popular and widespread the romanticized history of the Southwest had become. She did not discern evidence of past conflicts and environmental transformation but rather saw a landscape so immense it was removed from human influence, its inhabitants cloistered inside the safe confines of a historic narrative developed by the tourism industry.

Although the land encompassing the Forked Lightning Ranch was vast and rugged, like all of northern New Mexico, the Upper Pecos valley had experienced centuries of intensive human presence and use. The Forked Lightning Ranch had stood idle for five years after Tex Austin's bankruptcy, but when Buddy Fogelson purchased the land it once again became a working ranch. In the mid-1930s, Fogelson had visited fellow Texan Lyle Brush's deluxe guest ranch eleven miles up the canyon above Pecos village and developed an interest in owning property in the area. In 1938 Fogelson began negotiating the purchase of the unsold portion of Tex Austin's former holdings—the main ranch house and 135 surrounding acres.[3] He finalized the deal for the ranch house parcel in 1941. After Wilson C. Currier, in failing health, abandoned his hopes of finding oil, Fogelson also purchased Currier's land, which included most of the property between the river and Glorieta Mesa. Later that year, Fogelson bought the Los Trigos Ranch, the former land grant bordering the Forked Lightning Ranch to the south, from Bruce and Dorothy Strong. The combined land equaled a 10,000-acre ranch.[4]

Although Fogelson was new to the Upper Pecos valley, he quickly influenced local land-use patterns, much like Tex Austin and other Anglo landowners before him. Ranches like the Forked Lightning—large, commercial operations usually owned by Anglos—occupied much of the best rangeland around the headwaters of the Pecos River by the mid-twentieth century. The accumulation of land in the hands of a few wealthy Anglos forced all the other residents of the Upper Pecos valley to put their livestock on the Santa Fe National Forest. The resulting erosion from overgrazing affected all downstream communities and economic activities in the Pecos watershed.[5]

A native Nebraskan raised by well-educated Finnish immigrants, Fogelson made his fortune as an oil wildcatter in Texas.[6] Coming from an area steeped in cowboy culture and cattle, Fogelson saw the Forked Lightning as a vacation home but also a place to breed cattle as a hobby. Initially, he stocked it with a mix of purebred and commercial Horned Herefords purchased in Fort Worth, Texas. When the United States entered World War II in December 1941, Fogelson placed his new project on hold and volunteered for military duty. He was named chief of Eisenhower's petroleum planning division in Europe and served on the Allied War Reparations Commission after the German surrender.[7]

As the U.S. entered the war, Pecos had not recovered from the economic downturn during the Depression.[8] After the Tererro mine closed in 1939, the population of Pecos began to decline. Many local men who did not volunteer or get drafted pursued wartime employment opportunities on assembly lines in other parts of the West. They encountered a wider range of skilled labor positions and opportunities for geographic and occupational mobility.[9] Employment opportunities outside of San Miguel County continued to grow in the postwar period. Rather than returning to the Pecos area, many wage laborers settled in Denver, Tucson, Los Angeles, and other parts of New Mexico that offered employment in the defense and oil and gas industries.[10]

Young people composed the majority of the migrants who left northern New Mexico in the postwar years. With the population exodus, local agricultural production dropped by 70 percent. Those farmers who remained often sought supplemental wage labor in order to modernize their farms with trucks, tractors, and other equipment.[11] The population of the area did not rise again until the 1970s, when Pecos became a bedroom community for Santa Fe. The influx of new residents into other areas of New Mexico during the war years created an Anglo majority in the state for the first time, and the Fogelsons were part of that demographic shift. By the late 1940s, Fogelson was a decorated veteran and wealthy philanthropist. He already owned the Forked Lightning Ranch, and after meeting Greer Garson in 1948, Fogelson turned his energies to wooing the reluctant actress. She finally consented, and they married in Santa Fe in the summer of 1949. Together they began turning the Forked Lightning into their ideal of a Western ranch.

"I've Taken to Ranch Life like a Duck Takes to Water": Environmental Change on the Forked Lightning Ranch

Garson quickly developed a passion for ranching that rivaled Buddy's. The Fogelsons arrived at the ranch every June and stayed through Greer's birthday, September 29.[12] Shortly after their wedding, Buddy presented Greer with a section of the ranch for her very own. She called the parcel El Rancho Blanco and established a herd of Scottish-bred white shorthorns—six heifers and a bull—that reminded her of her British roots. "I've taken to ranch life like a duck takes to water," she wrote in a letter to a friend. "I've switched from bustles and bows to Levis and boots, and I think it's definitely a change for the better."[13] Ranch hands took to calling the parcel the "Greer Garson" pasture. Because the Fogelsons continued to maintain a commercial herd of Herefords, it was necessary to keep the purebred shorthorns away from the other cattle. Greer enjoyed immediate success at the New Mexico State Fair, where her shorthorns won many ribbons and awards. Soon the Forked Lightning Ranch developed a reputation in New Mexico as a first-rate cattle operation. In February 1951 Greer gave an address at the Cattle Growers Association Convention in Albuquerque—the first woman to do so.[14]

The Fogelsons relied on permanent employees to keep the Forked Lightning in operation year-round. They developed strong relationships with their staff built on mutual trust and friendship. Ranch foreman A. V. "Slim" Wasson, a former Texan who had been in the Pecos area since 1921, oversaw the ranch during Buddy's military service and was one of only a handful of attendees at the Fogelsons' private wedding in Santa Fe.[15] Wasson lived in a trailer van on the ranch in the 1940s. Eventually, the Fogelsons established a ranch foreman's residence and headquarters at Kozlowski's Trading Post.[16] Jay Kirkpatrick, a local born less than a mile south of Los Trigos, replaced Wasson as foreman in 1954 and later became a managing partner in the ranch. The Fogelsons also hired a veterinarian, Melvin Hinderliter. Another local man, Gilbert Ortiz, began working as a ranch employee under Hinderliter in 1963 and also received a college scholarship from the Fogelsons. Later he was promoted to ranch manager and lived at the Trading Post. Ortiz developed an extensive knowledge of bovine genetics, which he learned from Hinderliter.[17]

Forked Lightning cattle did not mingle with the herds on the Forest Service lands. The ranch offered plenty of quality grazing land, and the Fogelsons wished to keep the pedigree lines clean.[18] Cattle grazed on the land near the Pecos Pueblo ruins, in the pastures between State Highway 63 and the Pecos River, and in fenced pastures on the east side of the Pecos River. Most pastures had access to an arroyo that served as a water source for the animals.[19]

In the 1950s, the Fogelsons decided to switch from breeding Scottish shorthorns to Santa Gertrudis cattle. In 1958 Buddy impulsively bought "Gee-Gee," a $10,000 Santa Gertrudis bull, from his friend Winthrop Rockefeller in Arkansas. The King Ranch in Texas developed the Santa Gertrudis breed, formally recognized by the U.S. Department of Agriculture in 1940—the first breed of beef cattle to originate in the United States. After the hasty decision to purchase the sire, Fogelson consulted with Jay Kirkpatrick, who advised him to buy some heifers as well. Fogelson bought three and added thirty Santa Gertrudis cows the following summer, each purchased for an average price of $3,000. As the Santa Gertrudis operation grew, the Fogelsons sold their commercial Hereford cattle to provide more grazing pasture for the purebred livestock. By 1961 they owned seventy-five breeding age females. The Santa Gertrudis breed was noted for the ability to gain weight at a faster pace than other breeds. Although the breed was still unusual in the West in the 1950s, the Fogelsons were not the first to export Santa Gertrudis cattle to the arid high country. Tweet Kimball of the Cherokee Ranch in Douglas County, Colorado, stocked her ranch with the breed several years before the Fogelsons began their experiment in New Mexico.[20] The Fogelsons soon began using artificial insemination to improve the stock.[21] Artificial insemination had become popular in the dairy cattle industry in the 1940s. Cattle owners could manage the process easily with animals confined in barns. Using this technique for beef cattle that roamed across thousands of acres was challenging, but the separate pastures on the Forked Lightning Ranch allowed the employees to control, monitor, and separate the artificially inseminated animals with relative ease.[22]

The Fogelsons' experiments with cattle breeding occurred during a period of extreme climatic variability in New Mexico. In 1940 and 1941, New Mexico experienced an El Niño period of abnormally high precipitation, which resulted in flooding, killing frosts during the summer that damaged crops, and few fires throughout the state. A La Niña period immediately followed, and from 1942 to 1957 drought conditions ravaged the area. The 1950s was New Mexico's driest decade in 400 years. The year 1956 marked the climax of the dry period—as much as 60 percent of the state's crops failed in that year alone. As surface irrigation in the region declined due to drought, well drilling to access groundwater was accelerated to compensate. One Glorieta well digger claimed he had already drilled more than 50 wells in the area by 1950.[23] The drought affected not only agriculture but the livestock industry as well. As a result of the 1950s drought, range management scientists warned southwestern stockmen that drought planning should take precedence over all other grassland management practices.

The most abundant type of vegetation community at Pecos, piñon-juniper woodland, was vulnerable to climatic fluctuations. The wet years in the 1940s presented conditions favorable for piñon-juniper invasion in grazed grassland areas. Yet in the 1950s, severe drought conditions caused massive piñon and juniper die-offs in places such as the Pajarito Plateau west of Santa Fe and the Sevilleta National Wildlife Refuge.[24] Similar conditions around Pecos probably limited piñon-juniper expansion during the drought years. But in general, episodic climatic fluctuations over a number of decades, combined with continuing disturbance from livestock grazing, created conditions that altered the age structure and species composition of woodlands and accelerated piñon-juniper encroachment on grasslands.[25] The continued suppression of fire also affected piñon-juniper dynamics. Centuries of human activity radically affected plant communities, and that activity overlay a pattern of large-scale environmental change.

At the Forked Lightning Ranch, although the drought may have inhibited piñon-juniper encroachment to some extent, the ranch managers agreed that too many pastures were being overtaken by the trees. To expand grassland areas for grazing, land managers in the Southwest developed mechanical tree removal techniques as early as the 1930s. The most popular method involved the use of bulldozers with a chain stretched between them to rip out trees.[26] Until controlled burning methods emerged in the 1970s, mechanical removal was widely regarded as the most effective and safest method. Although burning removed a higher number of trees and allowed grasses to recover quickly, controlled burns were still uncommon. At Pecos the neighboring Forest Service, which controlled a vast amount of land in the valley, discouraged controlled burning. Despite developments in ecological science, many land managers did not yet understand the ecological causes of brush encroachment.[27]

The effects of mechanical clearing, grazing, drought, and fire suppression acted together to change the landscape of the Forked Lightning Ranch over time. The primary reason for clearing trees on the ranch in the 1960s was to maintain pasturage for the Santa Gertrudis cattle. However, the Fogelsons also wanted their ranch environment to be an attractive one. A professional article on piñon and juniper clearing suggested that "the resulting stands of grass surrounded by untreated woodland probably have as much aesthetic value to residents and travelers as does the typical piñon-juniper scenery." Actively managing the ranch environment created a landscape that was practical yet still visually appealing.[28]

"Don't Fancy This Place Up": *Turning the Forked Lightning Ranch into a Romantic Western Retreat*

Greer Garson recalled that shortly after marrying Buddy, who called her "Rusty" because of her red hair, he teasingly warned her not to turn the Forked Lightning Ranch into a Hollywood socialite's mansion. "Don't fancy this place up, Rusty," Buddy said. She promised instead that she would "respect the local environmental harmonies."[29] The cattle operation was the most significant impact on the landscape within and surrounding the Forked Lightning Ranch, but the aesthetic changes the Fogelsons made to the ranch were also noteworthy. The ranch house that John Gaw Meem built for Tex Austin already showcased the Spanish-Pueblo Revival architectural style promoted by Santa Fe tourism boosters, a style that intermixed Puebloan and Spanish elements and obscured the reality of Anglo economic power and interests in the region.[30] "The house was very plain and manly when I first saw it," Garson recalled. "Now, it's a little more Garson's style—nearly all white walls with brightly colored paintings and Indian rugs as accents."[31] In the 1950s the Fogelsons installed split-rail fencing along the highway and asked John Gaw Meem's firm to design a formal gateway at the Kozlowski's Trading Post entrance with "adobe" (cinder block) posts and massive walls bearing the Forked Lightning brand.[32] The Mandarin Orange paint used on the ranch house and fences (which faded to pink), and the Bismarck Blue trim and accents, instantly identified Forked Lightning lands and property. The Fogelsons' fanciful southwestern aesthetic could also be seen in nearby Pecos village after they donated the same paint to local residents for their homes and businesses.[33]

The cattle, known locally as "Fogelson's toys," were also as much a part of the Western scenery for visitors as they were a business investment.[34] Buddy liked to show them off for guests. Like most modern American postwar consumers, the Fogelsons had no direct relationship with their food supply, despite their proximity to nature at their ranch retreat. While many of their Hispanic neighbors in the Upper Pecos valley continued to keep small kitchen gardens, cows, and other farm animals to supplement their purchased food supplies, the Fogelsons grew no food on their property. As in the Tex Austin era, ranch employees transported all food to the ranch by jeep from Santa Fe, and the Fogelsons' cooks traveled with the couple and hired locals to assist them while in residence at the ranch.[35] Ranch hands also helped to maintain the landscaping around the ranch house complex, a pet project of Garson's. Because they did not need to grow vegetables or keep chickens, the Fogelsons enjoyed the luxury of a bluegrass lawn as well as ornamental trees and flowers planted around the ranch house.

Although no large-scale food production occurred at the ranch, Garson expressed interest in southwestern culinary traditions. She had a traditional adobe horno oven installed in the yard in the 1950s, where local Hispanic women taught her to bake bread. She also enjoyed hosting "chuckwagon" picnic lunches by the river on tables bedecked with blue denim cloths and red bandanna napkins. Guests hiked down steep concrete steps to the picnic area on the signposted "Niñas Trail," built just east of the ranch house in the 1960s.[36] In many respects, the Fogelsons' activities at the ranch seamlessly continued and expanded the inventions that Tex Austin had used so effectively to draw tourists to his dude ranch. The messier truth—a story of land use that also included unregulated resource extraction, soil erosion, water pollution, and struggle for survival and ownership of land—remained hidden behind this façade.

Activities at the Forked Lightning Ranch during the Fogelson era included a mix of serious business and picturesque leisure activities. Although the Fogelsons demonstrated benevolent interest in local affairs, they maintained their cultural and economic distance from the local population. A natural actress, Greer enjoyed her "role" as mistress of the manor, and her opinions strongly influenced activities at the ranch. For example, she and Buddy prohibited hunting and trapping on their property. Unlike Tex Austin and his guests, who had hunted wild game on the ranch and in the adjacent national forest, the Fogelsons and their family and friends shot clay disks on the private skeet range they built northwest of the ranch house in 1955. They allowed only limited fishing in the Pecos River as well. As a result, the ranch became a sanctuary for any wildlife that found favorable habitat conditions within the heavily grazed areas. Perhaps the predators discovered that game was plentiful. In a 1966 interview Garson fondly remembered a thrilling encounter with a "wolf"—presumably a coyote or fox—on the dirt road to the ranch house after a night at the Santa Fe Opera.[37] In interviews with the cattle trade press, she boasted of her contribution to roundups, riding fence to check damage to their enclosures after flash floods, and herding wild horses, as well as her regular duties supervising the house staff—butler, maid, and cook. She collected and displayed American Indian artifacts and rock specimens, patronized the arts in Santa Fe, and was involved with various charities.[38] Her connection to northern New Mexico, although enhanced by her flair for drama, was very real. She felt New Mexico gave her a sense of continuity and peace—a sanctuary in a landscape still somewhat removed from modern America. "There is an almost mystical strength about New Mexico," Garson wrote. "The longer you stay it seems to be the center of the world and everything else peripheral."[39]

"A Link to Bind the Past to the Present":
The Creation of the Pecos National Monument

Intrigued by the Spanish and American Indian history of New Mexico, Greer Garson visited the Pecos Pueblo ruins numerous times and showed them off to visitors. When the Fogelsons arrived at the Forked Lightning Ranch, the Pecos Pueblo and mission church ruins were a small, neglected testimony to nascent preservationist impulses in New Mexico. Efforts to protect archaeological sites had seen their first real successes in the early 1900s. The Antiquities Act of 1906 required the federal government to protect historically significant archaeological sites on federal lands as public resources, and the developing profession of archaeology brought attention to vandalism of ruins. The tourism industry also had a vested interest in the ongoing protection of New Mexico's American Indian and Spanish colonial history, although it tended to promote unfettered access to those historic places.

This wider social movement touched the Pecos Pueblo ruins in the 1920s. In 1920, the Gross Kelly Company deeded the site to Archbishop Albert T. Daeger of the Roman Catholic Archdiocese of Santa Fe. The Archbishop then conveyed the 62.6 acres to the shared custody of the Museum of New Mexico, the University of New Mexico, and the School of American Research in 1921. On February 20, 1935, New Mexico designated the ruins a state monument.[40] Preservation, interpretation, and recreation became official management priorities during this period. Archaeologist Alfred Kidder continued his work at the site until 1929, which provided some ongoing supervisory presence at the ruins, but lack of a permanent, on-site caretaker and adequate funding meant the transition to a publicly managed resource did not immediately result in increased protection for the property. The monument existed as a fragile, unprotected island of ruins in the rapidly changing landscape of the Upper Pecos valley, busy as it was with livestock production, logging, and a rural community struggling to make ends meet through the Depression, World War II, and the postwar years.

Pecos still remained a bit off the beaten path in the late 1930s and 1940s. After 1937, Route 66 connected Santa Rosa and Albuquerque directly, bypassing the original, roundabout "Santa Fe Loop" that included Pecos, Pigeon's Ranch, Glorieta, and Cañoncito. In 1941, the state of New Mexico redesignated the old Route 66 highway as State Route 50. Visitors could reach the monument and recreational opportunities in the Santa Fe National Forest via Route 50 and Highway 63. Nearby, Tom Greer continued to operate Pigeon's Ranch as a roadside tourist attraction on Route 50. As traffic and residential development increased on that road, so did threats to the aging structures at Pigeon's Ranch and the archaeological remains of the Glorieta Battlefield. The realignment of US 85 in the 1950s and the subsequent construction of Interstate 25 in 1964 greatly reduced traffic in the vicinity of the Civil War site—and also reduced visitors to Tom Greer's tourist enterprise. He closed the museum and other attractions in the 1950s and sold the property in 1971.[41] Despite changes in the major transportation routes, the Pecos Pueblo ruins remained a popular tourist site.

The circumstances of the Depression provided a temporary surfeit of workers for the state of New Mexico to undertake preservation work, but for the most part the state had little funding to devote to the monument. A similar situation existed across the country. A plethora of state and national monuments appeared following the passage of the 1906 Antiquities Act. Frequently, no provisions were made to provide funding for the upkeep of the monuments.[42] Although the Pecos State Monument remained underfunded, the landscape around the ruins was being integrated into the modern age. An entire infrastructure connected the Pecos region to the nation. Pecos had always been connected to other places, but much as the railroad had intensified those connections in the 1880s, developments in the 1940s and 1950s brought Pecos into a modern technological system that wove the country together. Improvements included paved roads, new highways, electricity, natural gas lines, and telephone lines.[43] Butane Gas Company of New Mexico, Pecos Light and Power Company, Benson Electric Company, and Pecos Telephone Company serviced local residents who could afford modernizing upgrades. For example, the Valencia Ranch, located in Pecos village north of the Forked Lightning Ranch, received electricity in its hacienda in 1951.[44]

The Museum of New Mexico, which oversaw operations at the monument, realized the facilities at the Pecos State Monument needed modernization, but the necessary funding remained unavailable. State officials had authorized the construction of caretaker quarters using Works Progress Administration labor in June 1941. The museum appointed F. W. King as the first caretaker of the Pecos ruins. Not long after King arrived, the well drilled on the monument grounds became contaminated. A second drilling attempt failed, and funding ran out before the Museum of New Mexico was able to complete the well. King left, and the lack of potable water and limited funding prevented the hiring of a new caretaker. Pecos State Monument was left untended between 1941 and 1950, leaving the site vulnerable to relic hunters, vandals, and careless tourists.[45]

Despite ongoing financial hardship, by 1950 the museum managed to scrape together enough money to enlarge the caretaker's residence, construct a small exhibit space, finish the well, and install telephone service and a single-phase power line along the south side of the entrance road.[46] The museum still could not provide a reasonable operating budget and adequate pay for a full-time employee throughout most of the decade. F. W. King returned as caretaker but left precipitously while the residence was still undergoing renovation, requiring the museum to contract with a local Pecos Light and Power employee, Lewis Stinett, who occupied the house temporarily as a substitute caretaker. A break-in when Stinett was away caused Mrs. Stinett and a friend to flee while the "marauders" stole mattresses and tools, thus ending their brief tenure at the monument. O. M. Clark took the post in 1951 and remained until 1956.

When Clark assumed his post, state and federal agencies throughout the country were paying more attention to facilitating visitor use and interpretation at historic sites. The National Park Service stood at the forefront of this project. By the postwar era, people were visiting state parks and historic sites, national forests, and other heritage areas in greater numbers and expected to find facilities and services similar to what they experienced in national parks. In 1952 Clark oversaw the completion of a marked, self-guided trail around the ruins under the supervision of archaeologist Stanley Stubbs from the Laboratory of Anthropology in Santa Fe. "As a result," Clark wrote to Boaz Long, director of the Museum of New Mexico, "visitors now spend about three times as much time on the grounds as before."[47] Additional improvements included a picnic area and comfort station for visitors. Picnic groups, including locals, continued to use the monument grounds for social gatherings, which required frequent garbage-hauling trips to the village dumping grounds four miles from the monument.[48]

Despite greater attention from caretakers, the ruins were in poor condition, and increased visitor access only worsened the problems. The museum did not establish regular visitation hours, which would have enabled better control of visitors at the ruins. Most of the caretaker's time was spent battling invasive weeds, trespassing livestock, and artifact hunters and curiosity seekers who threatened the archaeological treasures. The museum paid a crew of locals each year to clear the trails and ruins of invasive weeds by hand. After the hasty excavations and stabilization of the ruins by the School of American Research using Civilian Conservation Corps laborers in the late 1930s, which was performed to ready the site for the Coronado Cuarto Centennial in 1940, minimal archaeological work or preventive maintenance occurred until 1956, when Stanley Stubbs and Bruce Ellis excavated a kiva and portions of the "Lost Church" that was originally constructed by Fray Pedro Zambrano Ortiz in 1617.[49] Although the Pecos community had held the annual celebration of the Feast of Nuestra Señora de los Ángeles de Porciúncula at the ruins on the Sunday closest to August 2 since the last Pecos residents moved to Jemez in 1838, the celebration moved to St. Anthony's Parish in the village in 1953 because the rubble in the church was so deep. The ceremony didn't return to the historic mission church until 1969, when the nave was cleaned and stabilized.[50]

Struggling to provide adequate services and protection at the monument, the Museum of New Mexico began searching for an entity that could take over the management of the site. As early as 1947, the museum had offered Pecos to the National Park Service. The Park Service declined—in the immediate aftermath of the war, the agency was also suffering from decreased funding, personnel shortages, and a backlog of maintenance.[51] But the offer probably intrigued agency officials, as it came at a time when the Park Service was increasingly interested in historic sites, a change from earlier policies. In the first decades of the twentieth century, many Park Service officials and conservationists believed national park status should be reserved for land with outstanding scenic features such as Yellowstone or Glacier. National monuments, created under the auspices of the 1906 Antiquities Act, became the catchall category that absorbed sites of historic interest, unique natural features, and areas where presidential proclamation provided a surer means of preservation than the uncertain route of congressional designation. The monuments, managed by a range of agencies, generally were neglected and considered inferior to national parks.[52]

This attitude began to change in the 1930s. Horace Albright, first an assistant director and then director of the Park Service, felt his agency was the best equipped to manage sites protecting the nation's history. The Park Service already administered sites rich with historic resources. Albright hired Verne Chatelain as historian for the Division of Education, and Chatelain promoted the idea that the Park Service should develop a comprehensive interpretive program that offered visitors a sweeping view of the nation's history. At Colonial National Monument in the east, Chatelain argued that the historic landscape and buildings, in conjunction with an interpretive program, would "serve as a link to bind the past to the present and be a guide and an inspiration to the future." Other monuments could tell the same stories. Besides seeing the interpretive potential of the national monuments, Albright also wanted to broaden the Park Service's domain into areas untouched by its perennial rival, the Forest Service. In 1933 Albright's hopes were fulfilled when Franklin Roosevelt signed Executive Order 6166, which transferred all national monuments to the Park Service. The influx of workers and funding the Park Service received during the Depression allowed it to develop facilities at the national monuments, and the lines between a national monument and a national park began to blur. By the 1950s, the postwar economy was booming, and the United States Congress was prepared to commit an influx of funding to the Park Service to deal with the rapid surge in visitation to park sites and a backlog of maintenance, infrastructure, and development needs, including the addition of new units to the system. The addition of Pecos Pueblo to the national park system was now a realistic possibility.[53]

In 1958 Robert Utley, the southwest regional historian for the Park Service, officially recommended Pecos for inclusion in the national park system. The museum renewed negotiation with the Park Service for the transfer of the monument.[54] Despite becoming involved in some decisions, the Park Service did not immediately take over management of the ruins—the approval and planning process took eight years. In the meantime, the museum hired Vivian O'Neal as the new caretaker for the monument while they awaited the transition. O'Neal was an archaeology enthusiast with a long-standing interest in Pecos. A conscientious manager, she was determined to preserve Pecos as an important piece of history, and her husband, Edwin, contributed a great deal of time, labor, and ingenuity as well.[55] Unfortunately, when the state planners heard negotiations were underway with the Park Service for the transfer, the state cut off funding for the monument on June 30, 1961. Luckily, the O'Neals were financially secure and continued to live at the monument, occasionally using their own funds to purchase supplies.

Pecos finally achieved national monument status a few years later. On August 9, 1962, the Secretary of the Interior recommended approval for the designation of Pecos as a national monument, and President Lyndon Johnson signed it into law in 1965. The O'Neals provided basic security and maintenance during the planning phase until official designation occurred. The Park Service officially assumed management on January 1, 1966.[56] In the meantime, the monument acres received only the attention the O'Neals could provide in their informal, interim capacity.

The initial efforts to preserve the pueblo and mission ruins on the mesilla had been halting and piecemeal. The state of New Mexico struggled to manage the ruins and gratefully seized the opportunity to turn the monument over to the National Park Service, which, since the 1930s, had developed a broader mission that incorporated not only places of scenic beauty but areas of historical interest as well. In that era, as historian Hal Rothman describes it, the Park Service became "guardians of a cultural heritage." When the Park Service took over management of the Pecos Monument in 1965, they intended to develop the site in accordance with prevailing philosophies of providing facilities for visitors and interpreting the history of the monument. This mission would require a new phase of intensive management of the Pecos landscape.

"These Are Our Lands": *Conflict over Land Ownership in the Upper Pecos Valley*

In 1958 Buddy Fogelson expanded a pasture on the southern end of the Forked Lightning Ranch, known as the Pajarito pasture, with the purchase of an additional 608 acres on the west side of the AT&SF tracks and on the east side of the Pecos River.[57] The area was located in the former Los Trigos grant. The interstate divided the parcel after 1964, but local roads and a concrete underpass provided access to the pasture and the Pajarito community, located to the southeast of Rowe. In the late 1960s a group of local men from Pajarito began to interfere with access to the ranch's fenced, 4,000-acre Pajarito pasture. Pajarito residents claimed that because they were descendants and heirs of the original settlers on the grant, they were entitled to the use of that portion of the grant they recognized as common, unallotted pasture. On April 28, 1969, some local men accosted a ranch foreman on the pasture's access road and threatened him with injury if he returned. Three ranch employees returned one week later to repair the boundary fence, but six men turned them away with threats. The following spring, the same men turned away a surveyor hired by Fogelson to testify in the dispute. The locals, including Frank Salmeron and Esquipula Padilla, also removed one-half mile of boundary fence and allowed their livestock to graze on the Forked Lightning property.[58]

When the Park Service assumed management of the monument, they became players in the long-standing questions of who should control land in Pecos and how that land should be used. In the 1960s, the debate over land control in New Mexico attracted renewed attention and controversy when a group of *valientes* (militants) formed the *Alianza Federal de Mercedes* (Federal

Land Grant Alliance) to contest the history of unscrupulous transfers of Spanish land grant titles to United States' interests. Alianza founder Reies Lopez Tijerina "prospected" for new members among the nuevomexicanos and Puebloans in villages around the state and was in Pecos and Rowe in the late 1950s, where he attracted followers. In one impassioned speech, Tijerina shouted, "They took your land and gave you powdered milk, took your grazing and gave you Smokey the Bear, took your language and gave you lies in theirs. There are 1,715 land grants in the United States, and we will get them back."[59] Members of the Alianza drew on a tradition of anticolonial resistance that stretched back to the period following the Treaty of Guadalupe Hidalgo. *Corridos*, historic ballads, were passed down as oral tradition through generations and provided testimony of a history of lost property rights, as well as moments of resistance such as San Miguel County's short-lived *Gorras Blancas* (White Caps) alliance in the late 1800s. The Alianza also found inspiration in the postwar civil rights movement, which opened new opportunities for racial and ethnic groups to expose long, shared histories of discrimination and prejudice. While Tijerina and his followers recognized the contradiction of protesting U.S. colonization begun in 1848 while defending Spanish colonization of Puebloan and other native lands dating after 1598, they differentiated the two based on centuries of shared cultural and biological interconnections of Native Americans and nuevomexicanos, and their similar positions relative to the United States. Tijerina sought solidarity among the Puebloans and their Hispanic counterparts and referred to them collectively as Indo-Hispanos, an acknowledgement and embrace of the intermarriage and cultural exchange of the two groups, but one that also absolved Hispanos of any illegitimate claims to the lands of New Mexico.[60]

Supporters of the Alianza contested issues not only of land control but also land use. Often, controversy coalesced around the largest landholder in northern New Mexico, the U.S. Forest Service, which controlled many acres of former land grants and Puebloan land and set policies that affected access to traditional hunting, grazing, and harvesting territory. Despite decades of effort, the federal agency still confronted a grim ecological situation in New Mexico's forests. In 1949, New Mexico and Texas had signed the Pecos River Compact, which provided for equitable apportionment of water between the two states and created more regulatory pressure for upstream management. However, many early Forest Service management decisions were short-sighted or carried unanticipated consequences. The Forest Service experimented with watershed management techniques—primarily intensive forest management practices, including clearcutting—to increase streamflow yield as water demand grew and regional water supply considerations emerged.[61] In addition, the Soil Conservation Service planted trees, including non-native species, in the Santa Fe National Forest to reduce erosion in the early 1940s. Russian olive proved to be particularly invasive due to its low seedling mortality rate—by 1960, the species had crowded out much of the native vegetation and was a major component of the riparian woodland understory on the Middle Rio Grande and was likely becoming more common on the Pecos River.[62]

In the mid-twentieth century, ecological management policies emerged that underscored the growth of the livestock industry after 1880 as the major culprit of watershed damage on the Pecos River. The National Resources Planning Board, assembled by President Roosevelt, consulted experts in natural resource management at various federal agencies and authored a 1942 Pecos River Joint Investigation report that recommended reducing livestock in all parts of the watershed except portions of the Santa Fe and Lincoln National Forests, with reductions averaging from 15 to 50 percent of herds. The highest amounts of silt entered the river in the Pecos headwaters area, so the report proposed acquisition of 10,000 acres held by larger commercial grazing interests within the national forest. This acreage would be made available to those with limited numbers of livestock kept only for subsistence or cultural purposes.[63]

The Forest Service also had to balance the interests of a growing coalition interested primarily in the forests' recreational potential. For decades, the forests around Pecos had been a popular recreational destination for locals and tourists alike. Elliott Barker, the legendary director of the New Mexico Department of Game and Fish, had hunted in the Pecos high country; miners from Tererro had fished in the river; and visitors at the local dude ranches had enjoyed horseback riding through the forests. In the postwar era, the numbers of tourists grew due to increased affluence and leisure time, and recreational activities in the national forests also increased. In the Santa Fe National Forest, visitor numbers grew steadily from 78,200 in 1947 to 1.2 million in 1964.[64] Vacationers traveled to the Santa Fe National Forest from other states, but most visitors were nearby urban dwellers from New Mexico's rapidly growing cities. In addition to the impact of new trails and campgrounds, human-caused fires and erosion increased, and utilities created rights-of-way to bring services to rural communities, vacation destinations, and new public facilities. Tailings from three Tererro mine dump sites served as a convenient source of fill material for new construction projects throughout the Upper Pecos watershed, including the Lisboa Springs Hatchery, Forest Service campgrounds, state campgrounds, roads, and private projects.[65] As with clear-cutting and the introduction of non-native species, use of the tailings had unforeseen consequences, leading to soil contamination that was not discovered until decades later.

As the Forest Service strove to improve forest health while maintaining economic and recreational opportunities, it continued to come into conflict with locals over the use and control of the land. In the land grant communities of the Santa Fe National Forest, subsistence logging for fuel wood and other needs did not coexist easily with the growth of commercial timber sales and the demands of timber companies to have large areas of the forests opened to cutting. Geographer David Correia argues that the agency took a paternalistic approach to resolving the problem by encouraging locals to take wage labor jobs in the timber harvests. The Forest Service range managers often believed local cultural beliefs were the biggest challenge to resource protection. "Adjoining private land owners seem to feel that this area is theirs to use as they see fit, because they have historically done so," one report noted. Even as more members of the public became involved in influencing forest management, Hispanos were often left out. During a debate over livestock reduction in the 1950s, for example, the Forest Service hardly mentioned the subsistence permit holders. Although the Forest Service did try to keep resources available to locals, many Hispanos who continued to gather fuel wood and piñon nuts and relied on the forests for grazing land felt the professional bureaucracy and scientific management policies of the Forest Service excluded their input.[66]

In Pecos in their attempts to solve problems of overgrazing, the Forest Service eventually eliminated free-use permits on some allotments. On the Colonias allotment east of the village, free-use permits had long been more common than grazing under paid permit. Because of this long period of traditional forest use, trespass grazing was a persistent management issue before and after the reduction of free-use permits.[67] The Forest Service issued only three free-use permits in 1969 for the allotment, and by 1980 had phased them out entirely. The allotment provided marginal grazing land even for permitted animals—it contained only 445 acres suitable for grazing out of more than 20,000 total acres. After many decades of heavy use, the dense stands of piñon-juniper covering most of the allotment contained very little herbaceous understory for grazing.[68] Although there were penalties associated with trespass on Forest Service lands, many locals who depended on those lands for resources took their chances. On the Colonias allotment, the Forked Lightning property provided a boundary west of the forest, but trespass was inevitable from the east because no fencing separated private lands from the allotment.

Conflicts could also arise with individual landholders, as happened with the Fogelsons when Pajarito residents asserted their rights to former communal land enclosed within the Forked Lightning Ranch. In addition to travel between the villages, the residents of Rowe also used the road that ran through the old Los Trigos grant to the Pecos River to collect water before establishing a community water well in the 1960s. A bridge known as the Colonias bridge carried the road over the river, and the area adjacent to the bridge was also a popular fishing area.[69] The Colonias bridge received only sporadic maintenance and was already in poor condition by the early 1960s, its lumber stolen or burned. In March 1963 ranch manager and veterinarian Dr. Hinderliter asked Fogelson's attorney, F. A. Catron, to write to San Miguel District Attorney George Martinez and request that he recommend that the county commissioners close the unmaintained 1.5-mile portion of the Colonias Road across the ranch. Catron pointed out that locals used the road for "drinking parties and like activities." Catron argued abandonment of the road and bridge meant the right of way had reverted to Fogelson as the property owner of all adjacent lands on both sides. Nothing came of the request. District Attorney Martinez joined the Alianza movement, and the commissioners may have held Alianza sympathies as well because two years later they objected to closing the road.[70]

When Frank Salmeron and Esquipula Padilla cut fences on the Forked Lightning Ranch, the issue once again landed in the courts. But as in similar Spanish land grant disputes, the court cared only that the Fogelsons could produce a chain of title for the land going back to the 1909 patent of the Los Trigos grant, when Congress privatized the land. On April 8, 1970, H. Vearle Payne, a U.S. District Judge, ruled against Salmeron and Padilla "and all persons in active concert and participation with them," declaring that their rights under Spanish or Mexican law were unproven and extinguished by U.S. acquisition of the lands. Payne ordered them permanently restrained from interfering with use of the access road to the pasture, entering Fogelson's property, damaging or removing fences, and placing livestock on the ranch without consent.[71]

Like the Hispanos who remembered their claims to the land and their long struggle to retain those rights, the descendants of the Pecos also remembered their ties to their homeland. In 1951, the Pecos descendants at Jemez Pueblo joined with that pueblo in a lawsuit to try and receive a higher monetary compensation for the Pecos grant than had been awarded by the Pueblo Lands Board in 1930. The lawsuit cited the fact that the Pueblo Lands Board had not given any compensation for the water rights at Pecos. Filed under the auspices of the Indian Claims Commission Act of 1946, the Pecos's claim was part of a larger claim by the Jemez to the land around their own pueblo. In 1954 the United States government replied that Pecos Pueblo had no right to file a claim because the pueblo no longer existed. The government pointed to Pecos's merger with Jemez Pueblo in 1936 as proof that Pecos was no longer a separate entity. The government ignored the fact that joining with another pueblo did not erase Pecos descendants' identity or connections to their homeland. The lawyer for the Pecos and Jemez added Jemez Pueblo to the Pecos Pueblo suit, but the commission ruled against them in 1959.[72]

Despite official claims that Pecos Pueblo no longer existed, developments at Pecos in the 1970s provided new opportunities for Pecos descendants to access their ancient home. The Park Service's restoration of the mission ruins meant Pecos residents could once more hold the Feast of Nuestra Señora de los Ángeles de Porciúncula at the old church. The Park Service also commissioned historian John Kessell to write a history of Pecos Pueblo during the Spanish period. Although memories of this time had stayed alive in the oral traditions of Pecos descendants, Kessell's work, *Kiva, Cross, and Crown: The Pecos Indians and New Mexico, 1540–1840,* restored the history of the Pecos to a broader community awareness.

However, both the Museum of New Mexico and the Park Service focused on the archaeological and historical significance of the site as opposed to its link to a group of living Pecos descendants. There is no ready indication that the Park Service carried out any tribal consultation with the Pecos at Jemez Pueblo. The Park Service's southwest regional historian, Robert Utley, argued that Pecos Pueblo's historical significance came from its association with the history of Spanish colonial settlement and missionary activity, as well as how the site "vividly exemplifies" the Pueblos' "extermination by epidemic." Rather than acknowledging that the Pecos people lived on, with many cultural traditions intact, Utley's summation emphasized that the Pecos community was no more.[73]

Of course, the Pecos did remain, and during these decades, other Puebloan communities' legal successes at regaining access or control of land provided encouragement to the Pecos. Spurred on by Taos Pueblo's 1970 success in achieving title to Blue Lake, a sacred site, the Pecos Pueblo clan at Jemez used that legal precedent to negotiate with the New Mexico Department of Game and Fish to acknowledge their indigenous rights and interest in a sacred cave near Tererro that they continued to use for pilgrimages and initiations. Protection of the Pecos's access and attachment to the cave had become problematic in the twentieth century. Development of the mine and the growing population of Tererro interfered with the tribal members' ability to visit the cave for ceremonies without disturbance. A nearby dairy used the mouth of the cave as a cattle shelter, and the local community had only a casual understanding of the long-standing importance of the site to the Pecos. But starting in the 1970s, political awareness of these issues began to change. New legislation reflected growing acknowledgment of the environmental and social impacts of federal land use policies, and new requirements for consultation between federal lands administrators and Indian governments provided opportunities for protection of places of religious and cultural significance to indigenous people. In a victory for the Pecos, the Department of Game and Fish agreed to recognize the cave as a traditional cultural property important to the Pecos Eagle Society and eventually closed it to public access, barricading the entrance with a gate locked to all but the Pecos of Jemez.[74]

But unlike Puebloan communities like the Taos, who lived on in their traditional pueblo site, the Pecos struggled to maintain an acknowledgement of their ancestral connections from a distance at the Jemez Pueblo. In 1979 the parish council in the town of Pecos formally invited any interested Puebloans at Jemez to attend the annual Feast of Nuestra Señora de los Ángeles de Porciúncula. At the mass, Jose Toya, a Pecos descendant who lived at Jemez Pueblo, requested the chance to speak to the audience. His words revealed how deeply the conflict over the land had been embedded in people's memories. Toya castigated the local Hispanos for the way their ancestors drove the Pecos away in 1838. "Your people poisoned our water, killed our animals, ruined our crops, and drove us from these lands. But these are our lands, and we shall return to take them back," Toya said. During the speech, which Toya repeated in English, Spanish, and the Towa language, all of the Hispanos in the congregation left.[75]

During the 1960s and 1970s, the civil rights movement created a space that allowed Hispanos and Puebloans to forcefully voice their conviction that their claims to land in New Mexico remained valid. Although their attempts at gaining control of their old lands were often unsuccessful, those attempts did bring their stories to the attention of the public and made it more difficult for the history surrounding land ownership in New Mexico to be obscured and ignored. At Pecos, locals contested the Fogelsons' ownership of the Forked Lightning Ranch, and Pecos descendants spoke bitterly about the past. These events revealed the continuing tension and conflict over the environment in the Upper Pecos valley, conflict that had long been a part of Pecos history. As the National Park Service assumed management of Pecos National Monument, agency employees would have to decide how to interpret this history. They would also need to manage the environment of the monument. On paper, the monument had clearly defined borders, but in reality, nothing separated the monument from the surrounding environment and the continuing changes occurring there.

| # Enduring Spirits, Enduring Environment
1980–2019

DALLAS, 1989—Greer Garson Fogelson looked out her oversized window, not at the piñon-covered hills of Pecos but at the busy streets of Dallas far below her high-rise penthouse. At eighty-one years old, she was in poor health and had recently been hospitalized for heart surgery. Buddy had died two years before and left the Forked Lightning Ranch to Greer and his adopted son, Gayle. They no longer kept cattle, and Greer was considering selling the ranch. Earlier that year, a Florida developer named Jerry Crassas approached her and Gayle with an offer to buy the property. Imagining Crassas wanted to build something similar in scale to Tex Austin's old tourist resort, Garson had been considering the offer. But then the *Santa Fe Reporter* discovered that Crassas planned to develop the area on a much larger scale. The project would include residences for 20,000 people, an airstrip, a convention center, two 18-hole golf courses, a 454-acre shopping center, a medical facility, and several recreational areas. Reporters cornered Garson and Gayle Fogelson in Dallas, demanding to know if they really intended to let Crassas proceed with such a scheme. Gayle told the media, "Down here [in Dallas] the worst thing you can say about a man is that he left a town dry and then moved. I don't know where they would get the water for one golf course, let alone two. I think the whole thing sounds ridiculous."[1] But when Crassas offered to redesign his plans on a more limited scale, the Fogelsons reconsidered the deal.

Local opinions on the potential development varied. Some Pecos residents believed it would bring needed jobs, while others considered it only the latest example of a long line of outsiders who wanted to exploit the Pecos environment for their own benefit. But unlike in prior eras when people desired land in Pecos because they wanted to live there, farm, raise cattle, cut timber, or start a business, the existence of Pecos National Monument and the National Park Service meant that another option now existed—preserving the land and interpreting its history.

Certainly, the National Park Service did not want an extensive urban development on the doorstep of the national monument. In addition to the environmental impact, it would ruin the historic setting of the old Pecos Pueblo. The Fogelsons had been very supportive of the monument in the past and provided funding for its development. The Park Service hoped that instead of selling the land to a developer, Garson would choose to sell it to them instead. As the two decided what to do, the future of Pecos once again stood at a crossroads.

"Conceived in Harmony": The National Park Service at Pecos National Monument

By the 1980s, the Park Service had been established at Pecos for more than fifteen years and exercised an important influence over the local environment. The Park Service employees who worked at Pecos National Monument made decisions about managing the environment based on the broader philosophies and policies of the agency as a whole. Congress had established the national monument during a period of expansion known as the Park Service's Mission 66 program. Started in 1956 and running through 1966, Mission 66 responded to the tremendous increase in postwar tourism that created a pressing need for new visitor facilities at national parks.[2] As in other national parks during this time, Pecos National Monument suffered from an excess of visitors relative to its inadequate facilities. By 1962 the site received 14,000 visitors annually, mostly from out of state, with as many as 350 in a single day.[3] The Museum of New Mexico had installed basic visitor facilities near the southeast corner of the ruins, including a superintendent's residence, maintenance shed, checking station with exhibits, parking area, picnic site, and pit toilets.[4] Determined to improve the facilities at Pecos, the Park Service immediately turned to their first priority—a visitor center.[5] Although parks had featured museums and information centers before Mission 66, park planners developed the concept of the full-service visitor center during the Mission 66 program and soon considered it a necessity for every park. There was no question that Pecos would get a visitor center—but what exactly that visitor center would look like was another matter entirely.

Park Service architects had their own concept of the ideal visitor center. Influenced by the modernist architecture popular during the 1960s and 1970s, many Mission 66 visitor centers departed radically from the rustic designs previously favored by the Park Service. The new visitor centers employed modern, minimalist architectural features and materials to facilitate a controlled flow of visitors through interior spaces without drawing attention to the building design itself. Some of the new visitor centers, such as the one located in Beaver Meadows in Rocky Mountain National Park, were considered tasteful constructions in harmony with the landscape. Critics derided others, particularly the Jackson Lake Lodge at Grand Teton National Park, as unacceptably modernist intrusions into the natural scenery.[6] With so much attention focused on park architecture,

Park Service officials approached the design of the new Pecos visitor center carefully. The Washington office, the San Francisco Service Center (and later the Denver Service Center), the Southwest Regional Office, and the superintendent at Pecos, Thomas F. Giles (1966–1978), all provided input on the design.[7]

But the Park Service was not the only party with opinions about the visitor center and the influence to make those opinions heard. The Fogelsons had become important donors for the monument, and they were interested in helping fund the visitor center. Buddy and Greer had donated an additional 278.7 acres of the Forked Lightning Ranch surrounding the original state monument boundary in 1965, bringing the total acreage of the monument to 341.3 acres.[8] As the Park Service began trying to build better facilities for visitors to replace those operated under the state, the Fogelsons once again stepped forward with an offer to help. In 1971 Buddy Fogelson offered $600,000 in matching funds for the construction of a new visitor center.[9] Of course, accepting the money also meant pleasing the Fogelsons, who had definite ideas about the sort of visitor center they wanted built—one that echoed the romanticized traditionalism of the Forked Lightning Ranch, not the modernist architecture of the Mission 66 program.

Although opinions about the architectural design differed, both the Fogelsons and the Park Service hoped to build an environmentally conscious facility that would take into account the arid environment and incorporate alternative energy sources. Fogelson expected to use his considerable influence to foster a locally managed and contracted project that utilized solar-assisted heating. He remarked to the Southwest Regional Director, "I'm in the energy business myself; if the government doesn't start moving on this soon it will be too late!"[10] Solar energy was in abundance at Pecos, but water was not. Aridity had always been the limiting factor during the entire span of human settlement in the valley, and the Park Service operated within the same constraints. The visitor center and areas for housing, maintenance, and picnicking required a new well and water system with submersible pumps and pressure tanks. The planners were unsure about the effect of groundwater withdrawal on the recharge area. They also considered the potential effects of a new sewage system on vegetation types and quantity and surface water quality.[11] The Park Service hoped the visitor center would provide an example to the community of good environmental management and "tie present day environmental concerns to the 700-year human history of Pecos."[12] With the assistance of modern technology, the Park Service staff strove to recognize the limits of the environment.

As at many other Park Service sites, the Pecos visitor center was originally intended to provide an all-weather interpretive experience for those who might not wish to venture out onto the ruins trail on cold, windy days.[13] But the design directive also hoped to encourage visitors to explore the ruins by enticing them with a carefully managed series of views as they approached the monument by vehicle from various directions. The scenery was "a lure to all visitors to get out to the ruins and explore them—a motivation that could be instilled in no better way."[14] These early plans favored visitor access to the ruins over concerns about the impact visitors would have on the fragile site, reflecting a long history in the Park Service of accommodating tourists. Architect Bill Lumpkin's original visitor center design placed the facility on the east rim of the mesilla, in full view of the ruins, and incorporated indigenous building materials in the ubiquitous Spanish-Pueblo Revival style, a design sure to find favor with the Fogelsons.

The process for approving the visitor center design moved swiftly until a group of Park Service reviewers refused to support the plans because they felt the master plan and required environmental impact statement had been rushed and might violate various environmental protection laws, such as the National Environmental Protection Act. They also worried that the pseudo-historic design departed too far from the Park Service's new modernistic design paradigm that, in part, was meant to ensure that tourists would not confuse the visitor center with a historic building. Park Service officials continued to debate the location and size of the visitor center as well, and they considered off-monument sites in the village or on one of the interstate exchanges and in the grassy meadow east of the ruins, among other locations.[15]

At an impasse, the Park Service hired another architect, Tony Predock, to develop an alternative plan with a modernistic design incorporating solar technology.[16] Public reaction to that design, including the Fogelsons', was predictably unfavorable compared to the original Spanish-Pueblo Revival design. The stalled planning process frustrated Superintendent Giles, who felt "the original intent, direction, and momentum of the Pecos project has been perverted and destroyed." The delays and modernist design caused Buddy Fogelson to threaten to pull his support for the project. "I think we have lost Fogelson and his donations," Giles lamented. "These are two different things. Money might be provided through federal sources; but we can't buy good will from our only next-door neighbor. In the long run, that loss might be a greater one. It makes me sick."[17]

Although frustrated with the lengthy planning process, in the end the Fogelsons maintained their support for the project, and by 1975 all of the decision-makers had agreed on a simple adobe structure utilizing solar panels. The building was to be located on the north side of the mesilla. Planners felt the design was "conceived in harmony with traditional materials and forms . . . sympathetic with the site, terrain, and historic influences at Pecos," as well as "compatible with, but not imitative of, the architecture of the people who built pueblos and churches here."[18] But then the Advisory Council on Historic Preservation, a federal agency that is responsible for ensuring other federal agencies include preservation of historic resources in any project requirements, requested an in-depth comparative study of twelve potential visitor center sites before construction could begin. By this point, the Park Service had been forced to adjust all of its visitor center designs across the system after weathering public feedback regarding the unpopular Mission 66 buildings, and it had moved toward limiting visual impact on the historic scene. At Pecos, the agency no longer considered a view of the ruins from within the visitor center to be essential. Giles's successor, Superintendent John Bezy, signed the final recommendation for an unobtrusive location below and to the east of the rock escarpment of the mesilla, which screened the building from the ruins and provided adequate sun exposure for a passive solar design.[19] The delay and timing of the site selection, during which preservation interests within the Park Service gathered strength, thus determined how visitors experienced the landscape and ruins in the following decades.

But even with design approval, construction did not begin for several more years. Unhappy with the long delay, the Fogelsons interacted less frequently with the Park Service, although their unswerving dedication to the visitor center project impressed the monument staff. In 1974 the Fogelsons had donated another 23.5 acres to the national monument in two separate parcels, including a 3.5-acre site northeast of the ruins along Highway 63, which the Park Service initially reserved for a residential and maintenance area, although this was never built.[20] The long-awaited groundbreaking for the visitor center finally took place on August 7, 1983, and the Park Service dedicated the completed visitor center on August 2, 1987. Buddy Fogelson could not attend the dedication of his namesake building—coincidentally, he was hospitalized that same morning and died four months later in Dallas at the age of eighty-seven. The visitor center became a tribute to his memory for Greer Garson and their family and friends. Garson proudly showed off the new visitor center during her remaining years on the ranch and narrated the introductory film for the park. She also asked her friend Ricardo Montalban to visit from Los Angeles and narrate the Spanish-language version of the film. "[The Fogelsons] had a goal, a dream, a vision," remarked Superintendent John Bezy. "It was a personal commitment of the most significant kind. . . . The Rockefellers are responsible for the Grand Tetons. The Pecos National Monument is because of the Fogelsons."[21] In supporting the monument and donating land, the Fogelsons steered the Pecos environment toward one of preservation rather than development.

The ultimate choice of Spanish-Pueblo Revival architecture for the visitor center situated the building comfortably within the aesthetics of the Forked Lightning Ranch. Like the Fogelsons, the Park Service initially adopted the view of New Mexico as a landscape that had remained unchanged for hundreds of years. In his assessment of the site, park historian Frank Wilson provided only a superficial description of broader landscape changes since the Spanish mission era. "The mountains and rivers are still here, the trees may be growing a little closer to the ruins mesa," he wrote. "The ruts of the Santa Fe Trail are close by and the arroyo where the domestic water came from is still a short distance to the west. The many trails that must have led to the church are now covered over with grass. All is tranquil."[22] This image erased the centuries of extensive change and transformation at Pecos.

"Here Land Is Not a Product like an Automobile or a Hamburger": *The Sale of the Forked Lightning Ranch*

The Fogelsons had donated some land to the national monument, but the bulk of the Forked Lightning Ranch remained in their hands. In the last decade of the cattle operation, which ceased in 1988, the Forked Lightning Ranch kept an average of 110 mother cows and at least five bulls, as well as frozen embryos from five more sires for artificial insemination.[23] But in the year after Buddy's death, Greer and Gayle sold the remaining Santa Gertrudis cattle, and the pastures on both parcels were empty by December 1988.[24] When Garson then decided to sell the entire ranch in 1989, the Park Service was understandably interested in acquiring it. The Park Service already had studied the cultural and natural resources of the Forked Lightning Ranch in the hopes of eventually adding it to the historic site. The ranch would offer the Park Service the chance to interpret the history of cattle ranching in New Mexico and protect the archaeological ruins and Santa Fe Trail ruts on the property.[25]

The Fogelsons had considered donating the entire ranch to the Park Service when their involvement with the cattle operation declined during Buddy's illness.[26] However, in his will Fogelson conveyed the 5,500-acre northern parcel, which contained the ranch house, to Greer and left the 8,000-acre Los Trigos Ranch to his nephew and adopted son, Gayle David Fogelson.[27] In 1989 controversy erupted when Greer and Gayle began to negotiate the sale of their combined acreage to Jerry Crassas of Capital Developers International. Crassas envisioned "Santa Fe East 2001," a full-service resort community that would have rapidly urbanized the area. The exhaustive list of resort features included a ninety-two-acre hotel; an Olympic-size swimming pool; extended-stay cabins; a private airstrip; a 160-acre convention center; medical services; a 7,000-acre residential development for 20,000 permanent residents; a 454-acre shopping center; two 18-hole golf courses; a 419-acre shooting range; a hunting preserve stocked with quail, dove, grouse, pheasant, deer, rabbit, and elk; a racetrack for cars and motorcycles; and a 729-acre recreational center and athletic fields. Crassas, a wealthy Greek citizen and self-described wheeler-dealer, was the latest in a long line of fortune-seekers who approached the Upper Pecos valley with a limited understanding of the existing community and the ecological limits of the land. "I had never been west of the Mississippi River before," Crassas told a local paper. "But my partner told me I had to come and see this land. When I did, I fell in love with it."[28]

When the *Santa Fe Reporter* revealed Crassas's intentions for the property, some locals and environmentalists vehemently protested and organized to stop the development. The New Mexico Acequia Association's board members expressed "grave concern" about the plan, which they felt would deplete the water table and pollute the water on which the existing community relied.[29] George Adelo, the Pecos mayor, worried the village would lose its identity and the already overtaxed water and sewage systems would not support the sizeable new development.[30] Another local, A. Samuel Adelo, described Pecos as a refuge where people could live "under the cloak of its tranquility" and warned that the environment and culture in Pecos were fragile and worthy of protection. "In New Mexico, even today," he wrote, "the land has spiritual and community values. Here land is not a product like an automobile or a hamburger that are simply used to make money."[31] Just like the Pecos Indians and the original Spanish settlers, the late twentieth-century Upper Pecos valley residents continued to locate their cultural identity within the landscape.

Although Crassas failed to appreciate these long-held local values, he did make one correct assumption: the Pecos community understood that the resort would bring an abundance of wage-earning opportunities to the valley—an increase in jobs comparable to the railroad and mining booms of the 1880s and early 1900s. The National Park Service realized the importance of providing jobs to the local community when they assumed management of the monument in 1965. A 1962 study completed by the Park Service found that the population of the village of Pecos numbered less than 600, and about 2,700 people lived in the general area. Although some local residents remained active farmers and ranchers, they did so to maintain their cultural heritage and quality of life and required local wage labor opportunities with the Forest Service and other entities to make ends meet. Winter employment was particularly scarce when seasonal jobs in recreation declined. The Park Service, however, could offer only a limited number of positions.[32]

The relative isolation of the village created economic hardship, but it also preserved the sense of cultural continuity that inspired many to resist the resort plans in 1989. As a result, community opinion was split. The *Pecos Post* editors reasoned change should be welcomed, because the pueblo's first inhabitants had been the valley's first "developers," followed by the Spaniards and Anglos. "Life goes on and things change with or without our consent," the editors opined.[33] Cip Gonzales, a local school bus contractor and auto parts store owner, agreed. "What we have here is a lot of pretty country, and you can't get much income from that," he said. "So from the business standpoint, I'm in favor of it."[34] Others pointed out the new wage-earning opportunities would keep young people from moving away and help those residents forced to commute to Santa Fe or Las Vegas for work. Many, though, felt the development would be a disaster. Pecos resident Bob Hattle believed the new jobs would not be worth the price of the impact on village culture and the environment. "That's not the kind of job any of us wants to make a living—cleaning out a rich man's sewer," Hattle said.[35] Another local resident, Richard Roybal, agreed the potential for wages was akin to accepting scraps from "the rich man's table" and not worth the price of losing their water, increasing air and noise pollution, and transforming the village into a slum section of the new city.[36]

The "pretty country" Gonzales described had captivated the Fogelsons and their social circle since the 1940s. Like the Park Service, their approach to land stewardship fell somewhere between preservation and use. Although the Fogelsons defended their rights as private landholders and often mythologized local cultural traditions, they did value the long history of human activity in the valley and the living community still residing there. They steadfastly supported the national monument and had a strong philanthropic track record throughout the country. The monument staff and some residents feared that the Fogelsons' long-standing commitment was about to end abruptly. For a time, it appeared Garson might sell to Crassas. According to Garson's employee, M. S. Disimone, "[Crassas] came up with a proposal and a figure you just have to take a look at. There are some things you can't say no to."[37] Linda Stoll, the superintendent at Pecos, expressed surprise that the monument's main benefactor would consider the sale. She told the Santa Fe paper, "We have been fortunate that we have had a single landowner around us who has left the land alone. If the land is developed, it would put our viewshed at risk." Stoll and her staff also wondered how the cultural resources on the Forked Lightning Ranch property, including Kozlowski's Trading Post, the Santa Fe Trail ruts, the Hispanic homesteads, and additional pueblo remains could be protected in the midst of a large-scale development.[38]

As news of the potential sale spread in New Mexico, Garson was recovering from a hospital stay and dealing with another loss: a catastrophic fire had destroyed her Beverly Hills home and much of her Hollywood memorabilia. As a result, she was unaware of the controversy. In their initial negotiations, she and Gayle believed Crassas planned only to build a single home or a small-scale guest ranch, and if the Santa Fe Reporter had not leaked the resort plans, the transaction might have gone through. The village of Pecos also passed a resolution opposing the new development and prepared to pressure Garson to change her mind. After she left the hospital she announced that she and Gayle were reconsidering the sale.[39] But in the face of public opposition, Crassas agreed to present a scaled-down plan for consideration, and the Fogelsons temporarily faltered in their commitment to end the deal.[40]

As the Fogelsons wavered, Pecos residents looked for another alternative to development, and the presence of the Park Service and the national monument offered them one. The Pecos village resolution against the resort construction included a request to Secretary of the Interior Manuel Lujan Jr. and to their congressional delegation to "exercise all options" for the Park Service to take over the ranch and qualify the expanded site for national park status. Lujan, newly appointed under President George H. W. Bush, was born near the San Ildefonso Pueblo, grew up in Santa Fe as the son of the city's mayor, and graduated from the College of Santa Fe. He had served in Congress since 1968 as a prominent Hispanic Republican representing the concerns of New Mexico's American Indian population. Lujan labeled himself a moderate who balanced environmental protection with development, yet he advocated opening federal lands to mining, grazing, logging, and recreation as well as offshore oil drilling.[41] Although his reputation with the environmental community was mixed at best,

Lujan had a special interest in the fate of the Pecos area, and he did not want the site to be developed. After Crassas's development plans leaked, Lujan visited Pecos to assess the site, but he was not forthcoming with funding for purchasing the land because the ranch did not fit into the department's two priority categories—wetlands, and parklands in large urban areas. Further complicating the negotiation, the New Mexico congressional delegation had recently requested the purchase of two additional sites in New Mexico, and Lujan felt he could not support all three proposals. However, the Interior Department declared its willingness to accept the donation of the ranch for the national park system through an act of Congress.[42]

Before the Park Service could approach the Fogelsons about donating the ranch land, events took a new turn. The *Santa Fe Reporter,* which broke the initial story of Crassas's grandiose plans for the ranch despite his attempts to bribe them to hold it until after the sale, discovered that Florida police wanted Crassas on a felony warrant. Furthermore, Crassas had forty-eight convictions in his native Greece related to failed business dealings and had been wanted for fraud in Switzerland. The U.S. government considered him an "undesirable" alien and subject to deportation. The news about Crassas's record ended deal negotiations, and the *Reporter's* editor remarked, "Our local Greek tragedy has run its course."[43]

Although Crassas was no longer a threat, Pecos residents and the monument staff feared new developers would approach the Fogelsons. A few weeks later, Maurice Tripp, a California inventor with a questionable business reputation, contacted the Fogelsons about purchasing the land for a proposed manufacturing plant, but nothing came of it. In a separate deal, Gayle Fogelson sold Los Trigos in two parcels to local residents, the Cowles and the Lyons, who planned to raise Norwegian fjord horses and operate a guest ranch.[44] Hoping a private foundation would purchase Garson's portion of the ranch and donate it to the federal government, New Mexico's congressional delegation introduced legislation to create the 5,865-acre Pecos National Historical Park. Prompted by the controversial Crassas deal, historian William deBuys, who was working with the Conservation Fund, arranged a visit to Pecos for the fund's president and the director of the Richard King Mellon Foundation. His prompt response led the foundation to purchase the ranch for $4.5 million and lease it back to Greer Garson while Congress considered appropriations for operating funds.[45]

The debate and uncertainty over the old Forked Lightning Ranch's future finally ended in favor of preservation. On June 27, 1990, Congress established the new boundaries of the park to include the original 365-acre national monument and the addition of the 5,500-acre ranch.[46] The Mellon Foundation donated the land to the federal government in 1993. The new Pecos National Historical Park also included the two units encompassing part of the Glorieta Battlefield. Pigeon's Ranch, unoccupied since the late 1950s, had also been subject to development pressures. In the 1970s, a mobile home park developer wanted to purchase the site and bulldoze the historic structures, but the property owner rejected the offer and another concerned local resident, Linda Frye, purchased the ten-acre ranch property. To protect the historic area, Frye granted a twenty-year covenant to the New Mexico Preservation Bureau in 1981, and it was incorporated into the new national park in 1991.[47] At the same time, the Park Service also acquired the Cañoncito subunit, which included the location of the Confederate camp, in order to interpret the entirety of the Glorieta Battlefield, although four private homes, the AT&SF Railroad, and Interstate 25 presented unavoidable visual and auditory intrusions near the site.[48] In 1964 the remaining structure at Johnson's Ranch had been bulldozed to make way for the interstate.[49]

The transfer of property to the Park Service required new enabling legislation, which called for "the preservation and interpretation of [both] the cultural and natural resources" of the redesignated Pecos National Historical Park.[50] When Pecos was a national monument, the Park Service had emphasized the Spanish-colonial history of the site, but with the new acquisitions came expanded interpretive possibilities—and more complicated management decisions. Garson retained lifetime rights to the ranch house complex and ten contiguous acres and continued to make seasonal visits until she died on April 6, 1996, in Dallas.[51] Her passing marked the end of luxury ranching on the Pecos grant, but the Los Trigos grant parcels eventually transferred to new owners, Jane Fonda and Val Kilmer, both Hollywood actors like Garson. Fonda and Kilmer continued the tradition of managing the Forked Lightning property as private refuges for both people and wildlife.

Although the Pecos descendants at Jemez had not gotten involved in the debate over Pecos's future, their ties to the land remained, and as the Park Service began managing the expanded historical park, they recognized the Pecos Indians as stakeholders in the park's future. The Park Service also recognized residents of the Pecos village and members of several other pueblos besides Jemez as additional stakeholders. In 1994 the Park Service completed an ethnographic overview that involved consultation with Pecos descendants and solicited their opinions about the interpretation of the Pecos story.[52] The 1990 Native American Graves Protection and Repatriation Act also required cultural consultations that presented new opportunities for Pecos descendants to participate in the preservation of their history. In 1993 the Smithsonian Institution returned eighty-six sacred objects and religious artifacts to Jemez elders of Pecos descent.[53] Six years later, Harvard University's Robert S. Peabody Museum repatriated the remains of 1,922 people that Alfred Kidder excavated in the 1920s to the Pueblo of Jemez, to be returned to their original burial ground at Pecos Pueblo. The Pecos descendants walked from Jemez to Pecos with the remains to rebury them at the pueblo, a reversal of the route the last Pecos residents used when they moved to Jemez in 1838. Governor Raymond Cachupin of the Pueblo of Jemez stated, "By concluding this repatriation, we seek the restoration of the spiritual harmony and peace that the ancestors have been deprived of. We seek the reestablishment of the respect that all human beings deserve, and most of all, we seek confirmation of the concept that all men are created equal."[54] As the environment that had once harbored the Pecos at their pueblo transferred from private to public ownership, opportunities for the Pecos to once more participate in managing that land arose, although such opportunities depended on the commitment of the Park Service to the stakeholder concept.

"National Parks Are Not Pictures on a Wall":
The Park Service's Natural and Cultural Resource Management

With the creation of Pecos National Historical Park, the land ownership and management settled into the configuration it still possesses today. Although the Park Service became and remains the primary steward of the land within the national park, that did not mean the Pecos environment stopped changing. On the contrary, through its environmental management and interpretation of Pecos's history, the Park Service became an agent of change itself. And as Park Service officials made decisions about how to manage the new park, they were once more influenced by agency-wide policies and philosophies about the environment.

By the 1990s, the Park Service's attitude toward environmental management had changed drastically. For much of its history, the Park Service had given little thought to scientific management, concentrating instead on developing roads and buildings to facilitate tourism, expanding the park system, and adding educational programs and exhibits. This state of affairs changed in the postwar era as environmentalists pressured the Park Service to conduct scientific studies and monitor the ecological health of resources. The influential 1963 "Wildlife Management in the National Parks"—commonly referred to as the "Leopold Report" for its principal author, A. Starker Leopold—called for scientific management and research in the national parks based on sound ecological principles that prioritized the health of ecosystems. That same year, the National Academy of Sciences released a report on scientific research in the national parks. The committee supported many of the goals of the Leopold Report, stating that "national parks are not pictures on the wall; they are not museum exhibits in glass cases; they are dynamic biological complexes with self-generating changes."[55] Secretary of the Interior Stewart Udall championed the Leopold Report and directed Park Service Director Conrad Wirth, and his successor George B. Hartzog Jr. to develop new policies and administrative units reflecting restoration strategies that provided equal consideration of park ecosystems and visitor needs.[56]

A great deal of the Park Service's new scientific policies focused on parks recognized primarily for their natural landscapes, such as Yellowstone, as opposed to historic parks like Pecos. But many also recognized that just because parks were categorized as "historic" did not mean they lacked plants or wildlife or rivers.

All parks—not just ones encompassing large tracts of undeveloped land—were part of an ecological system. Ultimately, environmentalists pressured Congress to unite the three types of parks—natural, historic, and recreation areas—in the General Authorities Act of 1970.[57] The Park Service would have to manage all of them under the same mandates. Scientific management and research in the Park Service remained hampered by internal dispute, but slowly the agency culture began changing toward a more accepting view of ecology. Yet despite the fact that Pecos—and all parks—possessed landscapes that reflected the overlap and interdependence of "natural" and "cultural" resources, the Park Service continued to separate the resources and parks into distinct management categories. Even if Pecos was managed under the same directives, the agency considered it a historical park, distinct from a place such as Yellowstone, which was a "natural" park. Both, of course, encompassed landscapes that had been profoundly influenced by humans over thousands of years.

Trying to decide how to balance the "natural" and "cultural" sides of Pecos presented the Park Service with some quandaries. Park managers could, for example, decide to try to restore portions of the environment to an approximation of their appearance in past eras. But not all past uses of the land had been beneficial for the environment. Livestock presented one of the clearest examples—horses, cattle, goats, and sheep had all lived and grazed in the land the park encompassed, but they had also contributed to erosion and other problems. Park Service staff at Pecos had purchased horses for patrolling in areas with no roads and kept them at Kozlowski's Trading Post. Although the horses were rarely used, their pasture northeast of the trading post gave the animals access to the sensitive floodplain and riparian zone along Glorieta Creek. In the 1990s, Bobbi Simpson, the park's natural resources specialist, argued the pasture location violated the Park Service's wetlands and floodplains management guidelines. In 1995 park staff began a study to relocate the pasture and address negative-impact issues such as erosion, cowbird overpopulation (which affected other avian species), and invasive vegetation in the vicinity of the pasture.[58] Simpson noted the predominance of exotic vegetation species inside the corral, weakened bank structure where the horses could access the west side of Glorieta Creek, and the recovery of mostly native vegetation outside of the corral. "Overgrazing exacerbates our already profound exotic species and erosion problems," she wrote.[59]

Simpson suggested it might be necessary to sell the horses and keep no livestock at the park. But at the recommendation of Judy Reed, the park's cultural resource manager, the park also considered alterations to the existing management plan that would allow the park to keep the horses. "We suggest that the horses' contribution to the historic ranching landscape and usefulness to the staff in their performance of certain duties be compared to the animals' cost of maintenance when deliberating the fate of the Pecos horses," Reed argued. Suggested changes included expanding the size of the pasture, keeping the horses in the park only in the summer months, and corralling them away from the creek. Former Forked Lightning ranch manager Gilbert Ortiz, who had been hired by the Park Service after the ranch transfer, suggested moving the horses to a more ecologically stable portion of the park bordered by Highway 63 near the old Las Vegas Highway. This would have required installation of a water tank and additional fencing, as well as a survey for cultural resource impact.[60] The horses were briefly relocated to a refenced area of an old pasture, but keeping the horses required the ongoing provision of water and weed-free hay. Ultimately the park staff decided to sell the horses.[61] In this case, although horses had been a part of Pecos's history, park managers determined that ecological health trumped trying to recreate the past.

With the horses gone, park managers moved on to a full-scale restoration of the Glorieta Creek floodplain, 300 yards due east of Kozlowski's Trading Post. The area had been the site of a gravel-mining pit used for local road construction in the 1980s. Managers consulted with wetlands rehabilitation experts and in 1999 reshaped the 5.6-acre site into ponds, wet meadows, willow thickets, and cottonwood groves. The restoration included upland slope stabilization and extensive seeding and planting of herbaceous wetland plants and trees, such as sedges, rushes, bulrushes, willow, and cottonwood.[62] Although the floodplain and riparian corridor of the creek segment through the park already possessed more abundant and diverse vegetation than during recent historic periods, the restoration further improved conditions along the entire corridor. Following the restoration, normal flood cycles stimulated the reproduction of woody riparian species and improved native biodiversity.[63]

For other mammals and birds, the protected Park Service lands became a refuge in the 1990s and the twenty-first century. In the early years of Park Service management, deer and coyotes would occasionally enter the monument boundaries. Other mammal species documented in those early years included rabbits, skunks, and gophers.[64] Not all were welcome—pocket gopher burrows threatened archaeological resources around the ruins, and park employees began using snap traps in the burrows in 1994.[65] A faunal survey that same year documented twenty-four mammal species. Casual surveys in the early site-planning phases noted bird species such as piñon jays, juncos, sparrows, towhees, phoebes, bluebirds, meadowlarks, scaled quail, and, more rarely, roadrunners.[66] The noted phoebe species was probably Say's phoebe, a common summer resident in arid, open terrain. The ruins provided welcome habitat for this species, which prefers to nest on flat projections of vacant buildings.[67]

In the mid-1990s, the park began summer surveys looking for nesting or migratory activity of the endangered southwestern willow flycatcher. Surveys concentrated on the recovering willow stands under cottonwood overstory along Glorieta Creek and the Pecos River, but none of the birds were found within the park, perhaps because the willow stands had not yet achieved the desirable height of thirteen to twenty-three feet due to the lingering effects of cattle grazing. In 1992 someone spotted a nesting pair of willow flycatchers three miles upstream on the Pecos River near Monastery Lake. Because the ranch still contained short-grass grazing pastures, surveyors noted the problematic presence of brown-headed cowbirds, which practice brood parasitism on the flycatchers and other songbirds.[68]

Although they did not find willow flycatchers, bird surveyors did note feral dog packs roaming Park Service land. The packs preyed on the protected wildlife within the park boundaries, and ranchers in the Santa Fe National Forest also reported loss of calves due to dog packs.[69] In 1999 Marten Schmitz, the natural resource manager at the park, began a program in cooperation with San Miguel Animal Control to remove dogs from the park. Officials successfully removed 125 dogs in the first five years. As a result of the program, park staff noted an immediate improvement in wildlife sightings, including gray foxes, bobcats, porcupines, jackrabbits, desert cottontails, and mule deer. A ranger spotted the first ringtailed cat ever seen in the park.[70]

Park managers also needed to decide how to manage the ubiquitous piñon-juniper. Historically, the respective amounts of piñon-juniper and grasslands had varied considerably, influenced by grazing, wood-cutting, fires, and drought. Because the Forest Service had decades of experience with grassland restoration efforts in northern New Mexico, the Santa Fe National Forest Ranger District had provided expertise and equipment for prior restoration projects in the valley, including at the national monument and the Forked Lightning Ranch. In the summer of 1969, the Park Service had begun a grassland restoration project on the twenty-five acres in the historic trade encampment area east of the mesilla. Forest Service personnel used a drill and hydromulch machine to reseed the area with grassland species.[71] Park managers have continued piñon-juniper clearing projects in recent years.

Pecos may have been a "historical" park, but its landscape reflected and was influenced by contemporary changes and management decisions. Traditionally, the Park Service divided management into "natural" and "cultural" resources. Natural resources included wildlife, plants, and water, and managing them required scientific expertise in fields such as biology and botany. Cultural resources included historic structures and archaeological sites, with managers who possessed expertise in history, ethnology, and like subjects. Management documents rarely discussed the intersection of the natural and the cultural. In practice, of course, the two could not be separated. Understanding why certain species are present or absent in a park requires an understanding of the history of the site, just as understanding that history requires knowledge of past environmental conditions. Increasingly, the Park Service has recognized these intersections and moved toward a holistic stewardship ethic. For example, a 2012 Park Service report stated that "Parks exist as coupled natural-human systems. Natural and cultural resource management must occur simultaneously, and, in general, interdependently."[72] At Pecos, Park Service staff recognized these interconnections.

The environmental history report that served as the basis for this book arose from the staff's goal of managing cultural and natural resources together and overcoming artificial divides between them.

"There Are Spirits Everywhere; They'll Never Leave Us": Pecos in the Twenty-First Century

Park Service managers at Pecos operated within the boundaries of the national park, but in reality, nothing separated the environment within the park from the environment outside, and changes in the wider Upper Pecos valley influenced the park's environmental conditions. In the park's immediate vicinity, changing demographics and infrastructure in the late twentieth and early twenty-first centuries altered the character of the valley. In addition to the construction of I-25, commuter traffic and construction increased along State Route 50 and US 285. The new road development converted Pecos into a bedroom community for the growing capital city of Santa Fe. By 1988 the population of Pecos had doubled to 1,200, and it grew another 42.4 percent in the 1990s.[73] As of the 2010 census, Pecos had 1,392 residents.[74]

Development and population growth have particularly affected issues of water quality and quantity. When the Park Service acquired the original monument and later the Forked Lightning Ranch unit, these acquisitions did not include water rights to maintain adequate instream flows for habitat protection, and the state of New Mexico did not recognize wildlife habitat as a beneficial use of water. The lack of historical flow records and a supportive political climate hampered any potential application for water rights.[75] Upstream on Glorieta Creek, the Glorieta Baptist Conference Center, constructed in 1952, presented the greatest threat to water quality within the park boundaries. To meet the needs of its growing operation, the conference center expanded its wastewater treatment plant and added six sewage lagoons in 1977. The new lagoons malfunctioned and sewage effluent began to enter the creek, producing an overgrowth of algae and organic sludge deposits. After water quality tests in 1982, the New Mexico Environmental Improvement Division required the conference center to clean up the effluent problem, which temporarily improved the stream's water quality, although the lagoons remained an ongoing threat to the health of the creek.[76]

The remnants of the Tererro mine and its milling operation also affected water quality in the Pecos River. In 1980, federal Superfund legislation established liability for current and previous property owners of contaminated sites in the United States. Because the state of New Mexico had acquired the Tererro sites in 1950, it shared responsibility with AMAX, the successor to American Metal Company, for the cleanup of key metals and other contaminants at the mining and milling sites. Local groups such as La Gente del Rio Pecos and citizens in Pecos and Tererro raised concerns that led to initial studies of water and soil quality. In 1991, when a spring snowmelt moved contaminants into the Pecos

River and 90,000 fish died, public involvement in the cleanup grew. To avoid a Superfund listing, the responsible parties established a process that met all the requirements of the federal cleanup regulations but allowed it to take place under a site-specific administrative agreement. The process required a safety evaluation and remediation plan for the 50-acre mill and tailing ponds site on Alamitos Creek near the village of Pecos as well as the mine site, which involved testing, stabilization, and revegetation of the tailings, as well as cleanup of campgrounds and the fish hatchery, where mining waste had been used during construction and maintenance.[77]

With the cessation of mining and heavy grazing, in addition to changing management policies, riparian species began to recover. In 1980 the brown trout stocking program ended on the Pecos River, and in the 1990s the New Mexico Department of Game and Fish transplanted native Rio Grande cutthroat trout to the Upper Pecos, although with limited success. In the mid-1990s, non-native brown trout and rainbow trout continued to flourish in the park's stretches of Glorieta Creek and the Pecos River, but so did many native fish species, including the Rio Grande chub, longnose dace, white sucker, and fathead minnow.[78] Beaver activity also increased in the park in the mid-twentieth century. The population had recovered to 6,000 by 1967 after decades of restoration efforts.[79] Although the Fogelsons wrapped the base of cottonwoods with chicken wire mesh to prevent beaver herbivory, in 1994 park managers removed approximately one-third of the wire cages on some of the larger trees. A 1991 riparian survey along the Pecos River suggested the decline in cottonwood forest reproduction was likely the result of both beaver herbivory and impact from livestock grazing and erosion.[80] Although a 1996 faunal survey did not find any beaver within the park, they were already abundant in stretches of the river to the north. Park Service employee Eric Valencia reported that one of his neighbors had trapped thirteen beavers on their land north of the Lisboa Springs fish hatchery in the spring of 2009.[81]

New laws resulting from the environmental movement of the postwar era also affected the Pecos River watershed. In the 1960s, environmentalists had challenged both the Park Service and the Forest Service in regard to their management of wilderness. The extensive development of roads and facilities during Mission 66 had infuriated many who felt the Park Service was recklessly developing national parks. The Park Service protested that many parks included vast areas of undeveloped lands, but wilderness advocates countered that no legal measures existed to stop the Park Service from developing that land in the future. The Forest Service also faced criticism from environmentalists as it tried to defend intensive resource-use policies despite growing evidence of ecological damage. Wilderness advocates succeeded in passing the Wilderness Act in 1964, which created protected zones in national parks and national forests. The Wilderness Act reflected environmentalists' distrust of the agencies' stewardship. In 1964 Congress designated nearly 200,000 acres of land in the Santa Fe National Forest at the headwaters of the Pecos River and extending north into the Carson

National Forest as the Pecos Wilderness. After the prohibition of domestic sheep grazing in the area, the Forest Service successfully reintroduced Rocky Mountain bighorn sheep, absent since 1903. In 1980 an additional 55,000 acres were added. The first twenty miles of the Pecos River were designated as a National Wild and Scenic River in 1990.[82]

Although the establishment of the Pecos Wilderness set aside a portion of the forest for special protection and recreational enjoyment in a "primitive" setting, the demands for public access, recreational use, and timber cutting immediately outside its boundaries continued. In the 1970s officials in the Santa Fe National Forest proposed a "scenic highway" on Elk Mountain from Las Vegas to the Pecos Canyon, which would run along the southern boundary of the Pecos Wilderness. The proposal included access to potential ski slopes on Elk Mountain and additional logging of about sixty million board feet of old-growth ponderosa pine and Douglas fir. Environmentalists blocked the proposal using the National Environmental Protection Act, which required the Forest Service to assess and manage the watersheds within the national forests and produce environmental impact statements for development projects.[83] When the Forest Service and the state of New Mexico abandoned the project, it was a clear concession to the growing political power of environmentalists, even in the economically depressed region of northern New Mexico. The 1976 National Forest Management Act represented a turning point in this era because it created significant restrictions on destructive logging practices in order to protect the biodiversity of the forests. When the U.S. Fish and Wildlife Service declared the Mexican spotted owl an endangered species in 1993, environmental organizations used the 1973 Endangered Species Act's mandate to protect critical habitat as another effective means to force the Forest Service to consider broader ecological impact in its multiple-use management of New Mexico's forests.[84]

The Forest Service also began changing its fire management policies, transitioning from suppression to using thinning and prescribed burning to prevent large, uncontrolled fires. But this policy change emerged too late to prevent several large fires in the Pecos area. The year 2000 was the worst wildland fire year since 1910—there were 2,466 fires in New Mexico alone. In nearby Bandelier National Monument, the Park Service lost control of a prescribed burn and the resulting "Cerro Grande Fire" burned 47,650 acres and destroyed hundreds of homes in the Los Alamos area.[85] In the Pecos area, the "Monument Fire," probably started by a burning tire rim that ignited grasses bordering the interstate, burned the southwest portion of the Forked Lightning Ranch and crossed both LaJolla Road and Highway 63, eventually covering 160 acres. East of the Pecos River, the "Viveash Fire" burned 160 acres in the Cow Creek watershed. Both fires contributed to erosion and fish kills in the streams. Cyanide present in subsequent Pecos River water samples was likely due to the retardant used on the fire.[86] On the positive side, locals noticed deer recovery after the Viveash Fire as more desirable forage became available. Deer prefer several species that tend to resprout after a fire, including mountain mahogany, Wright silktassel, antelope bitterbrush, desert bitterbrush, serviceberry, blueberry elder, and black chokecherry.[87]

Climate change is now bringing further challenges to the Park Service's management of Pecos National Historical Park. A 2018 study, for example, noted that climate change will alter the bird community at the park. In the worst-case scenario, with no action taken to reduce climate change, some species will find the climate more favorable, some will find it less favorable, and some species, such as the killdeer and the willow flycatcher, could be extirpated from the park. Anticipating this scenario, park managers can mitigate the projected effects with habitat improvement, focusing on the most sensitive identified species.[88] Climate change will also force new considerations about vegetation management in a changing fire regime. Spring will arrive earlier, and summer will extend later in the year. Climate change will affect annual visitation and operating hours. All of these changes will result in budgetary adjustments and demand more flexibility in forecasting revenue needs. Adaptation to changing conditions will be the primary management tool, just as it has often been for inhabitants of the Upper Pecos valley.

The Park Service does not face the challenges of climate change alone, of course. Local Pecos village residents, for example, also face decisions about their environment's future. Today there is a growing interest in restoring local food production and acequia-centered communities in northern New Mexico, even though other uses have replaced some of the subsistence activities in places like the Upper Pecos valley. The Pecos village community's Hispanic identity remains strong, with 80 percent of residents identifying as Hispanic. The traditional acequia irrigation systems, with their historic and community values, are now being recognized for all of their "ecosystem services," including not only agricultural production but also their capacity to attract ecotourism, provide environmental education opportunities, and preserve cultural traditions. There are four active acequia associations in the village of Pecos: the Rincon Ditch, the East Ditch, the West Ditch, and the El Molino Ditch, collectively serving eighty-one irrigators and supporting 443 acres of irrigated agriculture. As of 2018, the village included among its priorities recognition of the long-standing historic use of valley floor agriculture in the ciénega and the need to conserve it.[89] The Upper Pecos Watershed Association, community members, and other organizations also joined together in 2019 to protest a proposal by a mining company to conduct exploratory drilling near the old Tererro mine.[90]

At the same time, the village is planning for tourism to continue as the mainstay for the local economy in the near future and seeks new opportunities to attract and provide services for tourists and adventure seekers who come through the village en route to the national park visitor center or the national forest campgrounds. Villagers are exploring instituting land use regulations that would limit the number of farm animals per parcel in the village or prohibit unsightly accumulation of junk or quasi-industrial uses.[91] Recognizing residents' connection to landscapes in the park, Park Service managers have opened the interpretive trail around the pueblo ruins to visitors with dogs and are also planning to open additional areas of the park for hiking for both tourists and locals alike. Park managers also sell fishing permits for those who want to try their hand at catching trout in the Pecos River within park boundaries. The program allows anglers to catch and keep non-native species, while catching and releasing native species.

Pecos descendants also remain involved with managing the site. For example, the Park Service works with a Pecos tribal liaison. The 2018 tribal liaison, Jeremy Moss, stated the Pecos Pueblo site should never be described as abandoned, because "abandoned means no one is here, no one cares, no one thinks about it. And that's not true." Pecos descendants also continue to attend the yearly celebration of the Feast of Nuestra Señora de los Ángeles de Porciúncula. As part of the 2018 celebration, participants carried an image of Our Lady of the Angels through the park to the front altar of the preserved mission church. Margaret Loretto, a Pecos descendant, had been attending the celebration since the 1960s. "There are spirits everywhere," Loretto said, "They'll never leave us."[92]

In 1989, Greer Garson's refusal to sell the Forked Lightning Ranch to a developer presented the opportunity for creating the current Pecos National Historical Park. In the decades since the park's creation, park managers have changed the environment based on ideas about the management of "natural" and "cultural" resources and finally a recognition that the two cannot be separated so easily. Transformations in the wider Upper Pecos valley and beyond also continue to affect the park. As we approach the five-hundred-year mark from when Bigotes led the delegation from Pecos to meet Coronado, Pecos's environment continues its long history of change. Bigotes, Fray Andrés Juárez, Juan de Dios Peña, Helen Kozlowski, Tex Austin, Greer Garson—all of these people and many more were a part of that change and a part of the Pecos environment. As a place, Pecos has never been and will never be static, although the precise shape of its future has yet to be determined.

NOTES

PREFACE

1. Cori Knudten and Maren Bzdek, "Crossroads of Change: An Environmental History of Pecos National Historical Park." Public Lands History Center, Colorado State University, August 2010.

CHAPTER 1. A POWERFUL AND PROSPEROUS PUEBLO

1. George P. Hammond and Agapito Rey, eds., *Narratives of the Coronado Expedition, 1540–1542* (Albuquerque: University of New Mexico Press, 1940), 324–325. Cicuye is variously pronounced see-KOO-yea and SEE-koo-yea as the best Spanish approximation of the name.
2. John L. Kessell, *Kiva, Cross, and Crown: The Pecos Indians and New Mexico, 1540–1840* (Albuquerque: University of New Mexico Press, 1987), 6–8.
3. Richard Flint and Shirley Cushing Flint, eds. and trans., *Documents of the Coronado Expedition, 1539–1542* (Dallas: Southern Methodist University Press, 2005), 381.
4. David J. Weber, *The Spanish Frontier in North America* (New Haven: Yale University Press, 1992), 45–49.
5. Kessell, *Kiva, Cross, and Crown*, 6–8.
6. Flint and Flint, *Documents of the Coronado Expedition*, 420.
7. Hammond and Rey, *Narratives of the Coronado Expedition*, 256–57, 289. Cicuye is also sometimes spelled "Cicuique."
8. Flint and Flint, *Documents of the Coronado Expedition*, 421.
9. Joe S. Sando, *Pueblo Nations: Eight Centuries of Pueblo Indian History* (Santa Fe: Clear Light Publishers, 1991), 22–26.
10. Genevieve N. Head and Janet D. Orcutt, eds., *From Folsom to Fogelson: The Cultural Resources Inventory Survey of Pecos National Historical Park*, vol. 1 (n.p.: National Park Service, 2002), 5–6.
11. Head and Orcutt, *From Folsom to Fogelson*, 1:6–8; Kessel, *Kiva, Cross, and Crown*, 11–12; see also Frances Levine, *Our Prayers Are in This Place: Pecos*

Pueblo Identity over the Centuries (Albuquerque: University of New Mexico Press, 1999), 6–10.

12. Head and Orcutt, *From Folsom to Fogelson*, 1:221–36; John V. Bezy, "The Geology of Pecos," in *Pecos Ruins: Geology, Archaeology, History, and Prehistory*, ed. David Grant Noble (Santa Fe: Ancient City Press,1993), 23–25; Frances Levine and Anna LaBauve, "Frontera: A View of Demographic Change in the Upper Pecos Valley from Sacramental Records at Nuestra Señora de los Ángeles, Pecos Pueblo and San Miguel del Vado," report prepared for Pecos National Historical Park, Pecos, New Mexico, 1994, file on copy, Pecos National Historical Park archives (hereafter, PNHP), 10–12.

13. Martin R. Rose, Jeffrey S. Dean, and William J. Robinson, *The Past Climate of Arroyo Hondo New Mexico Reconstructed from Tree Rings* (Santa Fe: School of American Research Press, 1981), 16–17.

14. Thomas Joseph Durkin III, "Prehispanic Land-Use Change in Pecos National Historical Park, New Mexico" (Master's thesis, Washington State University, 1999), 16–17.

15. Head and Orcutt, *From Folsom to Fogelson*, 1:165–166; Rose, Dean, and Robinson, *The Past Climate of Arroyo Hondo New Mexico Reconstructed from Tree Rings*, 93–100.

16. Head and Orcutt, *From Folsom to Fogelson*, 1:229–235.

17. Quoted in Kessell, *Kiva, Cross, and Crown*, 29.

18. Flint and Flint, *Documents of the Coronado Expedition*, 420.

19. Baltazar de Obregón, *Historia* (1584), quoted in Kessell, *Kiva, Cross, and Crown*, 29.

20. Kessell, *Kiva, Cross, and Crown*, 32–34.

21. Kessell, *Kiva, Cross, and Crown*,12, 32–34.

22. Flint and Flint, *Documents of the Coronado Expedition*, 420.

23. Suzanne K. Fish, "Farming, Foraging, and Gender," in *Women and Men in the Prehispanic Southwest: Labor, Power, and Prestige*, ed. Patricia L. Crown (Santa Fe: School of American Research Press, 2000), 172.

24. Durkin, "Prehispanic Land-Use Change in Pecos National Historical Park, New Mexico," 17.

25. William W. Dunmire and Gail D. Tierney, *Wild Plants of the Pueblo Province: Exploring Ancient and Enduring Uses* (Santa Fe: Museum of New Mexico Press, 1995), 21–23.

26. Fish, "Farming, Foraging, and Gender," 175–176; Sando, *Pueblo Nations*, 43; Colin G. Calloway, *One Vast Winter Count: The Native American West before Lewis and Clark* (Lincoln: University of Nebraska Press, 2003), 68–73.

27. Debra L. Martin, "Bodies and Lives: Biological Indicators of Health Differentials and Division of Labor by Sex," in Crown, *Women and Men in the Prehispanic Southwest*, 271.

28. Kurt Frederick Anschuetz, "Not Waiting for the Rain: Integrated Systems of Water Management by Pre-Columbian Pueblo Farmers in North-Central New Mexico" (PhD diss., University of Michigan, 1998), 115.

29. Anschuetz, "Not Waiting for the Rain," 90, 137–144.

30. Head and Orcutt, *From Folsom to Fogelson*, 1:123.

31. Head and Orcutt, *From Folsom to Fogelson*, 1:155.

32. Head and Orcutt, *From Folsom to Fogelson*, 1:196.

33. Head and Orcutt, *From Folsom to Fogelson*, 1:17.

34. Katherine A. Spielmann, *Interdependence in the Prehistoric Southwest: An Ecological Analysis of Plains-Pueblo Interaction* (New York: Garland, 1991), 109–111.

35. Quoted in Kessell, *Kiva, Cross, and Crown*, 29. Kessell questions the inclusion of cotton because little evidence exists to suggest that the Pecos grew cotton themselves.

36. George P. Hammond and Agapito Rey, eds., *The Rediscovery of New Mexico, 1580–1594: The Explorations of Chamuscado, Espejo, Castaño de Sosa, Morlete, and Leyva de Bonilla and Humaña* (Albuquerque: University of New Mexico Press, 1966), 278.

37. For examples of population estimates, see Alfred Vincent Kidder, *Pecos, New Mexico: Archaeological Notes* (Andover, Mass.: Phillips Academy, Robert S. Peabody Foundation for Archaeology, 1958), 133–136; Head and Orcutt, *From Folsom to Fogelson*, 1:223–226.

38. Head and Orcutt, *From Folsom to Fogelson*, 1:226.

39. Kessell, *Kiva, Cross, and Crown*, 489–492.

40. Frances Levine, Marilyn Norcini, and Morris Foster, "An Ethnographic Overview of Pecos National Historical Park," 1994, report on file, PNHP, 5-31 to 5-32; Katherine A. Spielmann, Margaret J. Schoeninger, and Katherine Moore, "Plains-Pueblo Interdependence and Human Diet at Pecos Pueblo, New Mexico," *American Antiquity* 55 (1990): 755; Calloway, *One Vast Winter Count*, 71–72.

41. Hammond and Rey, eds., *The Rediscovery of New Mexico, 1580–1594*, 278.

42. Kidder, *Pecos, New Mexico*, 81; Bezy, "The Geology of Pecos," 25.

43. Craig D. Allen, "Lots of Lightning and Plenty of People: An Ecological History of Fire in the Upland Southwest," in *Fire, Native Peoples, and the Natural Landscape*, ed. Thomas R. Vale (Wash. D. C.: Island Press, 2002), 145–148 provides a thorough argument for the primacy of lightning fires in the Southwest. Stephen J. Pyne, in *Fire in America: A Cultural History of Wildland and Rural Fire* (Princeton: Princeton University Press, 1982) argues for a more central human role.

44. Dunmire and Tierney, *Wild Plants of the Pueblo Province*, 164, 186, 190.

45. William W. Dunmire, *New Mexico's Spanish Livestock Heritage: Four Centuries of Animals, Land, and People* (Albuquerque: University of New Mexico Press, 2013), 4–5.

46. Kessell, *Kiva, Cross, and Crown*, 12–13.

47. Hammond and Rey, *Narratives of the Coronado Expedition*, 258.

48. National Park Service (NPS), "Water Resource Management Plan: Pecos National Historical Park," 1995, report on file, PNHP, 15.

49. Spielmann, *Interdependence in the Prehistoric Southwest*, 125.

50. Lang, Richard W., and Arthur H. Harris. *The Faunal Remains from Arroyo Hondo Pueblo, New Mexico: A Study in Short-Term Subsistence Change*. Vol. 5, *Arroyo Hondo Archaeological Series*. Santa Fe: School of American Research Press, 1984, 10–12.

51. Ramón A. Gutiérrez, *When Jesus Came, the Corn Mothers Went Away: Marriage, Sexuality, and Power in New Mexico, 1500–1846* (Stanford: Stanford University Press, 1991), 30–31.

52. Spielmann, *Interdependence in the Prehistoric Southwest*, 126–128.

53. Lang and Harris, *The Faunal Remains of Arroyo Hondo Pueblo*, 55–56, 63.

54. Lang and Harris, *The Faunal Remains of Arroyo Hondo Pueblo*, 126.

55. Sando, *Pueblo Nations*, 24–30; Dan Scurlock, "From the Rio to the Sierra: An Environmental History of the Middle Rio Grande Basin," General Technical Report, RMRS-GTR-5 (Fort Collins, Colo.: U.S. Department of Agriculture, Forest Service, Rocky Mountain Research Station, 1998), 82; Hammond and Rey, *Narratives of the Coronado Expedition*, 184; Levine, Norcini, and Foster, "An Ethnographic Overview," 2–4; Tracy Lynn Brady, "Kivas, Cathedrals, and Energy Seats: The Making of Religious Landscapes in the Upper Rio Grande Valley" (PhD diss., University of Colorado, 2004), 32–33, 49; Gutiérrez, *When Jesus Came*, 27–30.

56. Durkin, "Prehispanic Land-Use Change," 25–26; Roxanne Dunbar-Ortiz, *Roots of Resistance: A History of Land Tenure in New Mexico* (Norman: University of Oklahoma Press, 2007), 23; Calloway, *One Vast Winter Count*, 69.

57. Calloway, *One Vast Winter Count*, 69; Dunbar-Ortiz, *Roots of Resistance*, 27.

58. Gutiérrez, *When Jesus Came*, 8, 13, 23, 33; Calloway, *One Vast Winter Count*, 69, 92–93.

59. Gutiérrez, *When Jesus Came*, 14, 23.

60. Hammond and Rey, *Narratives of the Coronado Expedition*, 279–280.

61. Dunbar-Ortiz, *An Indigenous Peoples' History of the United States*, 22.

62. Spielmann, "Colonists, Hunters, and Farmers," 103; Spielmann, *Interdependence in the Prehistoric Southwest*, 217.

63. Spielmann, "Colonists, Hunters, and Farmers," 103.

64. Spielmann, *Interdependence in the Prehistoric Southwest*, 189.

65. Kessell, *Kiva, Cross, and Crown*, 8, 12, 22.

66. Kessell, *Kiva, Cross, and Crown*, 14–18.

67. Dunmire, *New Mexico's Spanish Livestock Heritage*, 24–28.

68. Richard Flint, "What's Missing from This Picture? The *Alarde*, or Muster Roll, of the Coronado Expedition," in *The Coronado Expedition: From the Distance of 460 Years*, ed. Richard Flint and Shirley Cushing Flint (Albuquerque: University of New Mexico Press, 2003), 57–80 and Harry C. Myers, "The Mystery of Coronado's Route from the Pecos River to the Llano Estacado," in *The Coronado Expedition: From the Distance of 460 Years*, ed. Richard Flint and Shirley Cushing Flint (Albuquerque: University of New Mexico Press, 2003), 140.

69. Myers, "The Mystery of Coronado's Route from the Pecos River to the Llano Estacado," 147.

70. Kessell, *Kiva, Cross, and Crown*, 17–23

71. Flint and Flint, *Documents of the Coronado Expedition*, 517.

72. Kessell, *Kiva, Cross, and Crown*, 25–26.

73. Kessell, *Kiva, Cross, and Crown*, 24–27.
74. Gutiérrez, *When Jesus Came*, 45–46.
75. Kessell, *Kiva, Cross, and Crown*, 41–62.

CHAPTER 2. SOWING THE SEEDS OF DISSENT

1. Andrés Resendéz, *The Other Slavery: The Uncovered Story of Indian Enslavement in America* (Boston: Houghton Mifflin Harcourt, 2016), 116–118; Kessell, *Kiva, Cross, and Crown*, 115, 152.
2. Andrew L. Knaut, *The Pueblo Revolt of 1680: Conquest and Resistance in Seventeenth-Century New Mexico* (Norman: University of Oklahoma Press,1995), 120–121, 142.
3. Quoted in Kessell, *Kiva, Cross, and Crown*, 131.
4. Alfred W. Crosby Jr., *Ecological Imperialism: The Biological Expansion of Europe, 900–1900* (New York: Cambridge University Press, 1986).
5. Dunmire, *New Mexico's Spanish Livestock Heritage*, 12–13.
6. Gutiérrez, *When Jesus Came*, 57.
7. Alfred W. Crosby Jr., *The Columbian Exchange: Biological and Cultural Consequences of 1492* (Westport, Conn.: Greenwood Publishing Company, 1972), 74–97; Gutiérrez, *When Jesus Came*, 30–31.
8. Weber, *The Spanish Frontier*, 81; Kessell, *Kiva, Cross, and Crown*, 68–71; Knaut, *The Pueblo Revolt of 1680*, 18.
9. Weber, *The Spanish Frontier*, 78.
10. Weber, *The Spanish Frontier*, 81; Kessell, *Kiva, Cross, and Crown*, 68–71; Knaut, *The Pueblo Revolt*, 18.
11. Crosby, *The Columbian Exchange*, 67.
12. Scurlock, "From the Rio to the Sierra," 293.
13. Weber, *The Spanish Frontier*, 57.
14. Weber, *The Spanish Frontier*, 57; Crosby, *The Columbian Exchange*, 5–15.
15. Kessell, *Kiva, Cross, and Crown*, 90.
16. Anschuetz, "Not Waiting for the Rain," 170.
17. Kessell, *Kiva, Cross, and Crown*, 89–90; Calloway, *One Vast Winter Count*, 150.
18. Kessel, *Kiva, Cross, and Crown*, 90–97; Weber, *The Spanish Frontier*, 88.
19. Crosby, *The Columbian Exchange*, 35–68, 96–97.
20. Quoted in John L. Kessell, *Spain in the Southwest: A Narrative History of Colonial New Mexico, Arizona, Texas, and California* (Norman: University of Oklahoma Press, 2002), 128.
21. Reséndez, *The Other Slavery*, 45.
22. Crosby, *The Columbian Exchange*, 35–68.
23. Kessell, *Kiva, Cross, and Crown*, 489–492, provides a summary of the various population estimates over the years.
24. Kessel, *Kiva, Cross, and Crown*, 47; Weber, *The Spanish Frontier*, 111; Rebecca Earle, *The Body of the Conquistador: Food, Race, and the Colonial Experience in Spanish America, 1492–1700* (New York: Cambridge University Press 2012), 5–17, 151.

25. Quoted in Kessell, *Kiva, Cross, and Crown*, 129.

26. Kessell, *Kiva, Cross, and Crown*, 170; Levine, *Our Prayers Are in This Place*, 18–19.

27. Knaut, *The Pueblo Revolt*, 134; Kessell, *Spain in the Southwest*, 110–111.

28. Elinore M. Barrett, *Conquest and Catastrophe: Changing Rio Grande Pueblo Settlement Patterns in the Sixteenth and Seventeenth Centuries* (Albuquerque: University of New Mexico Press, 2002), 68; Reséndez, *The Other Slavery*, 10, 136.

29. Phillip O. Leckman, "Meeting in Places: Seventeenth-Century Puebloan and Spanish Landscapes," in *New Mexico and the Pimería Alta: The Colonial Period in the American Southwest*, ed. John G. Douglass and William M. Graves (Boulder: University Press of Colorado, 2017), 87.

30. Quoted in Kessell, *Kiva, Cross, and Crown*, 124.

31. Kidder, *Pecos, New Mexico*, 106–109; Kessell, *Kiva, Cross, and Crown*, 104.

32. Weber, *The Spanish Frontier*, 133.

33. Knaut, *The Pueblo Revolt*, 77–79.

34. Gutiérrez, *When Jesus Came*, 77, 85; Kessel, *Kiva, Cross, and Crown*, 111; Calloway, *One Vast Winter Count*, 171.

35. Calloway, *One Vast Winter Count*, 152.

36. Gutiérrez, *When Jesus Came*, 55–57; Kessel, *Kiva, Cross, and Crown*, 12; David Hurst Thomas, "Materiality Matters: Colonial Transformations Spanning the Southwestern and Southeastern Borderlands," in *New Mexico and the Pimería Alta: The Colonial Period in the American Southwest*, ed. John G. Douglass and William M. Graves (Boulder: University Press of Colorado, 2017), 405.

37. Levine and LaBauve, "Frontera," 21; Dunmire and Tierney, *Wild Plants*, 41–42.

38. Robert MacCameron, "Environmental Change in Colonial New Mexico," In *Out of the Woods: Essays in Environmental History*, ed. Char Miller and Hal Rothman (Pittsburgh: University of Pittsburgh Press, 1997), 86.

39. Dunmire, *New Mexico's Spanish Livestock Heritage*, 35–39.

40. Levine and LaBauve, "Frontera," 161, 164; Carroll L. Riley, *Rio del Norte: People of the Upper Rio Grande from Earliest Times to the Pueblo Revolt* (Salt Lake City: University of Utah Press, 1995), 260.

41. Leckman, "Meeting in Places," 98.

42. Alden C. Hayes, *The Four Churches of Pecos* (Albuquerque: University of New Mexico Press, 1974), 26–29.

43. Riley, *Rio del Norte*, 258; Marc Simmons, "Why early New Mexico turned from cattle to sheep," *Santa Fe New Mexican*, April 15, 2016.

44. Kessell, *Kiva, Cross, and Crown*, 219.

45. Leckman, "Meeting in Places," 99.

46. James E. Ivey, "'The Greatest Misfortune of All': Famine in the Province of New Mexico, 1667–1672," *Journal of the Southwest* 36, no. 1 (1994): 77.

47. Levine, *Our Prayers Are in This Place*, 3.

48. Weber, *The Spanish Frontier*, 131–132.

49. Kessell, *Kiva, Cross, and Crown*, 109.

50. Kessell, *Kiva, Cross, and Crown*, 114.

51. Kessell, *Kiva, Cross, and Crown*, 110–112.

52. Reséndez, *The Other Slavery*, 119.

53. Weber, *The Spanish Frontier*, 125; Knaut, *The Pueblo Revolt*, 157.

54. Weber, *The Spanish Frontier*, 126.

55. Kessell, *Kiva, Cross, and Crown*, 321.

56. Kessell, *Kiva, Cross, and Crown*, 177–78.

57. Kessell, *Kiva, Cross, and Crown*, 178; Weber, *The Spanish Frontier*, 125.

58. Kessell, *Kiva, Cross, and Crown*, 188.

59. Kessell, *Kiva, Cross, and Crown*, 188.

60. Kessell, *Kiva, Cross, and Crown*, 147–49.

61. Weber, *The Spanish Frontier*, 107, 116.

62. Kessell, *Kiva, Cross, and Crown*, 123, 138. The painting is of the Pecos Pueblo's patron saint, Nuestra Señora de los Ángeles de Porciúncula (Our Lady of the Angels).

63. Knaut, *The Pueblo Revolt*, 69.

64. Kessell, *Kiva, Cross, and Crown*, 120–22.

65. Knaut, *The Pueblo Revolt*, 68–69.

66. Knaut, *The Pueblo Revolt*, 161.

67. Spielmann, "Colonists, Hunters, and Farmers," 107–08; Barrett, *Conquest and Catastrophe*, 77.

68. Quoted in Kessell, *Kiva, Cross, and Crown*, 212.

69. Quoted in Kessell, *Kiva, Cross, and Crown*, 212.

70. Spielmann, *Plains Pueblo Interdependence*, 759; Spielmann, "Hunters, Colonists, and Farmers," 110.

71. Ivey, "The Greatest Misfortune of All," 76; Reséndez, *The Other Slavery*, 167; Gutiérrez, *When Jesus Came*, 130.

72. Kessell, *Kiva, Cross, and Crown*, 229–243; Calloway, *One Vast Winter Count*, 174. See Knaut, *The Pueblo Revolt*, for a full overview of the causes of the revolt.

CHAPTER 3. STRIFE AND SETTLEMENT ON THE BORDERLANDS

1. Weber, *The Spanish Frontier*, 136.

2. In this chapter, we transition to using the terms "Hispanic" (adjective) and "Hispano" (noun) to describe the non-Puebloan inhabitants of the Upper Pecos valley in the late 1700s and early 1800s, as by this time a distinctive Hispanic identity had developed that was different from that of the Spanish settlers and Franciscans of earlier centuries.

3. Kessell, *Kiva, Cross, and Crown*, 243.

4. John L. Kessell and Rick Hendricks, eds, *By Force of Arms: The Journals of don Diego de Vargas, New Mexico, 1691–93* (Albuquerque: University of New Mexico Press, 1992), 424–433; James A. Vlasich, *Pueblo Indian Agriculture* (Albuquerque: University of New Mexico Press, 2005), 34.

5. Kessell, *Kiva, Cross, and Crown*, 238.

6. Weber, *The Spanish Frontier*, 18.

7. Kessell, *Kiva, Cross, and Crown*, 256–63.

8. Kessell, *Kiva, Cross, and Crown*, 295.

9. Weber, *The Spanish Frontier*, 140.

10. Pekka Hämäläinen, *The Comanche Empire* (New Haven: Yale University Press, 2008), 23; Reséndez, *The Other Slavery*, 174–175. Jack D. Forbes, in *Apache, Navajo, and Spaniard* (Norman: University of Oklahoma Press, 1960), 238–239, also suggests that friendly trade characterized the relationship between the Puebloans and the Plains Indians, stating that "In 1692 most of the Athapascans and Pueblos were friendly with each other."

11. Kessell, *Kiva, Cross, and Crown*, 263–266; Vlasich, *Pueblo Indian Agriculture*, 63. Ned Blackhawk, in *Violence over the Land* (Cambridge: Harvard University Press, 2006), 32, also argues that both Puebloan and Plains tribes "used the Spanish absence to enhance their own fortunes," with both groups engaging in intensified raiding.

12. John O. Baxter, *Las Carneradas: Sheep Trade in New Mexico, 1700 –1860* (Albuquerque: University of New Mexico Press, 1987), 13–17; Dunmire, *New Mexico's Spanish Livestock Heritage*, 47–48.

13. Kessell, *Kiva, Cross, and Crown*, 321.

14. Eleanor B. Adams and Fray Angelico Chavez, trans., *The Missions of New Mexico, 1776: A Description by Fray Francisco Atanasio Dominguez with Other Contemporary Documents* (Albuquerque: University of New Mexico Press, 1956), 213.

15. Charles Wilson Hackett, ed., *Historical Documents Relating to New Mexico, Nueva Vizcaya, and Approaches Thereto, to 1773*, vol. 3 (Washington D. C.: Carnegie Institution of Washington, 1937), 465–66.

16. Hayes, *The Four Churches of Pecos*, 9–11.

17. Hayes, *The Four Churches of Pecos*, 46–50.

18. Hayes, *The Four Churches of Pecos*, 53–58.

19. Hackett, ed., *Historical Documents Relating to New Mexico*, 465–66.

20. Kessell and Hendricks, *By Force of Arms*, 423; Kessell, *Kiva, Cross, and Crown*, 244–254.

21. Adams and Chavez, *The Missions of New Mexico*, 403.

22. MacCameron, "Environmental Change," 92.

23. Weber, *The Spanish Frontier*, 141, 306; Kessell, *Kiva, Cross, and Crown*, 319–339.

24. Hämäläinen, *The Comanche Empire*, 23–30; Stanley Noyes, *Los Comanches: The Horse People: 1751–1845* (Albuquerque: University of New Mexico Press, 1993), xix, xxiv. The Comanche maintained control of Comancheria until the 1860s and did not suffer their final defeat until 1875, when the U.S. government confined them to a reservation in Oklahoma.

25. Knaut, *The Pueblo Revolt*, 184–186.

26. Hämäläinen, *The Comanche Empire*, 33–36.

27. Blackhawk, *Violence over the Land*, 35.

28. Hämäläinen, *The Comanche Empire*, 43.

29. Kessell, *Kiva, Cross, and Crown*, 371, 372, 376, 359, 334; Calloway, *One Vast Winter Count*, 288.

30. Quoted in Kessell, *Kiva, Cross, and Crown*, 357.

31. Hayes, *The Four Churches of Pecos*, 53.

32. Blackhawk, *Violence over the Land*, 52.

33. Hämäläinen, *The Comanche Empire*, 38; William S. Kiser, *Borderlands of Slavery: The Struggle over Captivity and Peonage in the American Southwest* (Philadelphia: University of Pennsylvania Press, 2017), 8.

34. Kessell, *Kiva, Cross, and Crown*, 386, 357.

35. Kessel, *Kiva, Cross, and Crown*, 387–391.

36. Hämäläinen, *The Comanche Empire*, 46–74; Blackhawk, *Violence over the Land*, 53–56.

37. Kessell, *Kiva, Cross, and Crown*, 371, 392.

38. Quoted in Kessell, *Kiva, Cross, and Crown*, 395.

39. Kessell, *Kiva, Cross, and Crown*, 396.

40. Adams and Chavez, *The Missions of New Mexico*, 213.

41. Epidemics and evidence for them are summarized in Levine and LaBauve, *Frontera*, 48–49.

42. Levine and LaBauve, *Frontera*, 39–43.

43. Levine and LaBauve, *Frontera*, 61.

44. Weber, *The Spanish Frontier*, 204–224.

45. Kessell, *Kiva, Cross, and Crown*, 291, 395.

46. Adams and Chavez, *The Missions of New Mexico*, 213. The fact that Domínguez does not include Glorieta Creek in his list of water sources for Pecos suggests that it may have been an intermittent stream at this time or at least possessed a highly variable water flow.

47. Adams and Chavez, *The Missions of New Mexico*, 213.

48. Weber, *The Spanish Frontier*, 229.

49. Hämäläinen, *The Comanche Empire*, 109–120.

50. Hämäläinen, *The Comanche Empire*, 120–123; Kessell, *Kiva, Cross, and Crown*, 403–409, 436; John L. Kessel, *Miera Y Pacheco: A Renaissance Spaniard in Eighteenth-Century New Mexico* (Norman: University of Oklahoma Press, 2013), 161–162.

51. Kessell, *Kiva, Cross, and Crown*, 409; Hämäläinen, *The Comanche Empire*, 125–127.

52. Blackhawk, *Violence over the Land*, 104–105.

53. Hämäläinen, *The Comanche Empire*, 130–137, 206–207.

54. Kessell, *Kiva, Cross, and Crown*, 349.

55. MacCameron, "Environmental Change," 95–97.

56. G. Emlen Hall, *Four Leagues of Pecos: A Legal History of the Pecos Grant, 1800–1933* (Albuquerque: University of New Mexico Press, 1984), 12–13; Kessell, *Kiva, Cross, and Crown*, 439.

57. Malcolm Elbright, "New Mexican Land Grants: The Legal Background," in *Land, Water, and Culture: New Perspectives on Hispanic Land Grants*, ed. Charles L. Briggs and John R. Van Ness (Albuquerque: University of New Mexico Press, 1987), 15–26.

58. Hall, *Four Leagues of Pecos*, 11, 15.

59. Hämäläinen, *The Comanche Empire*, 171, 182–207; see Charles L. Kenner, *The Comanchero Frontier: A History of New Mexico–Plains Relations* (Norman: University of Oklahoma Press, 1994), for a detailed overview of comancheros

and ciboleros; Kessell, *Kiva, Cross, and Crown*, 415–421; Moises Gonzales, "The Genízaro Land Grant Settlements of New Mexico," *Journal of the Southwest* Vol. 56, No. 4 (Winter 2014), 583–602.

60. MacCameron, "Environmental Change," 92–93; Kelly L. Jenks, "Becoming Vecinos: Civic Identities in Late Colonial New Mexico," in *New Mexico and the Pimería Alta: The Colonial Period in the American Southwest* (Boulder: University Press of Colorado, 2017), 213–229.

61. Kessell, *Kiva, Cross, and Crown*, 415–421.

62. Hämäläinen, *The Comanche Empire*, 124.

63. Jared Orsi, *Citizen Explorer: The Life of Zebulon Pike* (Oxford: Oxford University Press, 2014), 207, 223–224; MacCameron, "Environmental Change," 85–86.

64. Hall, *Four Leagues of Pecos*, 17–22; National Register of Historic Places Inventory-Nomination, "Valencia Ranch Historic/Archaeological District, Pecos, New Mexico," 1981, 6.

65. Hall, *Four Leagues of Pecos*, 19, 26–27.

66. Hall, *Four Leagues of Pecos*, 24–27.

67. Hall, *Four Leagues of Pecos*, 26.

68. Epidemics and evidence for them are summarized in Levine and LaBauve, *Frontera*, 48–49; Kessel, *Kiva, Cross, and Crown*, 457.

69. Levine and LaBauve, *Frontera*, 39–43; MacCameron, "Environmental Change," 83.

70. Weber, *The Spanish Frontier*, 310.

71. Weber, *The Spanish Frontier*, 310–311; MacCameron, "Environmental Change," 87–88.

72. Ross Frank, *From Settler to Citizen: New Mexican Economic Development and the Creation of Vecino Society, 1750–1820* (Berkeley: University of California Press, 2000), 119–156, 224.

73. Weber, *The Mexican Frontier*, 16–18; Hall, *Four Leagues of Pecos*, 15–16.

74. See Frank, *From Settler to Citizen*, for a full discussion of the development of New Mexican society.

75. Weber, *The Mexican Frontier*, 6–14; Joseph P. Sánchez, Robert L. Spude, and Art Gómez, *New Mexico: A History* (Norman: University of Oklahoma Press, 2013), 121.

76. Weber, *The Mexican Frontier*, 34.

77. Weber, *The Mexican Frontier*, 16–17.

78. Hall, *Four Leagues of Pecos*, 33.

79. Hall, *Four Leagues of Pecos*, 36-40.

80. Hall, *Four Leagues of Pecos*, 40, 84.

81. Hall, *Four Leagues of Pecos*, 42–45.

82. Hall, *Four Leagues of Pecos*, 55.

83. Edgar L. Hewett, "Studies on the Extinct Pueblo of Pecos," *American Anthropologist* 6, no. 1 (Jan.–March 1904), 439; Joe S. Sando, *Nee Hemish: The History of Jemez Pueblo* (Albuquerque: University of New Mexico Press, 1982), 150–153.

84. Hall, *Four Leagues of Pecos*, 50–61; Levine, *Our Prayers Are in This Place*, 124–125; Barrett, *Conquest and Catastrophe*, 108.

85. Head and Orcutt, *From Folsom to Fogelson*, 2: 385–398; Hall, *Four Leagues of Pecos*, 63.

CHAPTER 4. CLAIMING THE LAND AND CONTESTING ITS FUTURE

1. D. Sloan, Architects with Cherry/See Architects, "Historic Structures Report: Trading Post, Forked Lightning Ranch House, Forked Lightning Pump House, Pecos National Historical Park, Pecos, NM," 2002, report on file, PNHP, 4–5. Note: Some sources suggest that prior to 1883, when a post office was installed at Pecos, the town was known as "Levy." We did not see this name noted on any period maps that we located, which all called the settlement "Pecos" if it was recorded. Robert Julyan, *The Place Names of New Mexico*, rev. ed. (Albuquerque: University of New Mexico Press, 1998), 260; Marc Simmons, "Polish Pioneers," *Santa Fe Reporter* May 3, 1989, 20.

2. Ancestry.com, *New Mexico, Territorial Census, 1885* [database online], Provo, Utah, USA: Ancestry.com Operations, Inc., 2010, page 58. Using this source entailed perusal of the birthplace of inhabitants in the village of Pecos in San Miguel County.

3. Weber, *The Mexican Frontier*, 125–129.

4. Josiah Gregg, *Commerce of the Prairies*, ed. Max L. Moorhead (Norman: University of Oklahoma Press, 1954), 13.

5. William deBuys, *Enchantment and Exploitation: The Life and Hard Times of a New Mexican Mountain Range* (Albuquerque: University of New Mexico Press, 1995), 92.

6. Roxanne Dunbar-Ortiz, *Roots of Resistance: A History of Land Tenure in New Mexico* (Norman: University of Oklahoma Press, 2007), 85–87.

7. See Susan Shelby Magoffin, *Down the Santa Fe Trail and into Mexico: The Diary of Susan Shelby Magoffin, 1846–1847*, ed. Stella M. Drumm (1962; repr., Lincoln: University of Nebraska Press, 1982), 99–100, for an example of one of the fictitious stories about Pecos Pueblo.

8. National Register Nomination, "Valencia Ranch," 6.

9. Don E. Alberts, *The Battle of Glorieta: Union Victory in the West* (College Station: Texas A&M University Press, 1998), 46; Andrew H. Young, "History of Ranching and Trading at Pecos National Historical Park: Pigeon's Ranch, Kozlowski's Trading Post, and Forked Lightning Ranch," 2001, report on file, PNHP, 21; Robert L. Spude, "Pigeon's Ranch Historic Structure Report," Intermountain Cultural Resource Management Professional Paper No. 74, Santa Fe, New M.: National Park Service, Intermountain Region Support Office, 2008; Jerry D. Thompson, *A Civil War History of the New Mexico Volunteers & Militia* (Albuquerque: University of New Mexico Press, 2015), 154.

10. Sloan, "Historic Structures Report," 4.

11. Young, "History of Ranching and Trading," 7; Hall, *Four Leagues of Pecos*, 122.

12. Head and Orcutt, *From Folsom to Fogelson*, 2: 401–402.

13. Marc Simmons and Hal Jackson, *Following the Santa Fe Trail: A Guide for Modern Travelers*, 3rd ed. (Santa Fe: Ancient City Press, 2001), 215.

14. Hämäläinen, *The Comanche Empire*, 294–296; Phyllis S. Morgan, *As Far as the Eye Could Reach: Accounts of Animals along the Santa Fe Trail, 1821–1880* (Norman, University of Oklahoma Press, 2015), 119, 123.

15. Nancy Langston, *Forest Dreams, Forest Nightmares: The Paradox of Old Growth in the Inland West* (Seattle: University of Washington Press, 1995), 57–59; deBuys, *Enchantment and Exploitation*, 92–97.

16. Ancestry.com. *1860 United States Federal Census* [database online]. Provo, Utah, USA: Ancestry.com Operations, Inc., 2009. Images reproduced by FamilySearch; Elbright, "New Mexican Land Grants," 23.

17. Elbright, "New Mexican Land Grants," 16–20.

18. John R. Van Ness, "Hispanic Land Grants: Ecology and Subsistence in the Uplands of Northern New Mexico and Southern Colorado," in *Land, Water, and Culture: New Perspectives on Hispanic Land Grants*, ed. Charles L. Briggs and John R. Van Ness (Albuquerque: University of New Mexico Press, 1987), 187; National Register Nomination, "Valencia Ranch," 8; David Hornbeck Jr., "Spatial Manifestations of Acculturative Processes in the Upper Pecos Valley, New Mexico, 1840–1880" (PhD diss., University of Nebraska, 1974), 113; MacCameron, "Environmental Change," 89

19. Hall, *Four Leagues of Pecos*, 47–48.

20. Hornbeck, "Spatial Manifestations," 61, 104–105; MacCameron, "Environmental Change," 87; deBuys, *Enchantment and Exploitation*, 128; James E. Vlasich, *Pueblo Agriculture* (Albuquerque: University of New Mexico Press, 2005), 106–108.

21. Weber, *The Mexican Frontier*, 208–211.

22. Throughout the Spanish period and through the mid-nineteenth century sheep were far more important for their mutton than their wool. The Civil War changed the dynamics of the sheep trade. Although it disrupted New Mexico's trade with California, the war created a demand for wool for use in uniforms. Hispanos began crossbreeding the churro with Merinos in order to produce a higher-quality wool fiber. Baxter, *Las Carneradas*, 21, 28–29, 109, 112, 148.

23. Baxter, *Las Carneradas*, 95.

24. William J. Parish, *The Charles Ilfeld Company: A Study of the Rise and Decline of Mercantile Capitalism in New Mexico* (Cambridge: Harvard University Press, 1961), 154–169.

25. Hall, *Four Leagues of Pecos*, 61–62.

26. Quoted in Hornbeck, "Spatial Manifestations," 118–119.

27. Hall, *Four Leagues of Pecos*, 167–168

28. MacCameron, "Environmental Change," 88–89; deBuys, *Enchantment and Exploitation*, 195; Elinore G. K. Melville, *A Plague of Sheep: Environmental Consequences of the Conquest of Mexico* (New York: Cambridge University Press, 1994), 9, 72–75, 114.

29. Hornbeck, "Spatial Manifestations," 120.

30. Richard White, *"It's Your Misfortune and None of My Own": A New History of the American West* (Norman: University of Oklahoma Press, 1991), 73–76.

31. Patricia Nelson Limerick, *The Legacy of Conquest: The Unbroken Past of the American West* (New York: W. W. Norton, 1987), 222.

32. Weber, *The Mexican Frontier*, 273–277.

33. Spude and Gómez, *New Mexico: A History*, 121.

34. Elbright, "New Mexican Land Grants," 29, 31; Hall, *Four Leagues of Pecos*, 70.

35. Hall, *Four Leagues of Pecos*, 71–83.

36. Robert W. Frazer, *Forts and Supplies: The Role of the Army in the Economy of the Southwest, 1846–1861* (Albuquerque: University of New Mexico Press, 1983), 1–11.

37. Surveys completed by Lieutenant George M. Wheeler in 1871 and 1876 show cultivated land extending the length of Glorieta Creek from Pigeon's Ranch to the pueblo ruins, perhaps remnants of fields first created by Valle. "Economic Features Part of Central New Mexico, Atlas Sheet No. 77 (B); Issued May 7th 1877; Weyss, Herman & Lang Del. Expeditions of 1871 & 1876 Under the Command of 1st. Lieut. Geo. M. Wheeler, Corps of Engineers, U.S. Army. U.S. Geographical Surveys West of the 100th Meridian," available at https://www.davidrumsey.com. Note: Search on "economic features New Mexico" and choose map 77B. Accessed September 16, 2009; Frazer, *Forts and Supplies*, 11, 102, 185–187.

38. Young, "History of Ranching and Trading," 33; Thompson, *A Civil War History*, 433; There were 13,262 "whites" counted in 1860 San Miguel County in the same territorial census. It was the most populous county at the time.

39. Frazer, *Forts and Supplies*, 114, 185–186.

40. Head and Orcutt, *From Folsom to Fogelson*, 2:403.

41. Reséndez, *The Other Slavery*, 228–230, 245–246.

42. Kiser, *Borderlands of Slavery*, 32–33.

43. Levine, *Our Prayers Are in This Place*, 139–141; Kiser, *Borderlands of Slavery*, 12–13.

44. Michael A. Morrison, *Slavery and the American West: The Eclipse of Manifest Destiny and the Coming of the Civil War* (Chapel Hill: University of North Carolina Press, 1997), 105–108; Kiser, *Borderlands of Slavery*, 34–35.

45. Kiser, *Coast-to-Coast Empire: Manifest Destiny and the New Mexico Borderlands* (Norman: University of Oklahoma Press, 2018), 183.

46. The following account of the Battle of Glorieta Pass is taken mainly from Alberts, *The Battle of Glorieta*. Thomas S. Edrington and John S. Taylor, *The Battle of Glorieta Pass: A Gettysburg in the West, March 26–28, 1862* (Albuquerque: University of New Mexico Press, 1998) and Hall, *Sibley's New Mexico Campaign*, also cover the battle.

47. Aspectos Culturales, ed., *Pecos mi Pecos* (Santa Fe: Aspectos Culturales, 2002), 22; John P. Wilson, *When the Texans Came: Missing Records from the Civil War in the Southwest* (Albuquerque: University of New Mexico Press, 2001), 131.

48. Quote from Wilson, *When the Texans Came*, 260.

49. Andrew E. Masich, *Civil War in the Southwest Borderlands, 1861–1867* (Norman: University of Oklahoma Press, 2017), 44–45; Reséndez, *The Other Slavery*, 278–284, quote on p. 279.

50. Masich, *Civil War in the Southwest Borderlands*, 39–45.
51. Masich, *Civil War in the Southwest Borderlands*, 112–113.
52. Jerry Thompson, ed., *Civil War in the Southwest: Recollections of the Sibley Brigade* (College Station: Texas A&M University Press, 2001), 81; Thompson, *A Civil War History*, 154–155.
53. Wilson, *When the Texans Came*, 259–260.
54. Wilson, *When the Texans Came*, 261.
55. Marc Simmons, *The Little Lion of the Southwest: A Life of Manuel Antonio Chaves* (Chicago: Sage Books, 1973), 183–184; Thompson, *A Civil War History*, 37–39, 157
56. Wilson, *When the Texans Came*, 265.
57. J. M. Chivington, "No. 3, Report of Maj. John M. Chivington, First Colorado Infantry," March 28, 1862, *The War of the Rebellion: A Compilation of the Official Records of the Union and Confederate Armies* (Washington, DC: Government Printing Office, 1883), Ser. 1, Vol IX, Chapter XXI; Thompson, *A Civil War History*, 37–39, 162–164.
58. Mark Fiege, *The Republic of Nature: An Environmental History of the United States* (Seattle: University of Washington Press, 2012), 210, 222.
59. Megan Kate Nelson, "The Difficulties and Seductions of the Desert: Landscapes of War in 1861 New Mexico," in *The Blue, the Gray, and the Green: Toward an Environmental History of the Civil War*, ed. Brian Allen Drake (Athens: University of Georgia Press, 2015), 46–48; Kenneth Noe, "Fateful Lightning: The Significance of Weather and Climate to Civil War History," in *The Blue, the Gray, and the Green: Toward an Environmental History of the Civil War*, ed. Brian Allen Drake (Athens: University of Georgia Press, 2015), 27. Noe claims that inclement weather had only minimal effect at Glorieta, although not "no effect," as was the case at Gettysburg.
60. Quoted in Young, "History of Ranching and Trading," 28–29. The government rejected Valle's claim.
61. Young, "History of Ranching and Trading," 32.
62. Alberts, *The Battle of Glorieta*, 21.
63. Richard Flint and Shirley Cushing Flint, "Three Ranches and the Battle of Glorieta Pass," New Mexico Office of the State Historian, http://dev.newmexicohistory.org/filedetails.php?fileID=21319 (accessed September 25, 2018).
64. Reséndez, *The Other Slavery*, 284–293, 305, 314; Masich, *Civil War in the Southwest Borderlands*, 262–263.
65. Simmons, "Polish Pioneers," 20.
66. John V. Bezy, and Joseph P. Sanchez, eds., *Pecos: Gateway to Pueblos and Plains; the Anthology* (Tucson: Southwest Parks and Monuments Association, 1988), 112–114.
67. Amy C. Earls, "Historic Land Use in the Rowe Area," 1980, report on file, PNHP, 15–17.
68. Head and Orcutt, *From Folsom to Fogelson*, 2: 403.
69. Head and Orcutt, *From Folsom to Fogelson*, 2: 400–405.

70. David A. Gillio, "Santa Fe National Forest Area: An Historical Perspective for Management," Cultural Resources Report No. 30 (Albuquerque: U.S. Department of Agriculture Forest Service Southwestern Region, 1979), 25–26.
71. Bezy and Sanchez, *Pecos: Gateway to Pueblos and Plains*, 114.
72. A. F. Bandelier, *Historical Introduction to Studies among the Sedentary Indians of New Mexico; Report on the Ruins of Pecos Pueblo* (Boston: A. Williams and Co., 1881; Milwood, N.Y.: Kraus Reprint Co., 1976), 100–101.
73. Hall, *The Four Leagues of Pecos*, 146.
74. "Economic Features Part of Central New Mexico, Atlas Sheet No. 77 (B); Issued May 7th 1877; Weyss, Herman & Lang Del. Expeditions of 1871 & 1876 Under the Command of 1st. Lieut. Geo. M. Wheeler, Corps of Engineers, U.S. Army. U.S. Geographical Surveys West of the 100th Meridian," available at https://www.davidrumsey.com. Note: Search on "economic features New Mexico." Accessed September 16, 2009.
75. Scurlock, "From the Rio to the Sierra," 128–129.
76. See William G. Robbins, *Colony and Empire: The Capitalist Transformation of the American West* (Lawrence: University Press of Kansas, 1994) for a discussion of how the railroads created eastern and international ties to the West.
77. Hall, *Four Leagues of Pecos*, 71–83.
78. Hall, *Four Leagues of Pecos*, 111–118.
79. Hall, *Four Leagues of Pecos*, 93–108.
80. Hall, *Four Leagues of Pecos*, 107.
81. Head and Orcutt, *From Folsom to Fogelson*, 2: 389–397; Vincent K. Jones, "Report on the Pecos Pueblo Grant, New Mexico, 1913, p. 18, in Folder 21, "Real Estate-Land Grants: Pecos Pueblo Grant, 1913," Francis C. Wilson papers, New Mexico State Archives, Santa Fe (hereafter, NMSA), 4.
82. Hall, *Four Leagues of Pecos*, 135–137.
83. Hall, *Four Leagues of Pecos*, 176, 188–189.
84. Andro Linklater, *Measuring America: How the United States Was Shaped by the Greatest Land Sale in History* (New York: Plume, 2002), 20, 84, 221, 233; Hall, *Four Leagues of Pecos*, 86–87.
85. Hall, *Four Leagues of Pecos*, 179–191.
86. Young, "History of Ranching and Trading," 6–7, 34–37; Peggy A. Gerow, "Cultural Resources Inventory of Pigeon's Ranch Subunit, Pecos National Historical Park, Santa Fe County, New Mexico," 2010, report on file, PNHP, 103.
87. See, for example, "Glorieta Battlefield, Glorieta, NM, June 1880," photo by Ben Wittick, original negative at Museum of New Mexico (hereafter, MNM), negative no. 15788, copy on file at PNHP; also "Pigeon's Ranch, Glorieta, NM, 1880," photo by Ben Wittick, original negative at MNM, negative no. 015781, copy on file at PNHP.
88. Marc Simmons and Hal Jackson, *Following the Santa Fe Trail: A Guide for Modern Travelers* 3rd ed. (Santa Fe: Ancient City Press, 2001), 215.
89. Spude, "Pigeon's Ranch Historic Structure Report," 9–10; "Old Stagecoach Relay Station on the Santa Fe Trail near Santa Fe, NM," original negative at MNM, negative no. 47936, copy on file at PNHP; "Canyoncito, NM, 1914,"

photo by Waldo Twitchell, original negative at MNM, negative no. 8834, copy on file at PNHP.

90. National Register of Historic Places Inventory-Nomination, "Nuestra Señora de Luz Church and Cemetery, Cañoncito, NM," 1995, p. 5.

91. Young, "History of Ranching and Trading," 8.

92. Head and Orcutt, *From Folsom to Fogelson* 2:402–404; Jones, "Report on the Pecos Pueblo Grant" 14; Vincent K. Jones, "Plat Showing the Cultivated Land of Tomas Koslosky within the Pecos Grant," 1913, in Folder 67, Drawer 12, Maps: Pueblo Land Grants, NMSA; Young, "History of Ranching and Trading," 8; "Court proceedings," *Las Vegas Gazette*, March 16, 1878, 4.

93. Hall, *Four Leagues of Pecos*, 176, 188–89.

94. Hall, *Four Leagues of Pecos*, 200.

95. Jones, "Report on the Pecos Pueblo Grant," 21; Cowley, Joseph, and Rhodes, "Cultural Landscape Overview," "Railroad and Tourism" map supplement; "Supplemental Plat, Private Claims within the Pecos Pueblo Grant Sections 1, 5, and 6," Approved 2/23/1934, Township 15 N, Range 11 and 12 E, available at https://www.glorecords.blm.gov. Note: Click on Search Documents, then click on Surveys to the left and enter New Mexico in the State field. Choose Supplemental Plat in the Survey Type field and Kimmel, Everett H. from the Surveyor field. Click on Search Surveys and choose the image for RECLOSING ON SANTO DOMINGO PUEBLO GRANT (accessed August 20, 2009).

96. Hall, *Four Leagues of Pecos*, 193–196, 209–219. Wilson was working all sides of the legal wrangling over the Pecos land for his own benefit, but he escaped prosecution because the U.S. Attorney's office dodged the issue.

97. Jones, "Report on the Pecos Pueblo Grant" 14; Jones, "Plat Showing the Cultivated Land of Tomas Koslosky within the Pecos Grant"; Young, "History of Ranching and Trading," 8; Head and Orcutt, *From Folsom to Fogelson* 2: 402; Census Place: Albuquerque Ward 3, Bernalillo, New Mexico; Roll: T624_913; Page: 14A; Enumeration District: 0012; FHL microfilm: 1374926, Ancestry .com. 1910 United States Federal Census [database online]. Lehi, UT, USA: Ancestry.com Operations Inc, 2006; B.A. Reuter, "Flour Mill Erected by Gov. Vigil and Other Mills of Pecos District." July 28, 1939. File: WPA 5-5-9 #7. WPA New Mexico Collection, Fray Angélico Chávez History Library, Santa Fe, New Mexico, U.S.A., 3–7, 11.

98. Hall, *Four Leagues of Pecos*, 216–17, 264.

99. Sarah Deutsch, *No Separate Refuge: Culture, Class, and Gender on an Anglo-Hispanic Frontier in the American Southwest, 1880–1940* (New York: Oxford University Press, 1987), 24–26; Mitchell, *Coyote Nation*, 18.

100. Head and Orcutt, *From Folsom to Fogelson* 2:404–406; Edward H. Spicer, *Cycles of Conquest: The Impact of Spain, Mexico, and the United States on the Indians of the Southwest 1533–1960* (Tucson: University of Arizona Press, 1967), 171.

101. "Pecos River Farmers to Place Head Lettuce on Market in Next Week," *Las Vegas Daily Optic*, June 27, 1925; "Pecos River Farmers to Market High Grade Crop of Lettuce First Time," *Las Vegas Daily Optic*, July 7, 1925.

102. Deutsch, *No Separate Refuge*, 13–40, 124.

103. Quoted in Courtney White and Earl Porter, "The Catanach Mill: A Grist Mill in the Upper Pecos Valley," 1996, report on file, PNHP, 2–4.

104. White and Porter, "The Catanach Mill," 2–4 through 2–6.

105. Head and Orcutt, *From Folsom to Fogelson* 2: 402.

106. "Glorieta Creek from Pecos Pueblo, Looking Northwest," 1915, Lothrop photo, original in MNM, negative no. 12330e, copy in Cowley, Joseph, and Rhodes, "Cultural Landscape Overview," 61; "Glorieta Creek Floodplain, Looking West toward Glorieta Mesa," 1915, Lothrop photo, original in MNM, negative no. 12325, copy in Cowley, Joseph, and Rhodes, "Cultural Landscape Overview," 61.

107. deBuys, *Enchantment and Exploitation*, 216.

108. Milton W. Callon, *Las Vegas: The Town that Wouldn't Gamble* (Las Vegas, N. Mex.: Las Vegas Publishing Co., Inc., 1962), 250; National Park Service Water Resources Division, "Pecos National Historical Park Water Resource Management Plan," 1995, 8.

109. deBuys, *Enchantment and Exploitation*, 280.

CHAPTER 5. MAKING A LIVING IN THE LAND OF ENCHANTMENT

1. "Tex Austin and His Pecos Ranch," photocopy in PNHP; "Annual Chicago Rodeo Expected to Go Over Big," *Las Vegas Daily Optic*, June 2, 1927.

2. Climax was a tobacco brand and Panatella a cigar brand.

3. "Clem Yore Writes of Early Life of Austin in Entertaining Way," *Las Vegas Daily Optic*, October 24, 1927; "Good Time Had by All during Austin Dinner," *Las Vegas Daily Optic*, October 22, 1927; "Tex Austin Day to be Asked in Paper Presented Council," *Las Vegas Daily Optic*, September 22, 1927; Victoria Carlyle Weiland, *100 Years of Rodeo Stock Contracting* (Reno, Nev.: The Professional Rodeo Stock Contractors Association, 1997), 26.

4. "Clem Yore Writes of Early Life of Austin in Entertaining Way"; Weiland, *100 Years of Rodeo Stock Contracting*, 26. Another reference to Tex Austin riding with Pancho Villa occurs in a biographical sketch written for the program of the rodeo held in London in 1924—again, a context where myth was far more important than fact. "First International Rodeo or Cowboy Championships," 1924, located in Austin, Texas, Rodeo Honoree Vertical Files, Dickinson Research Center, National Cowboy & Western Heritage Museum, Oklahoma City, Okla. (hereafter, DRC).

5. Adolph F. Bandelier, *The Delight Makers* (New York: Dodd, Mead and Company, 1890); John Urry, *The Tourist Gaze: Leisure and Travel in Contemporary Societies* (Newbury Park, Calif.: Sage Publications, 1990).

6. Victoria E. Dye, *All Aboard for Santa Fe: Railway Promotion of the Southwest, 1890s to 1930s* (Albuquerque: University of New Mexico Press, 2005), quote on page 27.

7. Sylvia Rodriguez, "Tourism, Difference, and Power in the Borderlands," in *The Culture of Tourism, the Tourism of Culture: Selling the Past to the Present in the American Southwest*, ed. Hal K. Rothman (Albuquerque: University of New Mexico Press, 2003), 185–188.

8. Rodriguez, "Tourism, Difference, and Power in the Borderlands," 194.

9. Head and Orcutt, *From Folsom to Fogelson* 1:21–27; Richard B. Woodbury, "From Chaos to Order: A. V. Kidder at Pecos," in *Pecos Ruins: Geology, Archaeology, History, and Prehistory*, ed. David Grant Noble (Santa Fe: Ancient City Press, 1993 and 1981), 15.

10. Dye, *All Aboard for Santa Fe*, 44–53.

11. Paul S. Sutter, *Driven Wild: How the Fight against Automobiles Launched the Modern Wilderness Movement* (Seattle: University of Washington Press, 2002), 19–27; Lawrence M. Lipin, in *Workers and the Wild: Conservation, Consumerism, and Labor in Oregon, 1910–30* (Urbana: University of Illinois Press, 2007), provides a specific case study of how automobiles altered workers' experience of the environment; Peter J. Schmitt, in *Back to Nature: The Arcadian Myth in Urban America* (New York: Oxford University Press, 1969), discusses the development of the outdoor recreation movement.

12. Sutter, *Driven Wild*, 27–30.

13. "Tex Austin's Forked Lightning Ranch," DRC.

14. "New Fight on Rodeo Act," *New York Times*, November 9, 1922; Louis S. Warren, *Buffalo Bill's America: William Cody and the Wild West Show* (New York: Alfred A. Knopf, 2005), 425. Warren discusses people's fascination with the frontier, in particular as it related to spectacles like rodeos or the Wild West show.

15. Young, "Ranching History," 10–11.

16. "Austin Buys a 6,000 Acre Tract of Land within Pecos Grant," *Las Vegas Optic*, September 15, 1925.

17. Head and Orcutt, *From Folsom to Fogelson* 2:389, 393–395.

18. "Supplemental Plat, Private Claims within the Pecos Pueblo Grant Sections 2–11, 14–17, and 20–23," Approved 2/23/1934, Township 15 N, Range 12 E; "Supplemental Plat, Private Claims within the Pecos Pueblo Grant Sections1–2, 6–8, 11–14, and 17–24," Approved 2/23/1934, Township 15 N, Range 12 E, both available at https://www.glorecords.blm.gov. Note: Click on Search Documents, then click on Surveys to the left and enter New Mexico in the State field. Choose Supplemental Plat in the Survey Type field and Kimmel, Everett H. from the Surveyor field. Click on Search Surveys and choose the image for RECLOSING ON SANTO DOMINGO PUEBLO GRANT (accessed October 2, 2009).

19. James Ivey, "A History of the Establishment of Pecos National Monument,"1987, report on file, PNHP, 5.

20. Sloan, "Historic Structures Report," 11–22; Chris Wilson, *The Myth of Santa Fe: Creating a Modern Regional Tradition* (Albuquerque: University of New Mexico Press, 1997); David Kammer, "Buildings Designed by John Gaw Meem, 1925-1959," available at www.newmexicohistory.org. Note: Click on People and then search for "Meem" to see the buildings he designed (accessed September 14, 2010).

21. White and Porter, "The Catanach Mill," 1-2 to 1-3.

22. Photos in Kidder, *Pecos, New Mexico*, 11–12, 57, 150, 205, 337.

23. "It's Always Cool at the Forked Lightning Ranch," Folder 1, Box 39, Real Estate Case Files, Tex Austin's Ranch, The Forked Lightning, 1933–37, Francis C. Wilson papers 1981-017, NMSA.

24. "Tex Austin and His Pecos Ranch" photocopy in "Tex Austin's Forked Lightning Ranch" folder, PNHP.
25. "It's Always Cool at the Forked Lightning Ranch."
26. "Eatments and Libations . . . at Tex Austin's," photocopy in "Tex Austin's Forked Lightning Ranch" folder, PNHP.
27. "Tex Austin and His Pecos Ranch."
28. "It's Always Cool at the Forked Lightning Ranch"; "Tex Austin's Forked Lightning Ranch."
29. Tex Austin's Forked Lightning Ranch."
30. Young, "Ranching History," 48; "Tex Austin and His Pecos Ranch."
31. "Tex Austin and His Pecos Ranch"; "Tex Austin's Forked Lightning Ranch."
32. "Tex Austin's Forked Lightning Ranch." A letter written in 1935, during the bankruptcy proceedings for Tex Austin's ranch, stated that a flood that summer had destroyed the bridge over Glorieta Creek that went to the ranch house. The letter continued to say the creek was "dry for practically the entire year," and thus the arroyo was "always passable." Around 1937, a new road to the ranch house was built that struck directly east from the main road as opposed to circling around Kozlowski's Trading Post. Reconstruction Finance Corporation to Mr. Grover Conway, State Highway Engineer, March 16, 1937, PECO unprocessed, Francis Wilson papers, PNHP; Cowley, Joseph, and Rhodes, "Cultural Landscape Overview," Railroad/Tourism map.
33. In 1937 Route 66 was realigned to pass directly from Santa Rosa to Albuquerque and no longer went through Pecos. Young, "History of Ranching," 9, 38–39; Bill Greer, interview by Andrew Young, January 12 and 13, 1998, transcript, Folder 17, Box 2, PECO 380, PNHP; Spude, "Pigeon's Ranch Historic Structures Report," 12–13; Jerry McClanahan, "The Lost Highway," *Route 66 Magazine* (Winter 1994/1995): 25–30; Peter B. Dedek, *Hip to the Trip: A Cultural History of Route 66* (Albuquerque: University of New Mexico Press, 2007).
34. Another business serving tourists in the Pigeon's Ranch area was the Arrowhead Lodge, built in the 1930s by an unknown entrepreneur. Serving the tourists who came to the valley to hunt, fish, and visit the area attractions, the complex consisted of a main lodge and seven cabins. In the 1960s it became a Methodist camp but by the early 1970s was a private residence. Young, "History of Ranching," 9, 38—39; Bill Greer, interview by Andrew Young; "Pigeon's Ranch, Glorieta, NM, ca. 1925," copy of photo in PNHP, original negative at MNM, negative #51739; "Glorieta, NM, ca. 1935," photo by T. Harmon Parkhurst, copy of photo in PNHP, original negative at MNM, negative #9690; "Pigeon's Ranch, Glorieta, NM, ca. 1935," photo by T. Harmon Parkhurst, copy of photo in PNHP, original negative at MNM, negative #9689; Gerow, "Cultural Resources Inventory of Pigeon's Ranch Subunit," 103,106; Spude, "Pigeon's Ranch Historic Structures Report,"13.
35. David A. Gillio, "Santa Fe National Forest Area: An Historical Perspective for Management," Cultural Resources Report No. 30 (Albuquerque: USDA Forest Service Southwestern Region, 1979), 26.

36. Gillio, "Santa Fe National Forest Area," 26–29; Harold K. Steen, *The U.S. Forest Service*, Centennial Edition (Durham, N.C.: Forest History Society, 2004), 71–75; Robert D. Baker, Robert S. Maxwell, Victor H. Treat, and Henry C. Dethloff, *Timeless Heritage: A History of the Forest Service in the Southwest* (n.p.: USDA Forest Service, 1988), 28.

37. Hays, *Conservation and the Gospel of Efficiency*, 2–4; Steen, *The U.S. Forest Service*, 3–20, 47–68, 78–81.

38. Jon T. Coleman, in *Vicious: Wolves and Men in America* (New Haven: Yale University Press, 2004), discusses the history of extermination campaigns against wolves. The USDA Biological Survey, a forerunner of the U.S. Fish and Wildlife Service, undertook many of the predator control activities in the twentieth century, but Forest Service rangers and local hunters and ranchers followed many of the same practices and held the same beliefs. Stephen Pyne, in *Year of the Fires: The Story of the Great Fires of 1910* (New York: Penguin Books, 2001), argues that the agency's policies of fire suppression originated as a way to justify their existence and thus became an unquestioned tenet of the agency.

39. deBuys, *Enchantment and Exploitation*, 219–222; Donald Lee Burtchin, "The Physical Geography of Pecos National Monument," (Master's thesis, University of Arizona, 1983), 66.

40. John W. Johnson, *Reminiscences of a Forest Ranger, 1914–1944* (Dayton: Brown and Kroger Publishing Co., 1976), 29.

41. "Tex Austin and His Pecos Ranch."

42. William D. Rowley, *U.S. Forest Service Grazing and Rangelands: A History* (College Station: Texas A&M University Press, 1985), 60–75.

43. Gillio, "Santa Fe National Forest Area," 29.

44. deBuys, *Enchantment and Exploitation*, 210.

45. Rowley, *U.S. Forest Service Grazing and Rangelands*, 92.

46. Johnson, *Reminiscences of a Forest Ranger*, 42–57.

47. "Elk Herd Found in Good Shape at Valley Ranch," *Las Vegas Optic*, April 23, 1915.

48. Johnson, *Reminiscences of a Forest Ranger*, 43.

49. DeBuys, *Enchantment and Exploitation*, 280; Lester Rainse, 6-74-5, "Lisboa Springs Fish Hatchery—San Miguel Count," May 13, 1936. WPA New Mexico Collection, Fray Angélico Chávez History Library, Santa Fe, New Mexico; Roy E, Barker, Chief, Fisheries Division, "New Mexico Builds Its Hatcheries," *New Mexico Wildlife* (Jan/Feb 1962, Vol. 7, no. 1, New Mexico 1912–1962 Golden Anniversary Issue).

50. Thomas P. Gable, "First Report of Game and Fish Warden for New Mexico, 1909–1910–1911," (Santa Fe: New Mexican Printing Company, 1912), 75; "More Fish, More Fun," in *New Mexico Wildlife*, New Mexico Department of Fish and Game Newsletter, vol. 54, no. 2 (Summer 2009).

51. Elliott S. Barker, *Beatty's Cabin: Adventures in the Pecos High Country* (Santa Fe: W. Gannon, 1977), 91–93.

52. Baisan and Swetnam, "Interactions of Fire Regimes," 14; Pyne, *Year of the Fires*.

53. Virginia T. McLemore, "Pecos Mine and Alamitos Canyon Mill," 1995, 1–2, Folder 2, Box 1, PECO 384, PNHP; Alice Bullock (?), "A Virtual Depression Goldmine," source unknown, October 17, 1976, photocopy of article in PNHP.

54. Leon McDuff, *Tererro* (Victoria, BC: Trafford Publishing, 2006), 3–14; "Much Timber Used by Metal Company Forester Reports," *Las Vegas Optic*, August 31, 1927.

55. McDuff, *Tererro*, 54–55.

56. Wes Darden, "Boom Camp of the Thirties," *New Mexico*, January 1967, photocopy in PNHP, 28.

57. Darden, "Boom Camp of the Thirties," 28; McDuff, *Tererro*, 101–174

58. McLemore, "Pecos Mine and Alamitos Canyon Mill," 1–2; Darden, "Boom Camp of the Thirties"; Bullock, "A Virtual Depression Goldmine."

59. McDuff, *Tererro*, 57–59; Bullock, "A Virtual Depression Goldmine," 16.

60. Hall, *Four Leagues of Pecos*, 256.

61. See Hall, *Four Leagues of Pecos*, 221–278, for a complete discussion of the 1924 Pueblo Lands Act as it pertained to Pecos; Levine, *Our Prayers Are in This Place*, 124–125.

62. Hall, *Four Leagues of Pecos*, 221–278.

63. Hall, *Four Leagues of Pecos*, 259, 267.

64. Hall, *Four Leagues of Pecos*, 221–278.

65. Hall, *Four Leagues of Pecos*, 221–278.

66. Letter from Cotton, Cotton Exchange Building, Oklahoma City to Francis C. Wilson, March 8, 1936, Folder 2, Box 39, Real Estate Case Files, Tex Austin's Ranch—The Forked Lightning, 1933–1937, Francis C. Wilson papers 1981-017, NMSA.

67. Letter from D. J. Leahy, Lawyer, to Francis C. Wilson, Attorney at Law, May 11, 1933, Folder 44, Box 12, Corporations, Tex Austin's Forked Lightning Ranch, Francis C. Wilson papers 1981-017, NMSA.

68. Sloan, "Historic Structures Report," 12; "Austin and Cowboys Back," *New York Times*, July 25, 1934.

69. Deutsch, *No Separate Refuge*, 162–164.

70. Aspectos Culturales, *Pecos, Mi Pecos*, 62–68.

71. Deutsch, *No Separate Refuge*, 162–164.

72. Deutsch, *No Separate Refuge*, 167.

73. Johnson, *Reminiscences of a Forest Ranger*, 68.

74. John R. Van Ness, foreword to *The Preservation of the Village: New Mexico's Hispanics and the New Deal*, by Suzanne Forrest (Albuquerque: University of New Mexico, 1989), vii.

75. Deutsch, *No Separate Refuge*, 174–199.

76. Johnson, *Reminiscences of a Forest Ranger*, 77, 85. The camp was designated New Mexico F-53, Company 2868; http://www.ccclegacy.org/CCC_Camps _New_Mexico.html (accessed January 20, 2019).

77. Letter from Francis C. Wilson to Messrs. Fisher, Boyden, Bell, Boyd and Marshall, August 1, 1934, Folder 1, Box 39, Real Estate Case Files, Tex Austin's

Ranch—The Forked Lightning, 1933–1937, Francis C. Wilson papers 1981-017, NMSA.

78. Letter from Cotton, Cotton Exchange Building, Oklahoma City to Francis C. Wilson, March 8, 1936, Folder 2, Box 39, Real Estate Case Files, Tex Austin's Ranch—The Forked Lightning, 1933–1937, Francis C. Wilson papers 1981-017, NMSA.

79. Young, "Ranching History," 48.

80. Young, "Ranching History," 49.

81. Johnson, *Reminiscences of a Forest Ranger*, 41, 66.

82. Young, "Ranching History," 49.

CHAPTER 6. MANAGEMENT AND MYTHOLOGY IN A POSTWAR LANDSCAPE

1. Linkletter is quoted in Michael Troyan, *A Rose for Mrs. Miniver: The Life of Greer Garson* (Lexington: University of Kentucky Press, 1999), 281. Troyan also provides a description of how the Fogelsons entertained at the ranch, which is summarized and embellished here.

2. Troyan, *A Rose for Mrs. Miniver*, 209–212.

3. The property known as Brush Ranch was previously known as Irvin's on the Pecos. Jerry Dorbin, "History and Archaeology of the Forked Lightning Ranch," 1991, report on file, Folder 22, Box 1, PECO 380, PNHP.

4. Young, "History of Ranching and Trading," 12–14; 56.

5. National Resources Planning Board, "The Pecos River Joint Investigation: Reports of the Participating Agencies" (Washington, D. C.: U.S. GPO, 1942), 248–249.

6. National Resources Planning Board, "Pecos River Joint Investigation," 248–249; Troyan, *A Rose for Mrs. Miniver*, 213.

7. Cowley, Joseph, and Rhodes, "Cultural Landscape Overview," 71.

8. National Resources Planning Board, "Pecos River Joint Investigation," 248–249.

9. Kenneth Ray Weber, "A New Mexico Village and the Metropolis: A Study of the Economy and Social Organization of a Rural Satellite" (Ph.D. diss., University of Oregon, 1972), 32–35.

10. Robert Kern, *Labor in New Mexico: Unions, Strikes, and Social History since 1881* (Albuquerque: University of New Mexico Press, 1983), 298–299; 1960 Census Preliminary Reports: Population Count for States, August 1960, available at https://www.census.gov (accessed April 20, 2010).

11. Dunbar-Ortiz, *Roots of Resistance*, 125.

12. Troyan, *A Rose for Mrs. Miniver*, 13; authors' interviews with former ranch employees, June 12, 2009.

13. Troyan, *A Rose for Mrs. Miniver*, 226.

14. Troyan, *A Rose for Mrs. Miniver*, 236, 243; Young, "History of Ranching and Trading," 16.

15. Troyan, *A Rose for Mrs. Miniver*, 225.

16. Cowley, Joseph, and Rhodes, "Cultural Landscape Overview," 71; Forked Lightning Ranch notes, Folder 10, Box 1, PECO 313, PNHP.

17. Dorbin, "History and Archaeology of the Forked Lightning Ranch," n.p.; authors' interviews with former ranch employees, June 12, 2009; Sloan, "Historic Structures Report," 24.

18. Authors' interviews with former ranch employees, June 12, 2009.

19. Meszaros, "Vegetation and Land Use," 14–15, 55; 1954 Land Use Map, Folder 22, Box 1, PECO 380, PNHP; Cowley, Joseph, and Rhodes, "Cultural Landscape Overview," Austin Period map; Head and Orcutt, *From Folsom to Fogelson*, 2:389 and figure 10.6.

20. "The History of Cherokee Ranch and Castle," cherokeeranch.org/cattle .html (accessed February 7, 2010); authors' interviews with former ranch employees, June 12, 2009.

21. Authors' interviews with former ranch employees, June 12, 2009; Young, "History of Ranching and Trading," 16; Troyan, *A Rose for Mrs. Miniver*, 280; "Purebred Santa Gertrudis Herd Established on Forked Lightning Ranch at Pecos, N.M.," *New Mexico Stockman*, September 1959, 40.

22. R. H. Foote, "The History of Artificial Insemination: Selected Notes and Notables," *Journal of Animal Science* 2002, 80:1–10.

23. Scurlock, "From the Rio to the Sierra," 77–80; Boaz Long, "Pecos Monument . . . Well Water," August 21, 1950, Folder 1950, Box 2, PECO 464, PNHP.

24. Scurlock, "From the Rio to the Sierra," 265.

25. Thomas W. Swetnam and Julio L. Betancourt, "Mesoscale Disturbance and Ecological Response to Decadal Climatic Variability in the American Southwest," *Journal of Climate*, 11, no. 21 (Dec. 1998), 3128–3147.

26. Aldo Leopold, "Review of H. M. Bell and E. J. Duksterhuis, 'Fighting the Mesquite and Cedar Invasion on Texas Ranges,'" *Journal of Forestry* 42, no. 1 (January 1946):63.

27. Robert E. Williams, "Modern Methods of Getting Uniform Use of Ranges," *Journal of Rangeland Management* (1954): 77–81.

28. Richard S. Aro, "Evaluation of Pinyon-Juniper Conversion to Grassland," *Journal of Range Management*, 1971, 193.

29. Troyan, *A Rose for Mrs. Miniver*, 226.

30. Wilson, *The Myth of Santa Fe*, 100–101.

31. Troyan, *A Rose for Mrs. Miniver*, 226.

32. Cowley, Joseph, and Rhodes, "Cultural Landscape Overview," figure 30; Sloan, "Historic Structures Report," 39.

33. Authors' interviews with former ranch employees, June 12, 2009; Sloan, "Historic Structures Report," 24.

34. Authors' interviews with former ranch employees, June 12, 2009; Troyan, *A Rose for Mrs. Miniver*, 38.

35. Authors' interviews with former ranch employees, June 12, 2009.

36. Troyan, *A Rose for Mrs. Miniver*, 280; see also Cowley, Joseph, and Rhodes, "Cultural Landscape Overview," figures 26 and 27.

37. Keith Easthouse, "Developers Seek Greer Garson Ranch for Huge Resort City Near Pecos," *Santa Fe Reporter*, December 20–26, 1989, 9–10; Troyan, *A Rose for Mrs. Miniver*, 281; Cowley, Johnson, and Rhodes, "Cultural

Landscape Overview," figure 26. Wolves have been extinct in New Mexico since the 1930s.

38. Troyan, *A Rose for Mrs. Miniver*, 264, 278–279; Cowley, Joseph, and Rhodes, "Cultural Landscape Overview," Figure 27.

39. Troyan, *A Rose for Mrs. Miniver*, 278.

40. National Park Service, "Pecos State Monument: An Area Investigation Report," (Santa Fe: National Park Service, Region Three, March 1962), report on file, PNHP, 11–12. Although the original church deed described the monument property as 80 acres, in 1964 the NPS discovered in survey research that the actual size was 62.6 acres. See Norman Herkenham, Southwest Region to John Catron, September 9, 1964, File L58-d-2, Pecos, N. Mex. 1961–64, SW Regional Office General Admin Files 1965–67, Box 64, 8NS-079-93-002, Record Group 79, National Archives and Records Administration - Rocky Mountain Region, Denver, Colo. (hereafter, NARA-RM).

41. Jerry McClanahan, "The Lost Highway," *Route 66 Magazine* (Winter 1994/1995), 39–40; Michael Wallis, *Route 66: The Mother Road* (New York: St. Martin's Press, 1990), 159; Gerow, "Cultural Resources Inventory of Pigeon's Ranch Subunit, Pecos National Historical Park," 41.

42. Hal Rothman, *America's National Monuments: The Politics of Preservation* (Lawrence: University Press of Kansas, 1989), xi–xvii.

43. Weber, "A New Mexico Village and the Metropolis: A Study of the Economy and Social Organization of a Rural Satellite," 32–35.

44. Marcus Flores, "Los Valencias," in *Pecos Mi Pecos*, 81; Boaz Long, "Pecos Monument . . . Well Water," August 21, 1950, Folder 1950, Box 2, PECO 464, PNHP.

45. Ivey, "A History of the Establishment of Pecos National Monument," 10; Report to C. T. McWhirter, State Purchasing Agent, August 7, 1951, in Folder 1951, Box 2, PECO 464, PNHP.

46. Ivey, "A History of the Establishment of Pecos National Monument," 10; Caretaker's correspondence, Folder 1950, Box 2, PECO 464, PNHP.

47. Clark to Long, August 6, 1952, Folder 1952, Box 2, PECO 464, PNHP; Ivey, "A History of the Establishment of Pecos National Monument," 11.

48. Clark to Long, August 5, 1952, PNHP.

49. Ivey, "A History of the Establishment of Pecos National Monument," 7–9. Head and Orcutt, *From Folsom to Fogelson*, 1:27–28.

50. Levine, *Our Prayers Are in This Place*, 124–125. The location of the celebration reverted to the monument in 1969 after the NPS completed stabilization of the seventeenth-century church.

51. NPS, "Pecos State Monument: An Area Investigation Report," 7.

52. Rothman, *America's National Monuments*, 52–71.

53. Rothman, *America's National Monuments*, 170, 187–188, 200–201.

54. Robert Utley was an expert in the U.S. Army and Indian relations in the West and later went on to become chief historian of the National Park Service. Norman Herkenham to Regional Chief, National Park System Studies, June 22, 1964, File L58-d-2, Pecos, NM 1961-64SW Regional Office

General Admin Files 1965-67, Box 64, 8NS-079-93-002, Record Group 79, NARA-RM.

55. Ivey, "A History of the Establishment of Pecos National Monument," 11.

56. Ivey, "A History of the Establishment of Pecos National Monument," 11, 21; NPS, "Pecos State Monument: An Area Investigation Report," 8, 12.

57. E. E. Fogelson Land Patent 020740, T.14N, R.12E, Sec. 1, Lots 1, 2, 3; Sec. 2, Lot 1, Sec. 3, Lots 1, 2, 3, 4; Sec.11, Lots 1, 2, 3; Sec.13, Lots 1, 2, 3, 5, 6, May 2, 1958, accessed April 26, 2010 at www.glorecords.blm.gov. Note: Search on State and Last Name (Fogelson), click on Search Patents, then click below Image to display the patent.

58. E. E. Fogelson vs. Frank Salmeron and Esquipula Padilla, U.S. District Court of New Mexico, civil case no. 8073, Box 1, Folder 22, PECO 380, PNHP.

59. Richard Gardner, ¡Grito! Reies Tijerina and the New Mexico Land Grant War of 1967 (Indianapolis: The Bobbs-Merrill Company, 1970), 79.

60. Lorena Oropeza, "Becoming Indo-Hispano: Reies López Tijerina and the New Mexican Land Grant Movement," in Formations of United States Colonialisms, ed, Aloysha Goldstein (Duke University Press, 2014), 181–184, 195.

61. Robert D. Baker et al., Timeless Heritage, 63–64.

62. Scurlock, "From the Rio to the Sierra," 264.

63. National Resources Planning Board, "The Pecos River Joint Investigation," 244–251; 260–261.

64. Baker et al, Timeless Heritage, 134.

65. LaCalandria Associates for Upper Pecos Watershed Association, "Upper Pecos Watershed Restoration Action Strategy," March 2007, www.env.nm.gov /swqb/wps/WRAS/UpperPecosWRAS.pdf (accessed February 28, 2010), 7.

66. David Correia, "The Sustained Yield Forest Management Act and the Roots of Environmental Conflict in Northern New Mexico," Geoforum 38, no. 5 (Sept. 2007): 1043–1044; "Narrative Report," 1 and "Range Environmental Analysis: Colonias Allotment, Reanalysis 1969," 2210 Range Management Planning, Folder 506 Colonias Allotment, Pecos RD, Santa Fe Forest Office, Santa Fe, N. Mex.; Carol Raish, "Historic and Contemporary Land Use in Southwestern Grassland Ecosystems," USDA Forest Service Gen. Tech. Rep. RMRS-GTR-135-vol. 1. 2004, 98.

67. Folder 2210 Range Management Planning, Folder 506 Colonias Allotment, Pecos Ranger District, Pecos RD, Santa Fe Forest Office, Santa Fe, N. Mex.

68. "Narrative Report," 1 and "Range Environmental Analysis: Colonias Allotment, Reanalysis 1969," 2210 Range Management Planning, Folder 506 Colonias Allotment, Pecos RD, Santa Fe Forest Office, Santa Fe, N. Mex.; Carol Raish, "Historic and Contemporary Land Use in Southwestern Grassland Ecosystems," USDA Forest Service Gen. Tech. Rep. RMRS-GTR-135-vol. 1. 2004, 98.

69. Authors' interviews with former ranch employees, June 12, 2009.

70. Correspondence, maps, and notes, Box 1, Folder 22, PECO 380, PNHP; Kevin Klein, "¡Viva la Alianza! Thirty Years after the Tierra Amarilla Courthouse

Raid," weeklywire.com/ww/06-13-97/alibi_feat1.html (accessed January 18, 2019).

71. E. E. Fogelson vs. Frank Salmeron and Esquipula Padilla, U.S. District Court of New Mexico, civil case no. 8073, Box 1, Folder 22, PECO 380, PNHP.

72. Hall, *Four Leagues of Pecos*, 283–285.

73. Ivey, "A History of the Establishment of Pecos National Monument," 13, 24–27.

74. R. C. Gordon-McCutchan, *The Taos Indians and the Battle for Blue Lake* (Santa Fe: Red Crane Books, 1991), 219; McDuff, *Tererro*, 133–135; "Pueblo Seeks to Save Cave," Albuquerque Journal, May 24, 2008; Todd Allin Morman, *Many Nations under Many Gods: Public Lands Management and American Indian Sacred Sites* (Norman: University of Oklahoma Press, 2018), 198–199.

75. Hall, *Four Leagues of Pecos*, 286–288; R. C. Gordon-McCutchan, *The Taos Indians*, 219; McDuff, *Tererro*, 133–135.

CHAPTER 7. ENDURING SPIRITS, ENDURING ENVIRONMENT

1. Easthouse, "Developers Seek Greer Garson Ranch"; "Actress Greer Garson Rethinking Land Sale," *Daily Times* (Farmington, N.M.), December 28, 1989; Tom Milligan, "Developer Still Considering Pecos Project," *Journal North*, January 3, 1990.

2. Ethan Carr, *Mission 66: Modernism and the National Park Dilemma* (Amherst: University of Massachusetts Press, 2007); Richard West Sellars, *Preserving Nature in the National Parks: A History* (New Haven: Yale University Press, 2009), 201–203.

3. Taffey Hall, "Inventory to the Glorieta Baptist Conference Center Collection, AR 795-564," Southern Baptist Historical Library and Archives. Nashville, Tennessee, 2009, 2.

4. NPS, "NPS Area Investigation 1962," 12.

5. NPS, *Pecos State Monument*, March 1963, 4–6.

6. Carr, *Mission 66*, 158–159, 162.

7. Thomas Giles to Russell E. Dickinson, NPS Deputy Director, February 27, 1974, Folder 13, PECO 462, PNHP.

8. Public law 89-54. The boundaries fell within sections 3 and 8 of Township 15 North, Range 12 East, sections 5 and 8. Deed of gift, December 15, 1964; Norman Herkenham to Regional Chief, National Park System Studies, June 22, 1964, RG79 NPS SW Regional Office General Admin Files, 1965-67, 8NS-079-93-002, Folder L58-d-2 Pecos, NM 1961-64, Box 64, NARA-RM.

9. Thomas Giles to Russell E. Dickinson, NPS Deputy Director, February 27, 1974, Folder 13, PECO 462, PNHP.

10. Regional Director, Southwest Region, to Deputy Director, WASO [Washington D.C. Area Support Office], November 6, 1973, Folder 14, PECO 462, PNHP.

11. The Park Service believed the new wells would "consume" 2.7 acre-feet of the area's surface water initially, which would be unlikely to have a major effect on surface streams. Planners believed that sewage effluence discharged into the ground would alter vegetation types and/or quantity in the construction area.

They also considered an evapotranspiration system for sewage, as well as using chlorinated effluent for irrigation and discharge into an arroyo. NPS, *Final Environmental Statement*, 1975, report on file, PNHP, 10, 11, 31.

12. NPS, "Pecos National Monument Management Objectives," 1971, Folder, 6 PECO 462, PNHP, 10.

13. NPS, *Preliminary Master Plan, Pecos National Monument*, 25.

14. NPS, "Master Plan for Pecos NM, 1965," Folder 4, PECO 462, PNHP, 1, 3, 7.

15. Thomas Giles to Assistant Director, Park Historic Preservation, WASO, November 5, 1975, Folder 8, PECO 462, PNHP.

16. In 1974 the Director of the National Park Service issued a directive requiring all new project designs to "consider the total energy requirements" and make use of new solar technologies. NPS Director to Regional Directors, DSC, and Harpers Ferry [Harpers Ferry Center, an NPS administrative unit], March 14, 1974, Folder 13, PECO 462, PNHP.

17. Thomas Giles to Russell E. Dickinson, NPS Deputy Director, February 27, 1974, Folder 13, PECO 462, PNHP.

18. NPS, *Preliminary Master Plan, Pecos National Monument*, 25.

19. "Analysis and Recommendation for Visitor Center Site—Pecos National Monument," August 7, 1981, report on file, PNHP.

20. NPS, *Final Environmental Statement*, 1975, 5.

21. Troyan, *A Rose for Mrs. Miniver*, 346–347.

22. Frank E. Wilson, "Part I Historic Structures Report: Pecos Mission Complex, Pecos National Monument," 1967, 7.

23. NPS, "Forked Lightning Ranch Addition to Pecos National Monument" (NPS Southwest Region, Summer 1983), report on file, Box 2, Folder 14, PECO 313, PNHP; NPS, "Management Analysis of Forked Lightning–Los Trigos Ranches," (NPS Southwest Region, October 1984), report on file, Box 2, Folder 13, PECO 313, PNHP.

24. Meszaros, "Vegetation and Land Use," 14.

25. NPS, "Forked Lightning Ranch Addition to Pecos National Monument"; NPS, "Management Analysis of Forked Lightning–Los Trigos Ranches," (NPS Southwest Region, October 1984), report on file, Box 2, Folder 13, PECO 313, PNHP.

26. Young, "History of Ranching and Trading," 55.

27. Young, "History of Ranching and Trading," 55; Meszaros, "Vegetation and Land Use," 3.

28. Easthouse, "Developers Seek Greer Garson Ranch."

29. "Pecos Development Threatens Acequias," *Journal North*, January 20, 1990.

30. Tom Milligan, "Pecos Ponders Future with Huge 'Ranch' Resort as Neighbor," *Journal North*, December 22, 1989.

31. A. Samuel Adelo, "When the Coyote Preaches, the Poor Are Unsafe," *New Mexican*, January 21, 1990.

32. NPS, "NPS Area Investigation 1962," 20, 30, 33, 37; Carol Raish and Alice M. McSweeney, "Traditional Ranching Heritage and Cultural Continuity in the Southwestern United States," in *Multifunctional Grasslands in a Changing World*,

Volume II; XXI International Grassland Congress; VIII International Rangeland Congress (Beijing: Guangdong People's Publishing House, 2008), 857.

33. Post Staff, "Editorially Speaking," *Pecos Post*, January 1990.
34. Post Staff, "Editorially Speaking," *Pecos Post*, January 1990; Milligan, "Pecos Ponders Future."
35. Tom Milligan, "Garson Balks at Ranch Resort Plans," *Journal North*, December 28, 1989.
36. Richard Roybal, "The Last Frontier," *Pecos Post*, January 1990.
37. Roybal, "The Last Frontier."
38. Easthouse, "Developers Seek Greer Garson Ranch."
39. "Actress Greer Garson Rethinking Land Sale," *Daily Times*, December 28, 1989; Tom Milligan, "Developer Still Considering Pecos Project," *Journal North*, January 3, 1990.
40. Miscellaneous media clippings, Folder 5, PECO 391 and Folder 1, PECO 394, PNHP.
41. "Manuel Lujan, Jr.," *Hispanic Americans in Congress*, http://www.loc.gov/rr/hispanic/congress/lujan.html (accessed May 15, 2010).
42. Milligan, "Garson Balks"; Milligan, "Developer Still Considering"; Steve Terrell, "Garson Stepson Vows Not to Sell Ranch," *Santa Fe New Mexican*, January 5, 1990; Paul R. Wieck, "Lujan Criticizes Efforts to Buy Garson Ranch," *Albuquerque Journal*, January 13, 1990.
43. Keith Easthouse, Steve Northrup, and Robert Mayer, "Crassas Has Long Criminal Record; Pecos Deal Now Unlikely," *Santa Fe Reporter*, January 17–23, 1990.
44. Steve Terrell, "California Inventor Not Likely to Get Garson's Ranch," *New Mexican*, February 7, 1990; Tom Milligan, "Garson May Consider Sale to Government," *Journal North*, March 14, 1990.
45. Editorial, "Pecos Monument Safe at Last," *Santa Fe Reporter*, July 4–10, 1990.
46. Public Law 101-313 (104 Stat. 278).
47. James Abarr, "The New Battle for Pigeon's Ranch," *IMPACT: Albuquerque Journal Magazine*, October 11, 1983.
48. NPS, "Draft Resources Management Plan," 1994, 19.
49. Mark Simmons, "Trail Dust: New Light on Johnson's Ranch," *Santa Fe New Mexican*, October 7, 1992.
50. 104 Stat. 278; Special Warranty Deed, 1990.
51. Young, "History of Ranching and Trading," 56–58.
52. Levine, Norcini, and Foster, *An Ethnographic Overview.*
53. Levine, *Our Prayers Are in This Place*, 131–132.
54. Aspectos Culturales, ed., *Pecos, Mi Pecos*, 7.
55. National Academy of Sciences, "A Report by the Advisory Committee to the National Park Service on Research," (Washington D. C.: National Academy of Sciences, 1963).
56. Sellars, *Preserving Nature in the National Parks*, 220; Advisory Board on Wildlife Management, *Wildlife Management in the National Parks: The Leopold Report*, March 4, 1963.
57. Sellars, *Preserving Nature in the National Parks*, 244–245.

58. Bobbi Simpson to Duane Alire, January 11, 1995 Folder 2, PECO 508, PNHP.

59. Bobbi Simpson to Chief Ranger, February 8, 1995, and Judy Reed to Linda Stoll, June 6, 1995, Folder 2, PECO 508, PNHP.

60. Bobbi Simpson to Chief Ranger, February 8, 1995, and Judy Reed to Linda Stoll, June 6, 1995, Folder 2, PECO 508, PNHP; Judy Reed to Linda Stoll, June 6, 1995, Folder 2, PECO 508, PNHP.

61. Authors' interview with former NPS employee, June 2009.

62. NPS, *Resources Management Plan*, PNM, 1988, 9; NPS Water Resources Division, "Water Resource Management Plan," 1995, 20; "Develop Feasibility Study/Restoration Design for Glorieta Creek Flood Plain/Reservoirs," Folder 14, PECO 175, PNHP; Rick Tate, "Pecos NHP Working to Turn Gravel Pits into Natural Wetlands," *Las Vegas Daily Optic*, August 31, 1999.

63. NPS Water Resources Division, "Water Resource Management Plan," 1995, 19.

64. NPS, "Preliminary Master Plan," 1973, 18.

65. Project Compliance Affirmation, February 10, 1994, Folder 11, PECO 397, PNHP.

66. NPS, "Preliminary Master Plan," 1973, 18.

67. J. Stokely Ligon, *New Mexico Birds and Where to Find Them* (Albuquerque: University of New Mexico Press, 1961), 96, 182–183, 204–205.

68. Willow flycatcher survey data, 1995–1997, Willow Flycatcher file, Natural Resources files, PNHP.

69. Carol Raish and Alice M. McSweeney, "Economic, Social, and Cultural Aspects of Livestock Ranching on the Española and Canjilon Ranger Districts of the Santa Fe and Carson National Forests: A Pilot Study," General Technical Report RMRS-GTR-113 (Fort Collins, Colo.: USDA Forest Service, Rocky Mountain Research Station, 2003), 18.

70. Natural Resource Management and Visitor Protection Division, 2003 Year End Report, Folder 6, PECO 384, PNHP; "Feral Dogs" folder, Natural Resource files, PNHP.

71. Superintendent to Regional Director, August 21, 1969, Folder 5, PECO 397, PNHP; NPS, *Final Environmental Statement*, 1975.

72. National Park System Advisory Board Science Committee, "Revisiting Leopold: Resource Stewardship in the National Parks," August 25, 2012, 9; Mark Fiege, "Nature, History, and Environmental History at Rocky Mountain National Park," *Park Science* 32, no. 2 (2016), 76–77.

73. Highway 50 Transportation Study, 26–27; NPS, *Resources Management Plan, PNM*, 1988, 40.

74. U.S. Census Bureau, "Annual Estimates of the Resident Population, 2018 Population Estimates, Pecos, New Mexico," https://factfinder.census.gov, accessed September 16, 2019.

75. Highway 50 Transportation Study, 11–12.

76. Jacobi and Smolka, New Mexico Health and Environment Department, "Upper Pecos River Water Quality Study 1980–81," July 1982, Folder 1, PECO 376, PNHP.

77. McDuff, *Tererro*, 173–174; William Paul Robinson, "Innovative Administrative, Technical, and Public Involvement Approaches to Environmental Restoration at an Inactive Lead-Zinc Mining and Milling Complex near Pecos, New Mexico," in *Proceedings of Waste Management '95*, University of Arizona/DOE/WEC, Tucson Ariz., March 1995.

78. NPS Water Resources Division, "Water Resource Management Plan," 1995, 15.

79. DeBuys, *Enchantment and Exploitation*, 97.

80. NPS Water Resources Division, "Water Resource Management Plan," 34; Muldavin, *Riparian and Wetlands Survey*, 1991, 27–29.

81. Parmenter and Lightfoot, "Field Survey of the Faunal Resources," 1996; authors' interview with Eric Valencia, 2009.

82. USDA Forest Service, "Wilderness Areas in the Santa Fe National Forest," www.fs.usda.gov/detail/santafe/specialplaces/?cid=fsbdev7_021062 (accessed May 27, 2010).

83. deBuys, *Enchantment and Exploitation*, 252–254.

84. J. R. Pegg, "Mexican Spotted Owl Entangled in Endangered Species Debate," Environmental News Service, October 3, 2003, www.ens-newswire .com/ens/oct2003/2003-10-03-10.html (accessed July 20, 2010).

85. U.S. Fire Administration, "2000 Wildland Fire Season," Topical Fire Research Series, Volume 1, Issue 2, October 2000 (Rev. December 2001).

86. J. Scott Hopkins, "Special Water Quality Survey of the Pecos and Gallinas Rivers Below the Viveash and Manuelitas Fires, 2000," Surveillance and Standards Section, New Mexico Environment Department, February 2001.

87. Authors' interviews with former ranch employees, June 12, 2009; Richard S. Aro, "Evaluation of Pinyon-Juniper Conversion to Grassland," *Journal of Range Management*, 1971, 194.

88. NPS Brief, "Birds and Climate Change: Pecos National Historical Park," 1–6, https://www.nps.gov/subjects/climatechange/upload/PECO_2018_Birds _-_CC_508Compliant.pdf (accessed November 12, 2018).

89. Architectural Research Consultants, Incorporated, "Village of Pecos Comprehensive Plan," February 2018, II-8, III-18, VI-4-5; William M. Fleming, José A. Rivera, Amy Miller, and Matt Piccarello, "Ecosystem Services of Traditional Irrigation Systems in Northern New Mexico," *International Journal of Biodiversity Science, Ecosystem Services & Management* 10, no. 4 (2014), 343–350.

90. Robert Nott, "Pecos Residents Unite against Proposed Mine," *Taos News*, August 19, 2019; stoptererromine.org (accessed October 27, 2019).

91. Architectural Research Consultants, Incorporated, "Village of Pecos Comprehensive Plan," VI 4–5.

92. Olivia Harlow, "Pecos Pueblo Descendants Keeping Traditions Alive," *Santa Fe New Mexican*, Aug. 5, 2018.

BIBLIOGRAPHY

ARCHIVAL COLLECTIONS

Francis C. Wilson Papers, New Mexico State Archives (NMSA), Santa Fe, New Mexico.

National Park Service, Southwest Regional Office General Administration Files, 1965–1967,

Record Group 79, National Archives and Records Administration: Rocky Mountain Region (NARA-RM), Denver, Colorado.

Pecos National Historical Park Collections, Pecos, New Mexico.

Tex Austin Files, Donald C. and Elizabeth M. Dickinson Research Center (DRC), National Cowboy & Western Heritage Museum, Oklahoma City, Oklahoma.

WPA New Mexico Collection, Fray Angélico Chávez History Library, Santa Fe, New Mexico.

GOVERNMENT PUBLICATIONS

Advisory Board on Wildlife Management. *Wildlife Management in the National Parks: The Leopold Report.* March 4, 1963. www.nps.gov/parkhistory/online_books /leopold/leopold.htm.

Aldon, Earl F., and Douglas W. Shaw, eds. *Managing Piñon-Juniper Ecosystems for Sustainability and Social Needs: Proceedings of the Symposium, April 26–30, 1993, Santa Fe, New Mexico.* Fort Collins, Colo.: USDA Forest Service, Rocky Mountain Forest and Range Experiment Station, 1993.

Ancestry.com. *New Mexico, Territorial Census, 1885* [database on-line]. Provo, Utah, USA: Ancestry.com Operations, Inc., 2010.

Architectural Research Consultants, Incorporated. "Village of Pecos Comprehensive Plan," February 2018, II-8, III-18, VI-4-5.

Baisan, Christopher H., and T. W. Swetnam. "Interactions of Fire Regimes and Land Use in the Central Rio Grande Valley." Research Paper RM-RP-330. Fort Collins, Colo.: USDA Forest Service, Rocky Mountain Forest and Range Experiment Station, 1997.

Baker, Robert D., Robert S. Maxwell, Victor H. Treat, and Henry C. Dethloff. *Time-less Heritage: A History of the Forest Service in the Southwest.* Intaglio, Inc., College Station, Tex. USDA Forest Service FS-409, August 1988.

Cowley, Jill, Maureen Joseph, and Diane Rhodes. "Cultural Landscape Overview, Pecos National Historical Park, New Mexico." Report on file, Pecos National Historical Park, Pecos, New Mexico, 1998.

D. Sloan, Architects, with Cherry/See Architects. "Historic Structures Report: Trading Post, Forked Lightning Ranch House, Forked Lightning Pump House: Pecos National Historical Park." Report on file, Pecos National Historical Park, Pecos, New Mexico, 2002.

Dorbin, Jerry. "History and Archaeology of the Forked Lightning Ranch." Report on file, Pecos National Historical Park, Pecos, New Mexico, 1991.

Earls, Amy C. "Historic Land Use in the Rowe Area, New Mexico." Report on file, Pecos National Historical Park, Pecos, New Mexico, 1980.

Eininger, Susan F., Genevieve Head, and Robert P. Powers. "Report on the Results of the 1994 Pilot Survey of the Forked Lightning Ranch, Pecos National Historical Park, San Miguel County, New Mexico." Report on file, Pecos National Historical Park, Pecos, New Mexico, 1995.

Fish, Suzanne K. "Pollen Results from Adobe and Mortar of the Pecos Mission." Draft report on file, Pecos National Historical Park, Pecos, New Mexico, 1994.

Gable, Thomas P. "First Report of Game and Fish Warden for New Mexico, 1909–1910–1911." Santa Fe: New Mexican Printing Company, 1912. Accessed on January 20, 2019, at https://archive.org/stream/firstreportofgam00newm/firstreport ofgam00newm#page/37/mode/1up.

Gerow, Peggy A. "Cultural Resources Inventory of Pigeon's Ranch Subunit, Pecos National Historical Park, Santa Fe, New Mexico." Report on file, Pecos National Historical Park, Pecos, New Mexico, 2010.

Gillio, David A. "Santa Fe National Forest Area: An Historical Perspective for Management." Cultural Resources Report No. 30. Albuquerque: USDA Forest Service Southwestern Region, 1979.

Haecker, Charles M. "Archaeological Remote Sensing Survey of the Civil War Site of Camp Lewis, Pecos National Historic Park, San Miguel County, New Mexico." Report on file, Pecos National Historical Park, Pecos, New Mexico, 1998.

Head, Genevieve N., and Janet D. Orcutt, eds. *From Folsom to Fogelson: The Cultural Resources Inventory Survey of Pecos National Historical Park.* 2 vols. Intermountain Cultural Resources Management Paper No. 66. Santa Fe: National Park Service, Intermountain Region Support Office, 2002.

Hoddenbach Consulting, Torrey, Utah. "Integrated Pest Management Plan: Pecos National Historical Park, Pecos, New Mexico." Photocopy on file, Pecos National Historical Park, Pecos, New Mexico, 1998.

Ivey, James E. "A History of the Establishment of Pecos National Monument." Report on file, Pecos National Historical Park, Pecos, New Mexico, 1987.

———. "Unique in All Respects": The Structural History of Pecos National Historical Park." Intermountain Cultural Resources Management Professional Paper No. 59. Draft report on file, Pecos National Historical Park, Pecos, New Mexico, 1996.

Jacobi, G. Z., and D. M. Jacobi. "Water Quality Assessment of the Pecos River and Glorieta Creek, Pecos National Historical Park, New Mexico." Santa Fe: National Park Service, Southwest Regional Office, 1998.

Johnson, K., G. Sadoti, G. Rácz, J. Butler, and Y. Chauvin. "Southern Plains Network Inventory Report for New Mexico Parks." N.p.: National Park Service, 2003.

Johnson, K., T. Neville, and R. E. Bennetts. "Natural Resource Condition Assessment for Pecos National Historical Park." Natural Resource Technical Report NPS/SOPN/NRR-2011/411. Fort Collins: National Park Service, 2011.

Johnson, Ross B. "Pecos National Monument New Mexico: Its Geologic Setting." USGS Geological Survey Bulletin 1271-E. 1967. https://www.nps.gov/parkhistory/online_books/geology/publications/bul/1271-E/intro.htm.

Knudten, Cori, and Maren Bzdek, "Crossroads of Change: An Environmental History of Pecos National Historical Park." Public Lands History Center, Colorado State University, August 2010.

Krumenaker, B. "Natural Resources Inventory of Pecos National Park." Report on file, Pecos National Historical Park, Pecos, New Mexico, 1992.

Levine, Frances, and Anna LaBauve. "Frontera: A View of Demographic Change in the Upper Pecos Valley from Sacramental Records at Neustra Señora de los Ángeles, Pecos Pueblo and San Miguel del Vado." Report on file, Pecos National Historical Park, Pecos, New Mexico, 1994.

Levine, Frances, Marilyn Norcini, and Morris Foster. "An Ethnographic Overview of Pecos National Historical Park." Report on file, Pecos National Historical Park, Pecos, New Mexico, 1995.

Muldavin, Esteban. *Riparian and Wetlands Survey: Pecos National Historical Park.* Albuquerque: University of New Mexico, 1991.

National Park Service. "Analysis and Recommendation for Visitor Center Site: Pecos National Monument." Report on file, Pecos National Historical Park, Pecos, New Mexico, 1981.

———. "Draft General Management Plan/Development Concept Plan: Environmental Impact Statement: Pecos National Historical Park." Denver: Denver Service Center, 1995.

———. "Draft Master Plan: Pecos National Monument." Report on file, Pecos National Historical Park, Pecos, New Mexico, 1972.

———. "Final Environmental Statement: Proposed Master Plan and Development Concept Plan, Pecos National Monument, New Mexico." Denver: U.S. Government Printing Office, 1975.

———. "Land Protection Plan: Pecos National Historical Park," Report on file, Pecos National Historical Park, Pecos, New Mexico, 1972.

———. "Master Plan: Pecos National Monument." Denver: U.S. Government Printing Office, 1975.

———. "Natural and Cultural Resource Management Plan: Pecos National Historical Park." Report on file, Pecos National Historical Park, Pecos, New Mexico, 1999.

———. "Pecos National Historical Park Interim Plan for Natural Resources Management FY 93–94." Report on file, Pecos National Historical Park, Pecos, New Mexico, 1993.

———. "Pecos National Historical Park Special Sites Study." Santa Fe: National Park Service, Southwest Regional Office. Report on file, Pecos National Historical Park, Pecos, New Mexico, 1992.

———. "Pecos National Monument, New Mexico: A Proposal." Santa Fe: National Park Service, Southwest Region, 1963.

———. "Pecos State Monument: An Area Investigation Report." Santa Fe: National Park Service, Region Three, 1962.

———. "Preliminary Master Plan: Pecos National Monument." N.p., 1973.

———. "Resources Management Plan: Pecos National Monument." N.p.: Southwest Cultural Resources Center, 1978.

———. "Resources Management Plan: Pecos National Monument." Photocopy on file, Southwest Regional Office, Santa Fe, 1988.

———. "Santa Fe National Historic Trail Comprehensive Management and Use Plan. Washington D.C., 1990.

———. "Statement for Management: Pecos National Monument." N.p.: U.S. Government Printing Office, 1976.

———. "Water Resources Management Plan: Pecos National Historical Park." 1995.

National Park System Advisory Board Science Committee, "Revisiting Leopold: Resource Stewardship in the National Parks," Washington, D.C.: U.S. Government Printing Office, August 25, 2012. https://www.nps.gov/calltoaction/PDF/LeopoldReport_2012.pdf. (accessed November 13, 2019).

National Register of Historic Places Inventory-Nomination, "Valencia Ranch Historic/Archaeological District, Pecos, New Mexico," 1984.

National Resources Planning Board. "The Pecos River Joint Investigation: Reports of the Participating Agencies." Washington, D.C.: U.S. Government Printing Office, 1942.

Parmenter, R. R., and D. C. Lightfoot. "Field Survey of the Faunal Resources on the Pecos National Historical Park, Pecos, New Mexico." Report on file, Pecos National Historical Park, Pecos, New Mexico, 1994.

Patraw, P. M. "Plants of Pecos National Monument, New Mexico." Report on file, Pecos National Historical Park, Pecos, New Mexico,1968.

Patten, K. A., and E. Frey. "Fishery Assessment and Regulation Recommendations for the Pecos River within Pecos National Historical Park." Report on file, Pecos National Historical Park, Pecos, New Mexico, 2004.

Perkins, D. H. Sosinski, K. Cherwin, and T. Zettner. "Southern Plains Network Vital Signs Monitoring Report: Phase 1." 2005.

Pittinger, J. S. "Fish Community Structure and Aquatic Habitat at Glorieta Creek, Pecos National Historical Park, San Miguel, New Mexico." 1997.

Raish, Carol, and Alice M. McSweeney. "Economic, Social, and Cultural Aspects of Livestock Ranching on the Española and Canjilon Ranger Districts of the Santa Fe and Carson National Forests: A Pilot Study." General Technical Report RMRS-GTR-113. Fort Collins, Colo.: USDA Forest Service, Rocky Mountain Research Station, 2003.

———. "Traditional Ranching Heritage and Cultural Continuity in the Southwestern United States." In *Multifunctional Grasslands in a Changing World*, Volume II;

XXI International Grassland Congress; VIII International Rangeland Congress, 857. Beijing, China: Guangdong People's Publishing House, 2008.

Rodriguez-Bejarno, D. "Preliminary Vegetation Classification, Pecos National Historical Park, New Mexico." Ms. on file, Pecos National Historical Park, Pecos, New Mexico.

Santa Fe Planning Associates. "Feasibility Study for Pigeon's Ranch: Glorieta Pass Battlefield, New Mexico." Report on file, Pecos National Historical Park, Pecos, New Mexico, 1985.

Scurlock, Dan. "From the Rio to the Sierra: An Environmental History of the Middle Rio Grande Basin," General Technical Report, RMRS-GTR-5. Fort Collins, Colo.: U.S. Department of Agriculture, Forest Service, Rocky Mountain Research Station, 1998.

Sivinski, Robert. "A Botanical Inventory of Pecos National Historical Park, New Mexico." Santa Fe: New Mexico Forestry and Natural Resource Division, Cooperative Agreement No. CA7029–2-0018, Report on file, Pecos National Historical Park, Pecos, New Mexico, August 1995.

Spude, Robert L. "Pigeon's Ranch Historic Structure Report." Intermountain Cultural Resource Management Paper No. 74. Santa Fe, New Mex.: National Park Service, Intermountain Region Support Office, 2008.

Stanislawski, Michael B. "The American Southwest as Seen from Pecos." Unpublished report on file, Southwest Regional Office, Santa Fe, New Mexico, 1983.

Stubbendieck, James, and Gary Willson. *An Identification of Prairie in National Park Units in the Great Plains.* National Park Service Occasional Paper No. 7. Washington, D.C.: U.S. Government Printing Office, 1986. https://irma.nps.gov /DataStore/DownloadFile/472539 (accessed November 13, 2019).

Swetnam, Thomas W., and Christopher H. Baisan. "Historical Fire Regime Patterns in the Southwestern United States since AD 1700." In *Fire Effects in Southwestern Forests, Proceedings of the Second La Mesa Fire Symposium,* edited by Craig D. Allen, 11–32. Fort Collins, Colo.: USDA Forest Service, Rocky Mountain Forest and Range Experiment Station, 1996.

Toll, Mollie S. "Plant Parts Found in Adobe Bricks at an 18th C. Spanish Mission, Pecos, NM: III." Report on file, Pecos National Historical Park, Pecos, New Mexico, 1995.

Torres-Nez, John. "Cultural Resource Inventory of the Glorieta Battlefield Interpretive Trail Project, Pecos NHP, Pecos New Mexico." Report on file, Pecos National Historical Park, Pecos, New Mexico, 2007.

Tucker, Edwin A. "The Early Days: A Sourcebook of Southwestern Region History, Book 1." Cultural Resources Management Report No. 7. Albuquerque: USDA Forest Service, Southwestern Region, 1989.

United States Department of Agriculture. "Soil Survey of San Miguel County, New Mexico." 1977.

United States Department of the Interior. "The Pecos River Joint Investigation: Reports of the Participating Agencies." National Resources Planning Board. Washington, D.C.: U.S. Government Printing Office, June 1942.

United States Geological Survey. "Bulletin 87: Mineral and Water Resources of New Mexico." Washington, D.C.: U.S. Government Printing Office, June 1965.

Western Region Sustainable Agriculture Research and Education, "Acequia Conservation Management" Project Report SW98–060, https://projects.sare.org/project -reports/sw98-060/. Accessed November 13, 2019.

White, Courtney, and Earl Porter. "The Catanach Mill: A Grist Mill in the Upper Pecos Valley." Report on file, Pecos National Historical Park, 1996.

White, Joseph Courtney. "Documentation of Original Architectural Fabric in the Church/Convento Complex at Pecos National Historical Park, 1988–1992." Report on file, Pecos National Historical Park, Pecos, New Mexico, 1993.

Wilson, Frank E. "Historic Structures Report: Pecos Mission Complex, Pecos National Monument." Part I. Draft report on file, Southwest Regional Office, Santa Fe, New Mexico, 1967.

Wooton, E. O., and Paul C. Standley. "Flora of New Mexico." In *Contributions from the United States National Herbarium*, vol. 19. Washington, D.C.: Government Printing Office, 1915.

Young, Andrew H. "History of Ranching and Trading at Pecos National Historical Park: Pigeon's Ranch, Kozlowski's Trading Post, and Forked Lightning Ranch." Report on file, Pecos National Historical Park, Pecos, New Mexico, 2001.

BOOKS AND ARTICLES

Abert, James W. *Abert's New Mexico Report, 1846–1847.* Foreword by William A. Keleher. Albuquerque: Horn & Wallace, 1962.

Adams, E. B., and Fr. A. Chavez, trans. *The Missions of New Mexico, 1776: A Description by Fray Francisco Atansio Dominguez, with Other Contemporary Documents.* Albuquerque: University of New Mexico Press, 1956.

Adler, Michael A., and Herbert W. Dick, eds. "Picuris Pueblo through Time: Eight Centuries of Change at a Northern Rio Grande Pueblo." Dallas: William P. Clements Center for Southwest Studies, Southern Methodist University, 1999.

Alberts, Don E. *The Battle of Glorieta: Union Victory in the West.* College Station: Texas A&M University Press, 1998.

———, ed. *Rebels on the Rio Grande: The Civil War Journals of A. B. Peticolas.* Albuquerque: University of New Mexico Press, 1984.

Allen Craig D. "Lots of Lightning and Plenty of People: An Ecological History of Fire in the Upland Southwest." In *Fire, Native Peoples, and the Natural Landscape,* edited by Thomas R. Vale, 143–193. Washington D.C.: Island Press, 2002.

Aro, Richard S. "Evaluation of Pinyon-Juniper Conversion to Grassland." *Journal of Range Management,* 1971, 188–197.

Aspectos Culturales, ed. *Pecos mi Pecos.* Santa Fe: Aspectos Culturales, 2002.

Ayer, Mrs. Edward E., trans. *The Memorial of Fray Alonso de Benavides, 1630.* Albuquerque: Horn and Wallace, Publishers, 1965.

Bahre, Conrad Joseph. *A Legacy of Change: Historic Human Impact on Vegetation in the Arizona Borderlands.* Tucson: University of Arizona Press, 1991.

Bandelier, A. F. *The Delight Makers.* New York: Dodd, Mead and Company, 1890.

———. *Historical Introduction to Studies among the Sedentary Indians of New Mexico; Report on the Ruins of Pecos Pueblo.* Boston: A. Williams and Co., 1881. Reprinted, Millwood, N.Y.: Kraus Reprint Co., 1976.

Barker, Elliott S. *Beatty's Cabin: Adventures in the Pecos High Country.* Santa Fe: W. Gannon, 1977.

Barrett, Elinore M. *Conquest and Catastrophe: Changing Rio Grande Pueblo Settlement Patterns in the Sixteenth and Seventeenth Centuries.* Albuquerque: University of New Mexico Press, 2002.

Baxter, John O. *Las Carneradas: Sheep Trade in New Mexico, 1700–1860.* Albuquerque: University of New Mexico Press, 1987.

Bezy, John V. "The Geology of Pecos." In *Pecos Ruins: Geology, Archaeology, History, and Prehistory,* ed. David Grant Noble, 23–25. Santa Fe: Ancient City Press, 1993.

Bezy, John V., and Joseph P. Sanchez, eds. *Pecos: Gateway to Pueblos and Plains; the Anthology.* Tucson: Southwest Parks and Monuments Association, 1988.

Blackhawk, Ned. *Violence over the Land.* Cambridge: Harvard University Press, 2006.

Brockway, Dale G., Richard G. Gatewood, and Randi B. Paris. "Restoring Grassland Savannas from Degraded Pinyon-Juniper Woodlands: Effects of Mechanical Overstory Reduction and Slash Treatment Alternatives." *Journal of Environmental Management* 64 (2002): 179–197.

Brooks, James F. *Captives and Cousins: Slavery, Kinship, and Community in the Southwest Borderlands.* Chapel Hill: University of North Carolina Press, 2002.

Brown, David E., and Neil B. Carmony. *Aldo Leopold's Southwest.* Albuquerque: University of New Mexico Press, 1995.

Callon, Milton W. *Las Vegas: The Town That Wouldn't Gamble.* Las Vegas, N.Mex.: Las Vegas Publishing Co., Inc., 1962.

Calloway, Colin G. *One Vast Winter Count: The Native American West before Lewis and Clark.* Lincoln: University of Nebraska Press, 2003.

Carr, Ethan. *Mission 66: Modernism and the National Park Dilemma.* Amherst: University of Massachusetts Press, 2007.

Cohen, Lizbeth. *A Consumer's Republic: The Politics of Mass Consumption in Postwar America.* New York: Knopf, 2003.

Cooke, Ronald U., and Richard W. Reeves. *Arroyos and Environmental Change in the American South-West.* London: Clarendon Press, 1976.

Coleman, Jon T. *Vicious: Wolves and Men in America.* New Haven: Yale University Press, 2004.

Correia, David. "The Sustained Yield Forest Management Act and the Roots of Environmental Conflict in Northern New Mexico." *Geoforum* 38, no. 5 (September 2007): 1040–1051.

Cronon, William. *Changes in the Land: Indians, Colonists, and the Ecology of New England.* New York: Hill and Wang, 1983.

———. "Modes of Prophecy and Production: Placing Nature in History." *Journal of American History* 76, no. 4 (March 1990): 1122–1131.

———. *Nature's Metropolis: Chicago and the Great West.* New York: W. W. Norton, 1991.

———. "The Uses of Environmental History." *Environmental History Review* 17, no. 3 (Autumn 1993): 1–22.

Crosby, Alfred W., Jr. *The Columbian Exchange: Biological and Cultural Consequences of 1492.* Westport, Conn.: Greenwood Publishing Company, 1972.

———. *Ecological Imperialism: The Biological Expansion of Europe, 900–1900.* New York: Cambridge University Press, 1986.

DeBuys, William. *Enchantment and Exploitation: The Life and Hard Times of a New Mexico Mountain Range.* Albuquerque: University of New Mexico Press, 1995.

Dearen, Patrick. *Bitter Waters: The Struggle of the Pecos River.* Norman: University of Oklahoma Press, 2016.

Dedek, Peter B. *Hip to the Trip: A Cultural History of Route 66.* Albuquerque: University of New Mexico Press, 2007.

Deutsch, Sarah. *No Separate Refuge: Culture, Class, and Gender on an Anglo-Hispanic Frontier in the American Southwest, 1880–1940.* New York: Oxford University Press, 1987.

Drake, Brian Allen, ed. *The Blue, the Gray, and the Green: Toward an Environmental History of the Civil War.* Athens: University of Georgia Press, 2015.

Dunbar-Ortiz, Roxanne. *An Indigenous Peoples' History of the United States.* Boston: Beacon Press, 2014.

———. *Roots of Resistance: A History of Land Tenure in New Mexico.* Norman: University of Oklahoma Press, 2007.

Dunmire, William W. *New Mexico's Spanish Livestock Heritage: Four Centuries of Animals, Land, and People.* Albuquerque: University of New Mexico Press, 2013.

Dunmire, William W., and Gail D. Tierney. *Wild Plants of the Pueblo Province: Exploring Ancient and Enduring Uses.* Santa Fe: Museum of New Mexico Press, 1995.

Dye, Victoria E. *All Aboard for Santa Fe: Railway Promotion of the Southwest, 1890s to 1930s.* Albuquerque: University of New Mexico Press, 2005.

Earle, Rebecca. *The Body of the Conquistador: Food, Race, and the Colonial Experience in Spanish America, 1492–1700.* New York: Cambridge University Press, 2012.

Edrington, Thomas S., and John S. Taylor. *The Battle of Glorieta Pass: A Gettysburg in the West, March 26–28, 1862.* Albuquerque: University of New Mexico Press, 1998.

Elbright, Malcolm. "New Mexican Land Grants: The Legal Background." In *Land, Water, and Culture: New Perspectives on Hispanic Land Grants,* edited by Charles L. Briggs and John R. Van Ness, 15–64. Albuquerque: University of New Mexico Press, 1987.

Fiege, Mark. "Gettysburg and the Organic Nature of the Civil War." In *Natural Enemy, Natural Ally: Toward an Environmental History of War,* edited by Richard P. Tucker and Edmund Russell, 93–109. Corvallis: Oregon State University Press, 2004.

———. "Nature, History, and Environmental History at Rocky Mountain National Park." *Park Science* 32, no. 2 (2016): 76–77.

———. *The Republic of Nature: An Environmental History of the United States.* Seattle: University of Washington Press, 2012.

Fish, Suzanne K. "Farming, Foraging, and Gender." In *Women and Men in the Prehispanic Southwest: Labor, Power, and Prestige,* edited by Patricia L. Crown, 169–196. Santa Fe: School of American Research Press, 2000.

Fleming, William M., José A. Rivera, Amy Miller, and Matt Piccarello. "Ecosystem services of traditional irrigation systems in northern New Mexico, USA."

International Journal of Biodiversity Science, Ecosystem Services & Management, 10:4, (2014): 343–350.

Flint, Richard. "What's Missing from This Picture? The *Alarde,* or Muster Roll, of the Coronado Expedition." In *The Coronado Expedition: From the Distance of 460 Years,* ed. Richard Flint and Shirley Cushing Flint, 57–80. Albuquerque: University of New Mexico Press, 2003.

Flint, Richard, and Shirley Cushing Flint, eds. and trans. *Documents of the Coronado Expedition, 1539–1542.* Dallas: Southern Methodist University Press, 2005.

———. "Three Ranches and the Battle of Glorieta Pass." New Mexico Office of the State Historian, http://dev.newmexicohistory.org/filedetails.php?fileID=21319. Accessed September 25, 2018.

Flores, Dan. *Coyote Nation: A Natural and Supernatural History.* New York: Basic Books, 2016.

Foner, Eric. *The Story of American Freedom.* New York: W. W. Norton and Company, 1998.

Foote, R. H. "The History of Artificial Insemination: Selected Notes and Notables." *Journal of Animal Science* 80 (2002):1–10.

Forbes, Jack D. *Apache, Navajo, and Spaniard.* Norman: University of Oklahoma Press, 1960.

Frank, Ross. *From Settler to Citizen: New Mexican Economic Development and the Creation of Vecino Society, 1750–1820.* Berkeley: University of California Press, 2000.

Frazer, Robert W. *Forts and Supplies: The Role of the Army in the Economy of the Southwest, 1846–1861.* Albuquerque: University of New Mexico Press, 1983.

Gardner, Richard. ¡*Grito! Reies Tijerina and the New Mexico Land Grant War of 1967.* Indianapolis: Bobbs-Merrill, 1970.

Gonzales, Moises. "The Genizaro Land Grant Settlements of New Mexico." *Journal of the Southwest* Vol. 56, No. 4 (Winter 2014): 583–602.

Gordon-McCutchan, R. C. *The Taos Indians and the Battle for Blue Lake.* Santa Fe: Red Crane Books, 1991.

Gottfried, Gerald J., and Rex D. Pieper. "Pinyon-Juniper Rangelands." In *Livestock Management in the American Southwest: Ecology, Society, and Economics,* edited by Roy Jemison and Carol Raish, 153–212. New York: Elsevier Science B.V., 2000.

Gregg, Josiah. *The Commerce of the Prairies* 1844. Edited by M. Moorhead. Reprinted, Norman: University of Oklahoma Press, 1954.

Gray, Stephen T., Julio L. Betancourt, Stephen T. Jackson, and Robert G. Eddy. "Role of Multidecadal Climate Variability in a Range Extension of Pinyon Pine." *Ecology* 87, no. 5 (2006): 1124–1130.

Gutiérrez, Ramón A. *When Jesus Came, the Corn Mothers Went Away: Marriage, Sexuality, and Power in New Mexico, 1500–1846.* Stanford: Stanford University Press, 1991.

Hackett, Charles Wilson, ed. *Historical Documents Relating to New Mexico, Nueva Vizcaya, and Approaches Thereto, to 1773 collected by Adolph F. A. Bandelier and Fanny R. Bandelier.* Vol. III. Washington D.C.: Carnegie Institution of Washington, 1937.

Hall, G. Emlen. *Four Leagues of Pecos: A Legal History of the Pecos Grant, 1800–1933.* Albuquerque: University of New Mexico Press, 1984.

Hall, G. Emlen, and David J. Weber. "Mexican Liberals and the Pueblo Indians, 1821–1829." 59 New Mexico Historical Review 5 (1984).

Hall, Martin Hardwick. *Sibley's New Mexico Campaign.* Austin: University of Texas Press, 1960.

Hämäläinen, Pekka. *The Comanche Empire.* New Haven: Yale University Press, 2008.

Hammond, George P., and Agapito Rey, eds. and trans. *Narratives of the Coronado Expedition, 1540–1542.* Albuquerque: University of New Mexico Press, 1940.

———. *The Rediscovery of New Mexico, 1580–1594: The Explorations of Chamuscado, Espejo, Castaño de Sosa, Morlete, and Leyva de Bonilla and Humaña.* Albuquerque: University of New Mexico Press, 1966.

Harris, Thomas A., Gregory P. Asner, and Mark E. Miller. "Changes in Vegetation Structure after Long-Term Grazing in Pinyon-Juniper Ecosystems: Integrating Imaging Spectroscopy and Field Studies." *Ecosystems* 6, no. 4 (June 2003): 368–383.

Hastings, Brian K., Freeman M. Smith, and Brian F. Jacobs. "Rapidly Eroding Piñon-Juniper Woodlands in New Mexico: Response to Slash Treatment." *Journal of Environmental Quality* 32 (2003): 1290–1298.

Hayes, Alden C. *The Four Churches of Pecos.* Albuquerque: University of New Mexico Press, 1974.

Hays, Samuel P. *Conservation and the Gospel of Efficiency: The Progressive Conservation Movement, 1890–1920.* Cambridge, Mass.: Harvard University Press, 1959.

Hewett, Edgar L. "Studies on the Extinct Pueblo of Pecos." *American Anthropologist* 6, no. 1 (January–March, 1904): 426–439.

Hirt, Paul. *A Conspiracy of Optimism: Management of the National Forests since World War Two.* Lincoln: University of Nebraska Press, 1994.

Huston, James L. "Property Rights in Slavery and the Coming of the Civil War." *Journal of Southern History* 65, no. 2 (May 1999): 249–286.

Hyde, Anne. *Empires, Nations, and Families.* Lincoln: University of Nebraska Press, 2011.

Ivey, James E. "'The Greatest Misfortune of All': Famine in the Province of New Mexico, 1667–1672." *Journal of the Southwest* 36, no. 1 (1994): 76–100.

Jackson, John Brinkerhoff. "Looking at New Mexico." In *Landscape in Sight: Looking at America,* edited by Helen Lefkowitz Horowitz, 55–67. New Haven: Yale University Press, 1997.

Jacobs, B. F., W. H. Romme, and C. D. Allen. "Mapping 'Old' vs. 'Young' Piñon-Juniper Stands with a Predictive Topo-Climatic Model." *Ecological Applications* 18, no. 7 (2008): 1627–1641.

Jacoby, Karl. *Crimes against Nature: Squatters, Poachers, Thieves, and the Hidden History of American Conservation.* Berkeley: University of California Press, 2001.

Jemison, Roy, and Carol Raish, eds. "Livestock Management in the American Southwest: Ecology, Society, and Economics." *Developments in Animal and Veterinary Sciences,* 30. New York: Elsevier Science B.V., 2000.

Jenks, Kelly L. "Becoming Vecinos: Civic Identities in Late Colonial New Mexico." In *New Mexico and the Pimería Alta: The Colonial Period in the American Southwest,* ed. John G. Douglass, William M. Graves, 213–238. Boulder: University Press of Colorado, 2017.

Johnson, John W. *Reminiscences of a Forest Ranger, 1914–1944.* Dayton: Brown and Kroger Publishing Co., 1976.

Julyan, Robert. *The Place Names of New Mexico,* rev. ed. Albuquerque: University of New Mexico Press, 1998.

Kenner, Charles L. *The Comanchero Frontier: A History of New Mexican–Plains Indian Relations.* Norman: University of Oklahoma Press, 1994.

Kern, Robert. *Labor in New Mexico: Unions, Strikes, and Social History since 1881.* Albuquerque: University of New Mexico Press, 1983.

Kessell, John L. *Kiva, Cross, and Crown: The Pecos Indians and New Mexico, 1540–1840.* 2nd ed. Albuquerque: University of New Mexico Press, 1987.

———. *Miera Y Pacheco: A Renaissance Spaniard in Eighteenth-Century New Mexico.* Norman: University of Oklahoma Press, 2013.

———. *Spain in the Southwest: A Narrative History of Colonial New Mexico, Arizona, Texas, and California.* Norman: University of Oklahoma Press, 2002.

Kessell, John L., and Rick Hendricks, eds. *By Force of Arms: The Journals of don Diego de Vargas, New Mexico, 1691–93.* Albuquerque: University of New Mexico Press, 1992.

Kidder, Alfred Vincent. *Pecos, New Mexico: Archaeological Notes.* Vol. 5. *Papers of the Robert S. Peabody Foundation for Archaeology.* Andover, Mass.: Robert S. Peabody Foundation for Archaeology, 1958.

Kiser, William S. *Borderlands of Slavery: The Struggle over Captivity and Peonage in the American Southwest.* Philadelphia: University of Pennsylvania Press, 2017.

———. *Coast to Coast Empire: Manifest Destiny and the New Mexico Borderlands.* Norman: University of Oklahoma Press, 2018.

Knaut, Andrew. *The Pueblo Revolt of 1680: Conquest and Resistance in Seventeenth-Century New Mexico.* Norman: University of Oklahoma Press, 1995.

Lang, Richard W., and Arthur H. Harris. *The Faunal Remains from Arroyo Hondo Pueblo, New Mexico: A Study in Short-Term Subsistence Change.* Vol. 5, *Arroyo Hondo Archaeological Series.* Santa Fe: School of American Research Press, 1984.

Langston, Nancy. *Forest Dreams, Forest Nightmares: The Paradox of Old Growth in the Inland West.* Seattle: University of Washington Press, 1995.

Lanner, Ronald M. *The Piñon Pine: A Natural and Cultural History.* Reno: University of Nevada Press, 1981.

Leckman, Phillip O. "Meeting in Places: Seventeenth-Century Puebloan and Spanish Landscapes." In *New Mexico and the Pimería Alta: The Colonial Period in the American Southwest,* ed. John G. Douglass, William M. Graves, 75–114. Boulder: University Press of Colorado, 2017.

Leopold, Aldo. "Review of H. M. Bell and E. J. Duksterhuis, 'Fighting the Mesquite and Cedar Invasion on Texas Ranges.'" *Journal of Forestry* 42, no. 1 (January 1946): 63.

Levine, Frances. *Our Prayers Are in This Place: Pecos Pueblo Identity over the Centuries.* Albuquerque: University of New Mexico Press, 1999.

Ligon, J. Stokely. *New Mexico Birds and Where to Find Them.* Albuquerque: University of New Mexico Press, 1961.

Limerick, Patricia Nelson. *The Legacy of Conquest: The Unbroken Past of the American West.* New York: W. W. Norton & Company, 1987.

Linklater, Andro. *Measuring America: How the United States Was Shaped by the Greatest Land Sale in History.* New York: Plume, 2002.

Lipin, Lawrence M. *Workers and the Wild: Conservation, Consumerism, and Labor in Oregon, 1910–30.* Urbana and Chicago: University of Illinois Press, 2007.

Lynch, Tom. *Xerophilia: Ecocritical Explorations in Southwestern Literature.* Lubbock: Texas Tech University Press, 2008.

MacCameron, Robert. "Environmental Change in Colonial New Mexico." in *Out of the Woods: Essays in Environmental History,* ed. Char Miller and Hal Rothman, 79–97. Pittsburgh: University of Pittsburgh Press, 1997.

Magoffin, Susan Shelby. *Down the Santa Fe Trail and into Mexico: The Diary of Susan Shelby Magoffin, 1846–1847.* 1962. Edited by Stella M. Drumm. Reprinted, Lincoln: University of Nebraska Press, 1982.

Martin, Debra L. "Bodies and Lives: Biological Indicators of Health Differentials and Division of Labor by Sex." In *Women and Men in the Prehispanic Southwest: Labor, Power, and Prestige,* edited by Patricia L. Crown, 267–300. Santa Fe: School of American Research Press, 2000.

Masich, Andrew E. *Civil War in the Southwest Borderlands, 1861–1867.* Norman: University of Oklahoma Press, 2017.

McDuff, Leon. *Tererro.* Victoria, BC: Trafford, 2006.

Melville, Elinore G. K. *A Plague of Sheep: Environmental Consequences of the Conquest of Mexico.* New York: Cambridge University Press, 1994.

Merchant, Carolyn. *The Columbia Guide to American Environmental History.* New York: Columbia University Press, 2002.

Miller, Christopher L., Russell K. Skowronek, and Roseann Bacha-Garaza, eds. *Blue and Gray on the Border: The Rio Grande Valley Civil War Trail.* College Station: Texas A&M University Press, 2018.

Mitchell, Pablo. *Coyote Nation: Sexuality, Race, and Conquest in Modernizing New Mexico, 1880–1920.* Chicago: University of Chicago Press, 2005.

Montgomery, Charles. *The Spanish Redemption: Heritage, Power, and Loss on New Mexico's Upper Rio Grande.* Berkeley and Los Angeles: University of California Press, 2002.

Morgan, Michèle E., ed. *Pecos Pueblo Revisited: The Biological and Social Context.* Cambridge, Mass.: Peabody Museum of Archaeology and Ethnology, Harvard University, 2010.

Morgan, Phyllis. *As Far as the Eye Could Reach: Accounts of Animals along the Santa Fe Trail 1821–1880.* Norman: University of Oklahoma Press, 2015.

Morman, Todd Allin. *Many Nations under Many Gods: Public Lands Management and American Indian Sacred Sites.* Norman: University of Oklahoma Press, 2018.

Morrison, Michael A. *Slavery and the American West: The Eclipse of Manifest Destiny and the Coming of the Civil War.* Chapel Hill: The University of North Carolina Press, 1997.

Myers, Harry C. "The Mystery of Coronado's Route from the Pecos River to the Llano Estacado." In *The Coronado Expedition: From the Distance of 460 Years,* ed. Richard

Flint and Shirley Cushing Flint, 140–150. Albuquerque: University of New Mexico Press, 2003.

Nelson, Megan Kate. "The Difficulties and Seductions of the Desert: Landscapes of War in 1861 New Mexico." In *The Blue, the Gray, and the Green: Toward an Environmental History of the Civil War,* ed. Brian Allen Drake. Athens: University of Georgia Press, 2015: 34–51.

———. *Ruin Nation: Destruction and the American Civil War.* Athens: University of Georgia Press, 2012.

Noe, Kenneth. "Fateful Lightning: The Significance of Weather and Climate to Civil War History." In *The Blue, the Gray, and the Green: Toward an Environmental History of the Civil War,* ed. Brian Allen Drake. Athens: University of Georgia Press, 2015:16–33.

Noyes, Stanley. *Los Comanches: The Horse People, 1751–1845.* Albuquerque: University of New Mexico Press, 1993.

Oakes, Yvonne R. "Pigeon's Ranch and the Glorieta Battlefield: An Archeological Assessment." Archaeology Notes 123, with contributions from Don E. Alberts and Betsy Swanson. Santa Fe: Museum of New Mexico, Office of Archaeological Studies, 1995.

Oropeza, Lorena. "Becoming Indo-Hispano: Reies López Tijerina and the New Mexican Land Grant Movement," in Aloysha Goldstein (ed.), *Formations of United States Colonialisms.* Durham: Duke University Press, 2014.

Orsi, Jared. *Citizen Explorer: The Life of Zebulon Pike.* Oxford: Oxford University Press, 2014.

———. "Construction and Contestation: Toward a Unifying Methodology for Borderlands History." *History Compass* 12, no. 5 (2014): 433–443.

Padget, Martin. *Indian Country: Travels in the American Southwest: 1840–1935.* Albuquerque: University of New Mexico Press, 2004.

Parish, William J. *The Charles Ilfeld Company: A Study of the Rise and Decline of Mercantile Capitalism in New Mexico.* Cambridge: Harvard University Press, 1961.

Pyne, Stephen J. *Fire in America: A Cultural History of Wildland and Rural Fire.* Princeton: Princeton University Press, 1982.

———. *Year of the Fires: The Story of the Great Fires of 1910.* New York: Penguin Books, 2001.

Reséndez, Andrés. "National Identity on a Shifting Border: Texas and New Mexico in the Age of Transition, 1821–1848." *Journal of American History* 86, no. 2 (1999): 668–88.

———. *The Other Slavery: The Uncovered Story of Indian Enslavement in America.* Boston: Houghton Mifflin Harcourt, 2016.

Riley, Carroll L. *Rio del Norte: People of the Upper Rio Grande from Earliest Times to the Pueblo Revolt.* Salt Lake City: University of Utah Press. 1995.

Robbins, William G. *Colony and Empire: The Capitalist Transformation of the American West.* Lawrence: University Press of Kansas, 1994.

Robinson, William Paul. "Innovative Administrative, Technical, and Public Involvement Approaches to Environmental Restoration at an Inactive Lead-Zinc Mining and Milling Complex near Pecos, New Mexico." In *"Proceedings of Waste Management '95,"* University of Arizona/DOE/WEC. Tucson, Ariz., March 1995.

Rodriguez, Sylvia. *Acequia: Water-sharing, Sanctity, and Place in Hispanic New Mexico.* Santa Fe: SAR Press, 2006.

———. "Tourism, Difference, and Power in the Borderlands." In *The Culture of Tourism, the Tourism of Culture: Selling the Past to the Present in the American Southwest,* edited by Hal K. Rothman, 185–205. Albuquerque: University of New Mexico Press, 2003.

Romme, William H., Craig D. Allen, John D. Bailey, William L. Baker, Brandon T. Bestelmeyer, Peter M. Brown, Karen S. Eisenhart, et al. "Historical and Modern Disturbance Regimes, Stand Structures, and Landscape Dynamics in Piñon-Juniper Vegetation of the Western U.S." Fort Collins: Colorado Forest Restoration Institute, Colorado State University, 2008. https://www.fs.fed.us/rm/pubs_other/rmrs_2008_romme_w001.pdf. (accessed November 13, 2019).

Rose, Martin R., Jeffrey S. Dean, and William J. Robinson. *The Past Climate of Arroyo Hondo, New Mexico, Reconstructed from Tree Rings.* Arroyo Hondo Archaeological Series, Volume 4. Santa Fe: School of American Research Press, 1981.

Rothman, Hal. *America's National Monuments: The Politics of Preservation.* Lawrence: University Press of Kansas, 1989.

Rowley, William D. *U.S. Forest Service Grazing and Rangelands: A History.* College Station: Texas A&M University Press, 1985.

Sánchez, Joseph P., Robert L. Spude, and Art Gómez. *New Mexico: A History.* Norman: University of Oklahoma Press, 2013.

Sando, Joe S. *Nee Hemish: A History of Jemez Pueblo.* Albuquerque: University of New Mexico Press, 1982.

———. *Pueblo Nations: Eight Centuries of Pueblo Indian History.* Santa Fe: Clear Light, 1991.

Schmitt, Peter J. *Back to Nature: The Arcadian Myth in Urban America.* New York: Oxford University Press, 1969.

Schott, M. R., and R. D. Pieper. "Succession of Pinyon-Juniper Communities after Mechanical Disturbance in Southcentral New Mexico." *Journal of Range Management* 40, no. 1 (Jan. 1987): 88–94.

Sellars, Richard West. *Preserving Nature in the National Parks: A History.* New Haven: Yale University Press, 1997.

Simmons, Marc. "Polish Pioneers." *Santa Fe Reporter,* May 3, 1989.

———. "Why Early New Mexico Turned from Cattle to Sheep." *Santa Fe New Mexican,* April 15, 2016.

Simmons, Marc, and Hal Jackson. *Following the Santa Fe Trail: A Guide for Modern Travelers.* 3rd ed. Santa Fe: Ancient City Press, 2001.

Spicer, Edward H. *Cycles of Conquest: The Impact of Spain, Mexico, and the United States on Indians of the Southwest, 1533–1960.* Tucson: The University of Arizona Press, 1962.

Spielmann, Katherine A. "Colonists, Hunters, and Farmers: Plains-Pueblo Interaction in the Seventeenth Century." In *Columbian Consequences: Archeological and Historical Perspectives on the Spanish Borderlands West,* vol. 1, edited by David Hurst Thomas, 101–114. Washington D.C.: Smithsonian Institution Press, 1989.

————. *Interdependence in the Prehistoric Southwest: An Ecological Analysis of Plains-Pueblo Interaction.* New York: Garland, 1991.

Spielmann, Katherine A., Margaret J. Schoeninger, and Katherine Moore. "Plains-Pueblo Interdependence and Human Diet at Pecos Pueblo, New Mexico." *American Antiquity* 55 (1990): 745–65.

Steen, Harold K. *The U.S. Forest Service: A History.* Centennial Edition. Durham, N.C.: Forest History Society, 2004.

Sutter, Paul S. *Driven Wild: How the Fight against Automobiles Launched the Modern Wilderness Movement.* Seattle: University of Washington Press, 2002.

Swetnam, Thomas W., and Julio L. Betancourt. "Mesoscale Disturbance and Ecological Response to Decadal Climatic Variability in the American Southwest." *Journal of Climate* 11, no. 12 (December 1998): 3128–3147.

Taylor, Morris F. *First Mail West: Stagecoach Lines on the Santa Fe Trail.* Albuquerque: University of New Mexico Press, 1971.

Thomas, David Hurst. "Materiality Matters: Colonial Transformations Spanning the Southwestern and Southeastern Borderlands." In *New Mexico and the Pimería Alta: The Colonial Period in the American Southwest,* ed. John G. Douglass and William M. Graves, 379–414. Boulder: University Press of Colorado, 2017.

Thompson, Jerry D. *A Civil War History of the New Mexico Volunteers & Militia.* Albuquerque: University of New Mexico Press, 2015.

————., ed. *Civil War in the Southwest: Recollections of the Sibley Brigade.* College Station: Texas A&M University Press, 2001.

Trigg, Heather. *From Household to Empire: Society and Economy in Early Colonial New Mexico.* Tucson: University of Arizona Press, 2005.

Troyan, Michael. *A Rose for Mrs. Miniver: The Life of Greer Garson.* Lexington: University Press of Kentucky, 1999.

Truett, Samuel, and Elliott Young, eds. *Continental Crossroads: Remapping U.S.-Mexico Borderlands History.* Durham: Duke University Press, 2004.

Tyler, Hamilton A. *Pueblo Gods and Myths.* Norman: University of Oklahoma Press, 1964.

Urry, John. *The Tourist Gaze: Leisure and Travel in Contemporary Societies.* Newbury Park, Calif.: Sage Publications, 1990.

Van Ness, John R. Foreword to *The Preservation of the Village: New Mexico's Hispanics and the New Deal,* by Suzanne Forrest, vii–x. Albuquerque: University of New Mexico, 1989.

————. "Hispanic Land Grants: Ecology and Subsistence in the Uplands of Northern New Mexico and Southern Colorado." In *Land, Water, and Culture: New Perspectives on Hispanic Land Grants,* edited by Charles L. Briggs and John R. Van Ness, 141–214. Albuquerque: University of New Mexico Press, 1987.

Vlasich, James A. *Pueblo Indian Agriculture.* Albuquerque: University of New Mexico Press, 2005.

Wallace, Susan E. *The Land of the Pueblos* (facsimile of the original 1888 edition). Santa Fe: Sunstone Press, 2006.

Wallis, Michael. *Route 66: The Mother Road.* New York: St. Martin's Press, 1990.

Warren, Louis S. *Buffalo Bill's America: William Cody and the Wild West Show.* New York: Alfred A. Knopf, 2005.

Weber, David J. *Bárbaros: Spaniards and Their Savages in the Age of Enlightenment.* New Haven: Yale University Press, 2005.

———. *The Mexican Frontier, 1821–1846: The American Southwest under Mexico.* Albuquerque: University of New Mexico Press, 1982.

———. *The Spanish Frontier in North America.* New Haven: Yale University Press, 1992.

Weiland, Victoria Carlyle. *100 Years of Rodeo Stock Contracting.* Reno, Nev.: The Professional Rodeo Stock Contractors Association, 1997.

Weisiger, Marsha L. *Dreaming of Sheep in Navajo Country.* Seattle: University of Washington Press, 2009.

White, Richard. *"It's Your Misfortune and None of My Own": A New History of the American West.* Norman: University of Oklahoma Press, 1991.

Will de Chaparro, Martina. *Death and Dying in New Mexico.* Albuquerque: University of New Mexico Press, 2007.

Williams, Robert E. "Modern Methods of Getting Uniform Use of Ranges." *Journal of Rangeland Management,* 1954, 77–81.

Wilson, Chris. *The Myth of Santa Fe: Creating a Modern Regional Tradition.* Albuquerque: University of New Mexico Press, 1998.

Wilson, John P. *When the Texans Came: Missing Records from the Civil War in the Southwest.* Albuquerque: University of New Mexico Press, 2001.

Woodbury, Richard B. "From Chaos to Order: A. V. Kidder at Pecos." In *Pecos Ruins: Geology, Archaeology, History, and Prehistory.* 1981. Edited by David Grant Noble, 15–22. Reprinted, Santa Fe: Ancient City Press, 1993.

Wooten, E. O. "New Mexico Weeds No. 1." Bulletin No. 13. New Mexico College of Agriculture and Mechanical Arts. Albuquerque: New Mexico Agriculture Experiment Station, October 1894.

———. "The Range Problem in New Mexico." Bulletin No. 66. New Mexico College of Agriculture and Mechanical Arts. Albuquerque: New Mexico Agriculture Experiment Station, April 1908.

———. "Trees and Shrubs of New Mexico." Bulletin No. 87. New Mexico College of Agriculture and Mechanical Arts. Albuquerque: New Mexico Agriculture Experiment Station, June 1913.

THESES AND DISSERTATIONS

Anschuetz, Kurt Frederick. "Not Waiting for the Rain: Integrated Systems of Water Management by Pre-Columbian Pueblo Farmers in North-Central New Mexico." PhD diss. University of Michigan, 1998.

Brady, Tracy Lynn. "Kivas, Cathedrals, and Energy Seats: The Making of Religious Landscapes in the Upper Rio Grande Valley." PhD diss. University of Colorado, 2004.

Burtchin, Donald Lee. "The Physical Geography of Pecos National Monument." Master's thesis. University of Arizona, 1983.

Durkin, Thomas Joseph III, "Prehispanic Land-Use Change in Pecos National Historical Park, New Mexico." Master's thesis, Washington State University, 1999.

Hornbeck, David Jr. "Spatial Manifestations of Acculturative Processes in the Upper Pecos Valley, New Mexico, 18401880." PhD diss., University of Nebraska, 1974.

Meszaros, Laura Victoria. "Vegetation and Land Use History of the Upper Pecos Area, New Mexico." Master's thesis, University of New Mexico, Albuquerque, 1989.

Weber, Kenneth Ray. "A New Mexico Village and the Metropolis: A Study of the Economy and Social Organization of a Rural Satellite." PhD diss. University of Oregon, 1972.

INDEX

acequia associations, 136, 148
acequias, 22, 36, 63, 65, 81, 136, 148
Acoma Pueblo, 22, 28, 31–32
Adelo, A. Samuel, 137
Adelo, George, 136
Advisory Council on Historic Preservation, 134
Aguilar, Juan de, 52
Alameda, 64
Alamitos Canyon mill, 106
Alamitos Creek, 106, 146
Albright, Horace, 123
Albuquerque, 15, 49, 80, 96, 104, 115, 120, 169n33
Alejandro (or Alexander) Valle grant, 52, 103. *See also* Cañon de Pecos grant
Alianza Federal de Mercedes, 124–25, 128
Allied War Reparations Commission, 114
Alvarado, Hernando de, 2–3, 9, 11, 14
AMAX (American Metal Company), 145
American Institute of Archaeology, 81
American Metal Company (AMAX), 105–6, 145
Antiquities Act, 120–22
Anton Chico, N.Mex., 65, 106
Anza, Juan Bautista de, 47–48
Apache Canyon, 71
Apaches: and attacks, 15; and Civil War, 75; and Comanches, 42, 47–48, 51; and corn, 34; and horses, 33–34, 42; and Navajos, 70; and Pecos Pueblo, 3, 42–44, 48; and Puebloans, 41–42; and raids, 28–29, 32–34, 42, 56, 68, 70;

and slavery, 14; and Spaniards, 32, 37, 39, 42, 44, 46, 48, 51; and trade, 13, 32–33, 38–40, 43; and U.S. Army, 67
archaeology: conferences, 99; discoveries, 3, 9, 13, 25, 40, 43, 77, 120; methods, 96; protection of sites, 120, 122; and tourism, 81, 96, 120, 122–23, 128, 136, 143–44
architecture, and parks and tourism, 95, 98, 118, 132–35
Arellano, Tristán de, 15
Arkansas River, 15
Armijo, Agustín, 64
Arránegui, José de, 40
Arrowhead Lodge, 169n34
Arrowhead Ruin, 4
Arroyo Hondo Pueblo, 10
Artillery Hill, 72–73
Asención, José María de la, 68
Atchison, Topeka & Santa Fe (AT&SF) Railroad, 75–77, 95–96, 98, 124, 140
Austin, John Van "Tex," 93–94, 97–100, 102, 106–12, 114, 118–19, 131, 149, 167n4, 169n32
automobiles, 96–97, 100, 136–37

Baca, Luis, 72
Bandelier, Adolph, 77, 96
Bandelier National Monument, 147
Barker, Elliott, 104, 126
Barlow and Sanders stage line, 75
Barreiro, Antonio, 63
bartering, 12, 52, 68

Baughl's Siding (also Baughl's Switch, Bowll's Switch), 76
Beaver Meadows, 132
Becknell, William, 61
Benavides, Alonso de, 20, 25–26
Benavídez, Luis, 55
Benson Electric Company, 121
Bernal, Diego González, 31, 33
Bernal, Juan, 33–34
Bezy, John, 135
Bigotes, 1–3, 5, 7, 9, 11–16, 149
birds, 10, 24, 83, 143–44, 148
bison, 2, 9, 12–13, 24, 31–33, 51
Blackhawk, Ned, 43
Black-on-White House, 4
Blue Lake sacred site, 129
bones, animal, 9–10
Bosque Redondo reservation, 75
Boston, Mass., 94, 97
Brush, Lyle, 114
Brush Ranch, 172n3
Bureau of Land Management, 98
Bursum bill, 107
Bush, George H. W., 138
Butane Gas Company of New Mexico, 121

Cachupin, Raymond, 140
Cádiz, Spain, 54
Calabaza, Gregorio, 56
Camp Lewis, 69
Cañada de los Álamos grant, 53
Cañoncito, 53, 80, 101, 120, 140
Cañon de Pecos grant, 36, 52–53, 77–79, 98, 128, 140. *See also* Alejandro (or Alexander) Valle grant
Capital Developers International, 136
captives, 13–16, 25, 38, 43, 68
Carleton, James, 75
Carson National Forest, 84, 102, 146–47
Case, J. J., 104–5
Castañeda de Nájera, Pedro de, 3, 5, 12
Castaño de Sosa, Gaspar, 16, 21
Catanach, Archibald D., 81, 83
Catholicism, 18, 22, 26, 32, 120
Catron, F. A., 127
Catron, Thomas B., 79
Ceballos, Bernardino de, 30
Cerro Grande Fire, 147
Chacón, Fernando, 51–52
Chacón, Rafael, 69

Chapman, Frank, 78–79
Charles Ilfeld Company, 64
Chatelain, Verne, 123
Chaves, Manuel, 70, 72–73
Cherokee Ranch, 116
Chicago, 93, 97
Chichimecas, 5, 16
Chivington, John M., 69, 71–73
Christianity, 2, 5, 16, 18–19, 26–27, 32, 35, 41–42
ciboleros, 51
Cicuye, 1, 3, 151n1
Civilian Conservation Corps (CCC), 110, 122
Civil Rights Act of 1866, 75
Civil War, 60, 67–75, 100
Clark, O. M., 121–22
climate change, 148
Collier, D. C., 81
Collier, John, 107–8
Collins, James, 72
Colonial National Monument, 123
Colonias allotment, 127
Colorado Fuel and Iron Company, 83
Columbus, Christopher, 21
Comanches, 32, 37–38, 41–51, 54, 56–57, 60, 64, 66–68, 70
Confederates, 68–75, 140
Conservation Fund, 139
Continental Life Insurance, 98
Córdoba, Spain, 18
corn, 6–8, 11–14, 21–22, 33–34, 67
Coronado, Francisco Vásquez de, 1–3, 11–17, 149
Coronado Cuarto Centennial, 122
Correia, David, 126
cotton, 7, 28, 31, 69, 153n35
Cow Creek, 147
Cowles, A. H., 105
Crassas, Jerry, 131, 136–39
Crews, E. R., 83
Cristóbal, 16
Crosby, Alfred, 20
Cuerno Verde, 47
Currier, Wilson C., 108, 111, 114

Daeger, Albert T. (archbishop), 98, 120
Dallas, Texas, 131, 135, 140
Daloh, 56
Darden, Wes, 105

Davidson, William Lott, 71
Davis Creek, 105
D. C. Collier and Co., 81
deBuys, William, 139
deer, 9–10, 33–35, 84, 94, 99, 102, 147
Denver & Rio Grande (D&RG) Railroad, 75
Denver Service Center, 133
Depression. *See* Great Depression
desert: and crops, 1, 6–7, 68; and hunting, 9–10; and livestock, 20, 28, 116; and parks development, 133; and water, 63, 75
Dick's Ruin, 4
disease, 7, 23–24, 34, 37, 39, 45–46, 53, 56
Disimone, M. S., 138
Dold, Andres, 79, 81
Domínguez, Francisco Atanasio, 40, 45–47, 159n46
Doroteo, Manuel, 64
Douglas County, Color., 116
drought, 5, 31, 33, 83, 117
Durango, Mexico, 41

ecological damage, 35, 52, 146
ecological imperialism, 20, 23
ecology, 102, 117, 125–26, 136, 141–43, 146–47
Ecueracapa, 47–48
Elbright, Malcolm, 66
Elk Mountain, 147
Ellis, Bruce, 122
El Niño, 117
El Paso, Texas, 37, 100
El Popé, 34–36, 38
El Ranchero restaurant, 109
El Rancho Blanco, 115
El Turco, 13–15
encomienda system, 30–32, 37, 40
Endangered Species Act, 147
Enos, Herbert M., 72
environmental change, 49, 83, 115, 117
environmentalists, 136, 141–42, 146–47
environmental management, 133, 141
environmental protection laws, 134, 138, 147
epidemics, 7, 23–24, 37, 43, 45–47, 53, 56, 129
Espejo, Antonio de, 16, 21

Eulate, Juan de, 29–30
expeditions, 1–7, 11–12, 14–16, 21–22, 42

farming, 5–7, 82–83, 109–10
Federal Land Grant Alliance. *See* Alianza Federal de Mercedes
Fernández, Domingo, 55
Fifth Texas Regiment, 71
Finney, Albert, 108
fires, 8–9, 102, 104, 110–11, 117, 147–48, 170n38
First Colorado Volunteers, 69
floods, 62, 65, 83, 102, 104, 117, 119, 169n32
Fogelson, Elijah E. "Buddy," 112–20, 124, 127–28, 130–39, 146
Fogelson, Gayle David, 131, 136, 138–39
Fonda, Jane, 140
forest management, 101–5, 110–11, 125–27, 147–48
Forest Service, 101–4, 110–11, 113, 116–17, 123, 125–27, 144, 146–47, 170n38
Forked Lightning Ranch, 89–90, 93–94, 97–100, 108–21, 124, 127–40, 143–49
Forked Lightning Ruin, 4
Fort Defiance, 70
Fort Leavenworth, 67
Fort Marcy, 67
Fort Union, 58, 67, 69–71, 74
Fort Worth, Texas, 114
Fragua, Juanita Kota, 56
Franciscans, 2, 14, 16, 18–22, 24–30, 32–34, 40–41, 49, 157n2
Fred Harvey Company, 96
Frye, Linda, 140
Fuenteovejuna, 18
fur trapping, 61–62, 104

Gable, Thomas, 103–4
Galisteo, 35, 41–43, 72
Galisteo Basin, 10
Garretson, John, 79
Garson Fogelson, Greer, *89*, 112–13, 115, 118–19, 131–33, 135–36, 138–40, 149
General Authorities Act, 142
Giles, Thomas F., 133–35
Glorieta, N.Mex., 103, 105, 108, 110–11, 117, 120, 164n27

Glorieta Baptist Conference Center, 145
Glorieta Battlefield, 120, 139–40
Glorieta Creek, 6, 9, 29, 46, *86*, *88*, *91*,
    146, 159n46, 169n32
Glorieta Mesa, 8, 10, 25, 72–73, 77, 82,
    85, 98–99, 111, 114
Glorieta Pass, 61–62, 69, 71–72, 74, 76,
    100; Battle of, 69–74, 78, 100
Godoy, Pedro Lucero de, 32
Gómez, Francisco, 31
Gonzales, Cip, 137
Goodrich-Lockhart Company, 105
Gorras Blancas, 82, 125
Grand Teton National Park, 132, 135
Gray, James, 58, 61–62
Great Depression, 104, 109–11, 114, 120,
    123
Greer, Bill, 100
Greer, Thomas Lacey, 88, 100, 120
Gregg, Josiah, 61
Gross Kelly Company, 81–82, 98, 107,
    120
Grzelachowski, Alexander, 73
Guadalupe, María, 68
Gutiérrez, Ramón A., 12

Hagerman, Herbert, 107
Hagus Canyon, 110
Haiashi, 56
Hall, G. Emlen, 50, 78, 108
Harrison, Benjamin, 101
Hartzog, George B., Jr., 141
Harvard University, 140
Háwikuh, 1–2, 13
Hebert, George, 80
highways. *See* roads
Hinderliter, Melvin, 116, 127
Hispanic and Hispano, use of terms, 157n2
historical parks, 140–42
historic sites, 113, 121–23, 136, 140, 144
Hobe-wagi, 38–39
Hobe-wagi (Rosa Vigil Pecos), 56
Hobson-Dressler site, 4
Hollywood, 94, 112–13, 118, 138, 140
Hopeh (Miguel Pecos), 56
Hornbeck, David, 65
horses: introduction of, 14, 17, 20, 33–34,
    42, 48; and Park Service, 142–43
hunting, 9–11, 27
Hyacinth Pigeon, 61

Indian Claims Commission Act, 128
Indian Creek, 105
Indian Detours tourism company, *87*, 96
Interior Department, U.S., 108, 139
intermarriage, 13, 55, 125
Irvin's Ranch, 172n3
Iturbide, Agustín de, 54

Jackson Lake Lodge, 132
Jaramillo, Juan, 16
Jemez people, 5, 12, 128, 140
Jemez Pueblo, 5, 11, 56, 70, 77–79,
    107–8, 113, 122, 128–29, 140
Jicarilla Apaches, 13
Johnson, Anthony P., 62, 67, 71, 74–75,
    80
Johnson, John W., 102–3, 109–11
Johnson, Lyndon, 124
Johnson's Ranch, 62, 71–72, 76, 80,
    140
Juárez, Andrés, 18–20, 23–26, 29, 31–32,
    35, 149
juniper trees, 8–9, 77, 109, 117–18, 144
Jupes, 48

kachinas, 10–12, 34
Kearny, Stephen Watts, 66–67
K'ela, 56
Kessell, John, 26, 37, 128, 153n35
Kidder, Alfred, 96, 99, 120, 140
Kilmer, Val, 140
Kimball, Tweet, 116
King, F. W., 121
Kingman Station, 76
King Ranch, 116
Kirkpatrick, Jay, 116
kivas, 12, 19, 35, *91*, 122
Kota, Francisco, 56
Kotsotekas, 48
Kozlowski, Helen, 58, 60, 62, 65, 67,
    69–70, 74–75, 80, 112, 149
Kozlowski, Joseph, 58
Kozlowski, Martin, 58, 60–62, 65, 67–68,
    70, 74–75, 77–81, 98, 106
Kozlowski, Thomas, 58, 81, 83
Kozlowski's ranch, 62, 67, 69–74, 78
Kozlowski's Trading Post, 58, 69, 76,
    98–99, 111, 116, 118, 138, 142–43,
    169n32
Kunkle, Jerome, 81

La Bajada Hill, 81
Laboratory of Anthropology, 122
La Cueva Road, 110
La Gente del Rio Pecos, 145
La Joya, 76
Lamy, N.Mex., 77
La Niña, 117
Las Vegas, N.Mex., 64, 71, 73, 76, 78–81, 83, 93, 96–97, 137, 147
Laub, John L., 80–81
Leopold, Aldo, 102
Leopold, A. Starker, 141
Leopold Report, 141
Levy, as town name, 161n1
Lewis, William H., 69
Limerick, Patricia, 66
Lincoln National Forest, 126
Lindbergh, Anne, 99
Lindbergh, Charles, 88, 99
Linkletter, Art, 112
Lisboa Springs Fish Hatchery, 103, 126, 146
Llano Estacado, 44
Loma Lathrop, 4
London, 93–94, 97, 167n4
Long, Boaz, 122
Long Walk, 75
Loretto, Margaret, 149
Los Alamos, 147
Los Trigos grant, 52–53, 55, 124, 127–28, 140
Los Trigos Ranch, 114, 136, 139
Los Trigos village, 52, 76, 116
Louisiana Territory, 48
Lowe, Howard, 106
Lujan, Manuel, Jr., 138–39
Lumpkin, Bill, 134

MacCameron, Robert, 49
Macomb, John N., 67
Mares, José, 48
Márquez, Bartolomé, 52
Martínez, Félix, 40
Martinez, George, 127–28
Ma-ta, 56
McFerran, J. C., 67
measles, 23–24, 46
Meem, John Gaw, 98, 118
Melgares, Facundo, 55
Mellon, Richard King, 139

Menchero, Juan Miguel, 41
Mendinueta, Pedro Fermin de, 45
Mendizábal, López de, 31
Mendoza, Gaspar Domingo de, 44
Merino, Buenaventura, 51–52
Mexada Oil Company, 110–11
Mexican-American War, 58
Mexico City, 16, 42, 44
Miguel, José, 68
Miller, John, 69, 71
mission ruins, *87, 88, 90*, 124, 128. *See also* Pecos Pueblo ruins
Mission 66 program, 132–33, 135, 146
Mollhausen, Baldwin, 65
Monastery Lake, 144
Montalban, Ricardo, 135
Monument Fire, 147
Moon Ranch, 99
Mosoyo, 30
Moss, Jeremy, 149
Museum of New Mexico, 120–22, 128, 132

Nambé Pueblo, 18
National Academy of Sciences, 141
National Environmental Protection Act, 134, 147
National Forest Management Act, 147
national forests, 101–2, 110–11, 113, 121, 126, 146–48
national monuments, 119, 121–24, 130–32, 135–36, 138–40, 142, 144, 147
national parks, 122–23, 132, 141, 145–46
National Park Service, 91, 97, 101, 110, 121–24, 128–49, 176n11, 177n16
National Resources Planning Board, 126
National Wild and Scenic River, 147
National Youth Administration, 110
Native American Graves Protection and Repatriation Act, 140
Navajos, 37, 68, 70, 75, 95
New Deal programs, 110
New Mexican Foot Volunteers, 69
New Mexico, as U.S. territory, 65–69
New Mexico Acequia Association, 136
New Mexico Department of Game and Fish, 104, 126, 129, 146
New Mexico Environmental Improvement Division, 145

New Mexico Preservation Bureau, 140
New Mexico State Fair, 115
New York, 79–81, 93–94, 97
Noriega, Manuel Antonio Chaves de, 70
Nuestra Señora de los Ángeles de
    Porciúncula (Our Lady of the Angels):
    church, 26, 49; Feast of, *92*, 107, 122,
    128–29, 149; painting, 56, *90*
Nuestra Señora de Luz, 80
Nuevo México, 18, 38

Obregón, Baltazar de, 5
Office of Indian Affairs, 78
oil, 109–11, 114–15, 138
Oñate, Cristóbal de, 21
Oñate, Juan de, 18, 21–24, 31, 41
O'Neal, Edwin, 123–24
O'Neal, Vivian, 123–24
Order of Santiago, 45
Oroz, Pedro, 16
Ortega, Pedro de, 25–26, 29–30
Ortiz, Gilbert, 116, 143
Ortiz, Juan Rafael, 55
Ortiz, Matías, 52
Ortiz, Pedro Zambrano, 25, 122
Otermín, Antonio de, 35
Our Lady of the Angels. *See* Nuestra
    Señora de los Ángeles de Porciúncula
Overland Mail route, 80

Padilla, Diego, 52, 55
Padilla, Esquipula, 124, 128
Padilla, Juan de, 14, 16
Pajarito, N.Mex., 124, 127
Pajarito Plateau, 117
Paleo-Indian period, 4
Panama-California Exposition Company,
    81
Pancho Villa, 94, 167n4
Park Service. *See* National Park Service
Pastor, Justo, 64
Payne, H. Vearle, 128
Pecos, Agustin Kota, 56
Pecos, Miguel, 56
Pecos, Rosa Vigil, 56
Pecos Canyon, 4, 147
Pecos ciénega, 6, 29, 36, 45, 49–50,
    52–56, 63, 84, 148
Pecos Conference on Southwestern
    Archaeology, 99

Pecos Eagle Society, 129
Pecos Light and Power, 121
Pecos National Historical Park, 56, 80, 92,
    139–41, 148–49
Pecos National Monument, 119, 130–32,
    135
Pecos Pueblo grant, 52–53, 75, 77–81, 98,
    101, 106–8, 128, 140
Pecos Pueblo ruins, 61, 77, *85*, *91*, 94–95,
    99, 107, 113, 116, 119–21. *See also*
    mission ruins
Pecos Reserve, 101
Pecos River, 9, 36–37, 56–57, 80–84, *85*,
    93–94, 126–27, 145–47. *See also* Río
    Pecos
Pecos River Canyon, 11, 104
Pecos River Compact, 125
Pecos River Forest Reserve, 101
Pecos River Joint Investigation report, 126
Pecos River Mining Company, 105
Pecos State Monument, 121
Pecos Telephone Company, 121
Pecos Wilderness, 147
Pedrosa, Juan de la, 35
Peña, Juan de Dios, 36–38, 47, 49–50,
    52–54, 57, 149
People's Party, 82
Peralta, Pedro de, 19, 23, 25, 29
Pigeon's Ranch, 61–62, 67, 71–74, 76, 80,
    86, *88*, 100, 110, 120, 139, 169n34
Pike, Zebulon, 52, 60
Pike's Peakers, 69, 71
Pino, Juan Estevan, 64–65
piñon nuts, 1, 8, 19, 24, 29, 31–32, 35,
    40, 65, 127
piñon trees, 8–9, 40, 43, 77, *91*, 117, 144
Polk, James K., 65
Pove, 56
Predock, Tony, 134
Promontory, Utah, 75
Pueblo, Colo., 69
Pueblo Lands Act, 108
Pueblo Lands Board, 106–9, 128
Pueblo Revival style. *See* Spanish-Pueblo
    Revival style
Pueblo Revolt, 24–25, 42
Pyron, Charles L., 71–72

Quintana, Benigo, 56, 98
Quivira, 13–16

raids, 13, 32–33, 37, 42–49, 68, 158n11
railroads, 60, 75–77, 80, 82, 84, 94–95, 109
Raton Pass, 76
Reed, Judy, 142
repartimiento system, 30
Reséndez, Andrés, 25, 75
Revolutionary War, American, 47
Richard King Mellon Foundation, 139
Rio Grande, 9, 15, 22, 66, 76, 96, 104, 126, 146
Río Pecos, 51. *See also* Pecos River
Rivera, Anicieto, 78
Rivera, Miguel, 55
roads, 67, 96, 100, 110, 121, 124, 126–28, 146
Robert S. Peabody Museum, 140
Robledo, Francisco Gómez, 31
Rockefeller, Winthrop, 116
Rocky Mountain National Park, 132
rodeos, 93–94, 97–98, 167n4, 168n14
Rodriguez, Sylvia, 95
Roman Catholic Archdiocese, 120
Roosevelt, Franklin Delano, 109, 123, 126
Rosas, Luis de, 28
Rothman, Hal, 124
Route 66, 100, 120, 169n33
Rowe, N.Mex., 4, 76, 124–25, 127
Roybal, Richard, 137
Ruiz, José Mariano, 56
Ruíz, Pedro, 78, 98
Ruter, B. A., 82

Salmeron, Frank, 124, 128
San Antonio, 74
San Cristóbal, 35
San Diego, 81
San Felipe Pueblo, 73
San Gabriel de Yunge, 22
Sangre de Cristo Mountains, 62, 77, 83
San Ildefonso Pueblo, 138
San Juan Pueblo, 34
San Miguel, Francisco de, 22
San Miguel County, N.Mex., 67, 69, 82, 104, 106, 115, 125, 127, 161n2
San Miguel del Vado, N.Mex., 36, 50–53, 55–56, 68, 73, 144
Santa Fe, 25, 32, 35, 43–45, 47–49, 61, 69–71, 95
Santa Fe de Nuevo México, 18

Santa Fe National Forest, 101, 114, 120, 125–26, 144, 146–47
Santa Fe Railroad, 105
Santa Fe Trail, 58, 60–65, 67, 71–73, 75–76, 135; ruts, 62, 136, 138
Santa Gertrudis cattle, 112, 116–17, 136
Santa Rosa, N.Mex., 99, 120, 169n33
Santo Domingo, 18
scenic highway, 147
Schmitz, Marten, 144
School of American Research (Santa Fe), 120, 122
Scurry, William R. "Dirty Shirt," 72–74
Second New Mexico Infantry, 73
Second Texas Mounted Rifles, 71
Se-h-ng-pae (Juan Antonio Toya), 56
Sena, Tomás de, 45
Sesa-whi-ya (Agustin Kota Pecos), 56
Sevilleta National Wildlife Refuge, 117
Sharpshooter's Ridge, 73, *86*, 100
sheep, 15–21, 28, 64–65, 102
Shi-to-ne, 56
Shongopovi, 31
Shoshone, 42
Shynj-dyu-kinu, 56
Sibley, Henry Hopkins, 69–70, 74
Simpson, Bobbi, 142
slavery, 13–16, 19, 22–23, 25, 60, 68, 70, 75
Slough, John P., 69–74, 78–79
smallpox, 23–24, 35, 46–47
Smithsonian Institution, 140
Sntyu-wagi, 56
Soil Conservation Service, 125
Sopete, 13–14
Southern Athabaskan nomads, 13
Spanish-Pueblo Revival style, 98, 118, 134–35
Spanish Reconquest, 24, 38
St. Anthony's Parish, 122
Stinett, Lewis, 121
St. Louis, 61–62, 98
Stoll, Linda, 138
Strong, Bruce, 114
Strong, Dorothy, 114
Stubbs, Stanley, 122
Sutter, Paul, 97

Taber, Sarah, 80
Taber, Walter, 80
Tabu-taa, 56

Tanos rebels, 35
Taos, 11, 31, 39, 43–44, 48, 129
Taos Pueblo, 11, 39, 129
Taovayas, 43
Tappan (lieutenant), 73
Tererro mine, 104–6, 109, 114, 126, 129, 145, 148
Tewa, 34
Texas Mounted Rifles, 71
Tiguex, 15
Tijerina, Reies Lopez, 125
timber, 28, 31, 40, 76–77, 80–81, 83, 109–11, 126–27, 147
Toh-wagi (Juanita Kota Fragua), 56
Toon-kanu, 56
Towa language, 5, 129
Toya, Jose, 129
Toya, Juan Antonio, 56
Toya, Pablo, 107
Toya, Simona, 56
transcontinental railroad, 75
Treaty of Guadalupe Hidalgo, 66, 125
tribute system, 1–2, 19, 23, 25–26, 29–34, 37
Trigo, Manuel de San Juan Nepomuceno y, 40
Tripp, Maurice, 139
Trist, Nicolas, 66
Trujillo, Francisco, 52
Tsa-aku, 56
Tyi-koon wachu, 56

Úbeda, Luis de, 16
Udall, Stewart, 141
United States v. Joseph, 79
University of New Mexico, 120
Upper Pecos Watershed Association, 148
U.S. Army, 60, 65–67, 69–70, 110
USDA Biological Survey, 103, 170n38
U.S. Department of Agriculture, 116
U.S. Fish and Wildlife Service, 147, 170n38
U.S. Forest Service. See Forest Service
Utes, 42–44, 46, 48, 68, 70, 75
Utley, Robert, 123, 129

Valdez, Juan Bautista, 64
Valencia, Eric, 146
Valencia Ranch, 121

Valle, Alexander, 52, 61–62, 67, 71, 74–75, 77, 80, 103
Valley Ranch, 103
Van Ness, John R., 110
Van Norstrand, Clarence, 97. See also Austin, John Van "Tex"
Vargas, Diego de, 37–41, 46
Velasco, Fernando de, 34–35
Velasco, Juan Bautista de, 23
Vélez Cachupín, Tomás, 43–44
Vigil, Donaciano, 54, 66, 77, 81
Vigil, Jose Miguel, 56
Villanueva, Vicente, 52–53, 55
Viveash Fire, 147

Wa-kin (Francisco Kota), 56
Ward, John N., 78
Warner, Louis H., 108
Warren, Louis, 98
Warsaw, Poland, 61
Wasson, A. V. "Slim," 115–16
Wayu, 56
Weber, David J., 22
wheat, 18–21, 24, 32–35, 40–41, 45
Wichitas, 13, 15, 42
Wilderness Act, 146
Wild West show, 168n14
Willow Creek, 105–6
Wilson, Francis C., 81, 107–8, 110–11, 166n96
Wilson, Frank, 135
Windmill Hill, 72
Wirth, Conrad, 141
Woodruff, Ariz., 100
Works Progress Administration, 110, 121
Wright, J. Whitaker, 79

Xabe, 13–15

Yamparikas, 48
Ye, Juan de, 39
Yellowstone, 122, 141–42
Yore, Clement, 93–94
Young, Andrew, 99

Zacatecas, 16, 21
Zeinos, Diego de la Casa, 24, 40
Zer-wakin (Jose Miguel Vigil), 56
Zuñis, 1–2

CPSIA information can be obtained
at www.ICGtesting.com
Printed in the USA
LVHW032117040821
694540LV00010B/1636